Also by Diana Kennedy

THE CUISINES OF MEXICO
THE TORTILLA BOOK
RECIPES FROM THE REGIONAL COOKS OF MEXICO

NOTHING
FANCY

Recipes and Recollections of Soul-Satisfying Food

By Diana Kennedy

NORTH POINT PRESS
San Francisco 1989

The following recipes have been reprinted by permission from
Harper & Row:
"Philadelphia Snapper Soup" from *American Regional Cookery*, by
Sheila Hibben. Copyright 1946 by Sheila Hibben. Copyright ©
renewed 1974 by Jill Hibben Hellendale. Reprinted by permission
of McIntosh and Otis, Inc.
"Alice B. Toklas's Veal and Pork Loaf" from *The Alice B. Toklas
Cookbook*. Copyright 1954 by Alice B. Toklas.
"Shrimps in Pumpkin-Seed Sauce" from *Recipes from the Regional
Cooks of Mexico*, by Diana Kennedy. Copyright © 1978 by Diana
Kennedy.
"Flambéed Mangoes" ("Mangos Flameados") from *The Cuisines of
Mexico*, by Diana Kennedy. Copyright © 1972 by Diana Kennedy.
"Pierre Franey's Ragoût Toulousaine" from *The New York Times
International Cook Book* by Craig Claiborne. Copyright © 1971 by
The New York Times Company.

Illustrations by Jerry Joyner

LIBRARY OF CONGRESS CATALOGING-IN-PUBLICATION DATA
Kennedy, Diana.
    Nothing fancy : recipes and recollections of soul-satisfying food
    by Diana Kennedy ; [illustrations by Jerry Joyner].
        p.   cm.
    Reprint. Originally published: Garden City, N.Y. : Dial Press,
    1984.
    Bibliography: p.
    Includes index.
    ISBN 0-86547-374-9
    1. Cookery.   I. Title.
TX714.K46   1989
641.5—dc19   88-34884

North Point Press
850 Talbot Avenue
Berkeley, California
94706

To my mother, first of all, and to everyone who has helped or taught me along the way, especially Craig, Jacques, Peter, and my sister Jean, and to all the wonderful young American chefs of today—may they not forget the "soul food" of yesterday.

CONTENTS

ACKNOWLEDGMENTS

It is one of the happiest circumstances to have had the same editor for all my books, and I should like to thank her most sincerely. Frances McCullough, my dear friend and exceptional editor, guides me gently and lets it be *my* book.

My sincere thanks to Elaine Chubb, a fellow countrywoman, a most meticulous and painstaking copy editor, who not only understood all the British references but contributed to them in no small way.

I am also most grateful to Larry Alexander for his sensitive and intelligent approach to designing this book.

Additional thanks go to all my friends and other cookbook writers who have been generous enough to share their recipes with me—which I have acknowledged individually with their recipes—and to all my friends in Mexico and New York who have helped me along the way, particularly Gladys and Jean Delmas, Alvin and Marjorie Jackson, and Sally Sloan.

And especially to Jerrie Strom, chief guinea pig, who let me take over her kitchen and gave me her invaluable advice, my warmest thanks.

Special thanks to the Bridge Company and Casa Moneo for loaning equipment to be sketched.

INTRODUCTION

Nothing Fancy: Recipes and Recollections of Soul-Satisfying Food is just that, with a few fancy exceptions, of course. It is a collection of recipes that are, or have been at one time or another, part of my culinary life—favorite dishes that I love to eat and remember friends by. Some of the recipes come from my rather traditional upbringing in England, others stem from ideas that I have picked up while traveling and eating, and some I have just plain invented in my search for new textures and tastes to go along with the old.

Mrs. Beeton included in her famous book on household management home remedies for measles, scarlet fever, croup, and diarrhea, and Martha Washington the same, while my Mexican "bible," *La Cocinera Poblana,* states clearly on the title page that it includes: "varied recipes, secrets of the dressing table and domestic medicine to preserve good health and prolong life." And now that there is a more holistic approach to good health and food, I shall include, raised eyebrows notwithstanding, a few little natural remedies that have become part of my everyday life.

I love to cook the occasional complicated recipe purely as a culinary exercise, following the instructions to the letter, and then, inevitably, I begin to improvise. I have so often heard, "I have *improved* on so-and-so's recipe"—to me that smacks of arrogance, when one knows only too well what goes into the making of an "honest" cookbook. I prefer to use the phrase "adapted to suit my own palate or circumstance," because each one of us brings a particular experience or talent into the kitchen.

I have done my years of entertaining—show-off dinners, as I call them—and I am sure I sent my guests home with a good case of *foie.* Now I prefer to sit down with good friends—old or new—who understand what eating is all about: that food is an adventure which doesn't always come off, but that it should always be cooked with love and with the freshest ingredients that the place can offer, no matter how simple. For the more you cook, the less confident you are that things *will* turn out perfectly—adequately, perhaps—but then, perfection is rare because it is all tied up with you and the elements, that unfathomable alchemy which the slightest change in moisture, wind, or phase of moon can upset. But when it does happen, one has a right to be ecstatic and boastful. A meal prepared with all these elements speaks for itself, transcending barriers of language. What an effective new diplomatic language it could be and perhaps, to some extent, already is.

The former British Ambassador in Mexico, Sir Crispin Tickell, loved to tell the story that the Belgian statesman Paul-Henri Spaak, a well-known gourmet, always said that the most important person in any embassy was the cook, the second the ambassador's wife, and only third the ambassador himself.

For some years now Frances McCullough, my editor and good friend, has been trying to cajole me—sometimes twisting my arm in her gentle way—into writing this book. I was astonished when she first mentioned it: "Why would anybody want to have my personal recipes?" . . . "Just begin by writing down what you have cooked for me over the years," she persisted. And so, one day when comparative calm reigned in my somewhat turbulent life, I began making a list—I find most things get achieved by making a list. I began leafing through old books that had recipes printed in faded type, and others written in a dozen different hands. Sometimes the pages were stuck together with a blob of egg yolk, or a squashed raisin, or the unmistakable smear of chocolate—I am sure you know the type of thing—an irreplaceable record of one's early cooking years. I began thinking about the food I like to eat every day and on special occasions, about the easy recipes for when I am in a hurry and those that I make with unerring regularity. Some were from other people's books, recipes that I had modified to suit my tastes or to substitute ingredients that I could lay my hands on more easily.

It was quite an experience, rather like opening up a box of old clothes long since forgotten. "Will they still fit?" "Do you think I could get away with it today?" "How on earth did I get by with this one?" There were many surprises, delights, and disappointments. The sight of them began to evoke memories of other times—it seemed like other lives, not mine—and occasions, of journeys, and above all of old friends who had contributed to my culinary knowledge and tastes through the years. Most particularly, it brought back vivid memories of my late husband, Paul. He would collect recipes for me when I couldn't accompany him on his travels through Central America and the Caribbean. For instance, I found a faded piece of paper with ragged edges typed in his inimitable, terse way: *"Sancocho* (Dominican National Dish) 2 meats (pork/chicken), (pork/beef), (goat/chicken), etc. Season with garlic, onions, salt. Saute in fat and water, when boiling add yams, yucca, platino verde, potatoes, pumpkin, season salt, black pepper, dash viniger, bouquet garni let simmer, the longer warm the richer." This was followed by: *"Haiti Bouillon:* same ingredients less pumpkin, add water cress and small amount spinach (more w/cress than spinach) served with pieces of lemon peel." His typing was no better than mine, his spelling far worse—like me, he was always in a hurry. My mind wandered back to our last journey together from Mexico to New York when he was fighting against advancing cancer. We were in a motel dining room somewhere in Texas. Paul laid his knife and fork down soon after he had started his meal. "I don't know whether to thank you or not," he bellowed. "Most of my life I could eat anything anywhere, but now look what you have done to me. This damned rubbish . . ." With that he pushed his plate back in disgust.

It was quite a gastronomic adventure searching through those books. I found recipes that I hadn't cooked for fifteen years or more. I remember they were perfectly clear at the time, but now they seemed vague when I tried to recreate them in my Mexican kitchen. So I began to write letters to friends I hadn't seen or heard from for years. "Did you really mean *two* pounds of butter?" "Should the texture be slightly grainy?" "What sort of peppers do they use in your part of Yugoslavia?" "Do you by any chance have Aunt Maud's recipe for spiced beef?" It seemed like Christmas all over again as letters and cards began to arrive. "That soup was *my* invention. I do have time to cook, you know [she thought I thought she was too busy being a professional], often to the distress of my family. . . ." "No we ain't got no recipe for yon 'spiced beef' that you believe me mum used to cock up," came the reply from Scotland. "Lovely to hear from you but I don't have the slightest recollection of giving you that recipe." And so on. I found a gazpacho recipe—one out of a hundred that I really like—typed by an old friend and colleague of Paul's at *The New*

York Times, Sam Brewer. ("Damn good correspondent," Paul would growl whenever Sam's name came up.) "This comes from Antonio Olazcoaga, a fine old Basque glutton . . . who was a good friend of Paul's and mine when we were in Spain together." Then there was Ruth's duck-egg sponge, which I had admired on a visit to her house in Cheltenham in the sixties. It was one of those real old-fashioned chewy sponge cakes that you hardly ever find nowadays when "soft and downy" flour and double-acting baking powder, God forbid, are all the rage. I had some difficulty with that one, but I'll tell you about it later on.

It was not easy "cooking" this book—especially the recipes that had been so much a part of my life when Paul was still alive—in an ecological house in the mountains of Mexico. There were no cultivated mushrooms—only the glorious wild ones during the rainy season; not one bottle of decent sherry was available, let alone Madeira; there were no pickling cucumbers and no ox tongue. (The local custom here is to barbecue the whole head of the animal, so no amount of money or persuasion could get me a tongue.) I did finally track down some saltpeter, for corning beef, at one of the busiest drugstores in town. "Yes, I do have some," said the harassed owner, running his hand through his permanently tousled hair, "but I have to look for it, so come back tomorrow." I got the same answer every day for a week. In despair, I let ten days elapse before returning to the store, and when I finally did go there, he met me with a hurt smile. "Here it is. It has been waiting for you for two weeks. Why didn't you come in before?"

Building and adapting an ecological house of adobe to suit my needs took years of time and patience . . . in fact, in 1980 I moved into what I now realize was an incomplete shell, and even some of that shell had to be altered and rebuilt. There is no main water supply to the house. All the water that there is, is captured in a large tank during the rainy season, and woebetide anyone who even leaves the tap dripping, let alone open, for more than a few seconds. Hot water to the kitchen is nonexistent, since the solar heater was placed over the guest bathroom, which, though mostly unused receives a plentiful supply of hot water, while the kitchen is at the end of a lukewarm line. So we have to compromise and heat a zinc tub full of water covered with plastic in the sun to wash the dishes. The three main burners of the large masonry hacienda-type stove were, until recently—and for most of the cooking for this book—optimistically connected to the methane gas supply from the digester under the cow shed. The cows do their part magnificently, but the pressure, design, or something is wrong, so no gas.

For the first two and a half years of living in my house I had no refrigerator and no car to go and get last-minute supplies, and to make things worse, Zita the cat filled herself up during the daytime with forbidden fish from the aquiculture tank and slept at night while the mice were at play. It was not easy, and I thought longingly of the places where I had test-cooked some of these recipes: Peter Kump's compact and alphabetically ordered kitchen in New York, or Jerrie Strom's magnificent array of stoves, pots, and counters, with a pair of efficient Mexican hands along with it all to make the dirty dishes disappear as fast as they were used.

I did have a small electric oven, but an erratic supply of electricity because the bad storms that year kept hitting our power line—just at the time, of course, when there was hardly a breath of wind and my air generator was sluggish.

"How lucky you are to lead such a peaceful life in the country!" (when I am not working and touring in the United States, of course) is a general comment from unsuspecting friends and acquaintances. I usually nod in agreement because it is easier to agree than to go into all the reasons why it isn't.

For instance, I am just beating up the egg whites when neighbor Don Zenón yells from the gate, which is a good hundred yards downhill—it is the only way of communicating because he and my large dog, Guardian, do not get along. I have to go down and find out what he wants. It turns out to be a contribution to the local fiesta. I give him all the reasons why I don't approve of the debauchery and filth that go along with it, and ten minutes later he leaves and I find that I have agreed to contribute a considerable amount of men's clothing to put on top of the greasy pole that the young bloods will attempt to climb. Back in the kitchen once more, I realize to my horror that here I am contributing generously to the *machos* of the village—not one of the girls I could think of would be caught dead climbing up a greasy pole. Too late! He has gone, and the eggs have fallen flat beyond resurrection.

On another occasion the dough for the hot cross buns had just risen to perfection for baking when Elisorio, the general factotum around my place, came to report that the male goat was frothing at the mouth and running around in circles. This obviously required immediate action, so off I went—to this day there is dried dough on the steering wheel—leaving my beautifully risen buns to their own devices.

Interruptions of this sort prompted me to change my cooking time to the late afternoon and evening, when everyone had gone home and it was relatively quiet. But I hadn't taken into account that the afternoon storms during the rainy season might cause a cut in the electricity. They always came in from the east, however, and I could see them from my kitchen window. Of course, one day I was fooled. The coffee sponge had had twelve minutes in the oven when the lights went out—a storm had blown in unseen from the north. I watched anxiously with a flashlight as the cake that had risen to the top of the pan held . . . I prayed to the tenth muse . . . and it held there serenely until the lightning passed and the oven whirred into life again.

Later that week I made the mistake of putting the newly candied peel out in the sun to dry. About an hour later I heard a shout and smelled smoke. There were Elisorio and his son fanning a small bonfire into life. The bees had swarmed in their thousands all over the peel and he was trying to convince them to go back to their hives.

One night, I forget what I was making, but I had all the appliances going full blast when everything went dark, including the light over the front door by the fuse box. I found a new fuse easily enough, and with a small flashlight between my teeth I pulled the lever down to disconnect the incoming current. Just in time the warning of Marcemio, Elisorio's oldest son, flashed into my mind: "But that still doesn't disconnect the current from the windmill," he had told me. Obviously what I needed was a rubber glove, so I went upstairs to find one. I stopped dead in my tracks, for there above my desk was the largest deadly scorpion I had ever seen. The fuse was forgotten. Where was the spray?—the only nonecological permitted in the house, because I refuse to admit fleas and scorpions into my ecological cycle. I went down to the kitchen and groped around for the spray. Of course the scorpion had gone when I got back, but I doused the area thoroughly anyway. Now for the rubber glove, I had almost forgotten it. Down I went again and tugged and tugged at the fuse capsule, which refused to budge, and since I believe in signs, I gave up. This obviously was not my night to cook. I left the mess of doughs, pots and pans, and greasy spoons and went off to bed.

THE MAKING OF A PALATE

A corn tortilla eaten the moment it comes off an earthenware comal set over a wood fire can be ambrosial . . . the Mexican peasant is as exigent about how his corn is prepared for that tortilla as any Frenchman is about his finest soufflé.

I suppose you could say that my sister and I were brought up in a middle-class home—not clearly upper or lower, but somewhere in between—on the outskirts of London. There was never much money around for luxuries, but because my mother was so versatile in the kitchen, despite her full-time teaching job, we ate extremely well from a variety of foods of such good quality that it would be difficult to match them today. I was her biggest fan and always looked forward to her meals: she made even liver and bacon seem like a very special dish, and her braised stuffed veal breast would earn a cordon bleu in my book. Occasionally she would give us money to buy what we fancied for supper—I suppose we were about ten and eleven then—and we would invariably come back with a rich, gloriously unpasteurized Camembert cheese and a hunk of liver sausage.

I remember we used to go to Sainsbury's in Edgware, where the foods fascinated us. The walls were of gleaming white tile and on each side was a spotless and orderly counter—one with a display of countless cuts of bacon, "green" (salted) or well-smoked, from Denmark or England mostly, next to the cold meats and pies; on the other, huge slabs of butter from Ireland, New Zealand, Denmark, Normandy, and different parts of Britain. I can still smell that freshly churned butter as it was hewn off from the main slabs with ridged wooden pats that were constantly dipped into cold water, and the rough shape was slapped deftly into a small, even block—you could buy the smallest amount. At the end of the store was a display of gunnysacks full of different types of sugar from all over "the Empire": Barbados, a soft brown; Demerara, fine brown crystals; "pieces," another lumpy brown; castor, a fine granulated; and loaf sugar for tea. We always had jars of several sugars in the house, each for a different recipe.

I also remember those afternoons when a neighbor's maid would look after me. She knew my passion only too well, and when we returned from a walk with the dog she always brought back a bag of six warm, dark brown, yeasty doughnuts coated with granulated sugar. The best part of eating them was getting to the middle and that luscious pocket of real raspberry jam. I would eat five out of the six and thought I had gone to heaven.

At weekends we always had visitors to tea. It seemed that we were forever cutting bread and butter. It was often an exasperating business when the bread was too new and that carefully cut slice would collapse as soon as you cut through to the bottom crust, or the butter was not soft enough to spread evenly. I never liked all these visitors because it disturbed my reading—I was an avid reader in those days and would work my way through the shelves of the library: cowboy stories, romantic novels, the Brontës, Dickens, Thackeray; whatever the book might be, it was unkindly interrupted by that seemingly endless round of teas.

It was at about that time that I won a scholarship to a fancy girls' school in Hampstead. My rich godmother helped out and bought my uniform for me. I wish I had made more of my time there. I was shy and giggly and must have been an unbearably irritating student. But I did have my bright moments, topping all in French and Latin, as well as being quite a good painter. While the rest of the curriculum fell on deaf ears, I did attend and worked hard in the cooking class. We had a wonderfully equipped kitchen, and it was there that I learned—and have never forgotten—the basic principles of pastry making. I had always watched Mother, who was an accomplished pastry maker, making short crust, flaky, puff, and occasionally choux pastry, but that experience was reinforced in the school kitchen: cold ingredients—and there were no refrigerators then—light handling, and always using a metal implement to stir. I once nearly failed my cooking exam when I was caught using a wooden spoon to mix the pastry dough. We learned all sorts of uninteresting things, too, like making tapioca pudding—my bête noire with all those glutinous lumps—white sauce for vegetables, milk puddings, and the like. But they all came in useful because throughout our growing years we were expected to cook at home: it was part of growing up.

The latter years of World War II were spent in the Forestry Corps of the Land Army, which took me to South Wales and Wiltshire, and it was then that I began to appreciate the freshness of local country foods: freshly baked breads from peat-fired brick ovens, home-cured hams and local cheeses with strong cider for harvest suppers, as well as trout and salmon straight out of the small rushing rivers a stone's throw from our door. After some postwar years in Dumfriesshire, Scotland, and London, where I first started to cook with more interest, I began to spend vacations abroad on a shoestring budget. I remember I was fascinated by long, leisurely meals in restaurants facing out onto Las Ramblas in Barcelona; my first beef tartare and fondue in an Austrian skiing village—although these are not typically Austrian; a "seafood holiday" around the coasts of Normandy and Brittany before France became so chic to travel in; Provençal food in the South of France: they were new and great gastronomic adventures to me.

I then took myself off to Canada, where eating was a revelation after the stringent rationing of wartime and postwar Britain. For the first time I ate honest, ethnic peasant foods and crusty bread and made use of produce from Mennonite farms. From there I made my first trip around the United States in the fifties. I ate my first so-called Mexican food and drank my first margarita in Los Angeles' Olvera Street—I thought more kindly of it then than now. I dined at Antoine's and Galatoire's in their heyday with the president of the Vieux Carré Commission of New Orleans, and later ate my first West Coast salmon in Vancouver. It was darker in color than I was used to, but meaty and delicious. Everything was new and exciting except for tea in Boston: I arrived there with my head full of images of the Boston Tea Party, longing for a good cup of tea, only to be served with what I was later to know as standard American tea—a slender tea bag hanging limply from a thick mug of lukewarm water.

My wanderings then took me to the Caribbean to attend the first Casals Festival in Puerto Rico, where I lived with a local family and had a chance of trying the native dishes at their best. After a brief stopover in the Dominican Republic—which was then still under the subduing heel of Trujillo—I landed in Haiti. One of the first people I met there was Paul Kennedy. He was a foreign correspondent for *The New York Times* based in Mexico City. We fell in love, and I needed no second invitation to join him there.

I was overwhelmed when I first visited the Mexican markets—chilies of all shapes and sizes, wild greens and herbs I had never encountered before, and a profusion of tropical fruits of all hues. It was then that I first began to appreciate that ever present and haunting smell of fresh tortillas as they puffed up on the comal, and tasted my first spongy white tamales wrapped in corn husks as they were drawn from huge improvised steamers at the entranceway of the market. The bakeries, too, were a revelation with their crusty rolls *(bolillos)* and fifty or more varieties of sweet yeast breads that were constantly being replenished fresh from the oven throughout the day.

It was in Mexico that I began to develop new tastes, completely different from any I had experienced before: the piquancy and surprising flavors of the different chilies; the muskiness of the herbs; the sweet density of the tropical fruits, both delicate in flavor and fascinating in texture. No two were alike. Yes, it was the textures above all that stood out, and then the contrasts of flavors that enhanced one another: spices and charred chilies with soused fish, onion wilted in bitter orange juice with musky oregano, the crunch of *salsa mexicana* (finely chopped white onion, green chilies, coriander, and tomato) with raw seafood, pigs' feet with crisp lightly pickled vegetables, and the shredded meats in all the exciting chili sauces. They immediately became a passion and in no time at all joined the ranks of my personal "soul food."

I am constantly asked how to train one's palate. It would be presumptuous of me to set down any hard-and-fast rules. I can only suggest that one should perhaps start with, for instance, a salad dressing, taking time to taste several different oils, vinegars, mustards, and so on. Mix various blends of them and then try to decide how successfully they complement each other and the salad greens you are going to use. And this is just one simple example.

My manuscript for this book came back marked: "Feet, tongue, noses, ears . . . explain your passion for these!" "Textures, flavors, something different," I responded. After all, how dull to be always eating chicken breast and fillet of beef. Cut a tomato into quarters and another into slices and try both . . . there is a difference in flavor, because of the texture, subtle though it may be. Mashed potatoes are anathema to me; riced potatoes are something else again. For preference I would choose julienned or sliced potatoes, with the skins on, of course, or better still, a good baked potato with a crusty skin—no foil, thank you! Why eat that spongy, tasteless rice—precooked, converted, predigested, whatever— when for a quarter of an hour more you could have a good chewy plate of rice, white or brown? There are many more instances like these.

Brillat-Savarin devotes several pages of *La Physiologie du Goût* (translated as *The Philosopher in the Kitchen*) to the "Analysis of the Sensation of Taste"; here he is on the process of tasting:

> *A man who eats a peach, for example, is first of all agreeably impressed by the smell emanating from it; he puts it into his mouth and experiences a sensation of freshness and acidity, which incites him to continue; but it is not until the moment when he swallows and the mouthful passes beneath the nasal channel, that the perfume is revealed to him, completing the sensation that every peach should cause. And finally, it is only after he has swallowed that he passes judgment on the experience, and says to himself, "That was delicious".*

I thought of that passage this past summer in Italy. On a bus trip up to a small hillside vineyard the road was lined with cherry trees laden with rich, red bunches of cherries. I could not get down from the bus fast enough and with unseemly haste crammed my mouth full of them. The sensation of biting through those taut skins into the juicy flesh beyond was as sensual an experience as any I could remember.

EQUIPMENT I SIMPLY CANNOT DO WITHOUT

> *Never before in history have more people had more kitchens, more equipment, more ingredients to cook with and more time to cook than the average American today . . . so why not relax and try a few recipes that span over four days.*

Cooks in the United States are without doubt the most catered to in the whole world—if they have the cash. They have a bewildering choice of machines, gadgets, pots, dishes, and knives—most of which will never be sharpened—to choose from. Much is of excellent quality and design, while there is a good share of junk, too—my pet aversions are that thin enameled ware in absurd shapes painted with flowers that resemble camouflaged chamber pots, and light, fancy kitchen knives—but be that as it may, the American public is very fortunate. Across the country from coast to coast there are hundreds of cookware stores, large and small, encouraging the cook to make more adventurous meals.

Three giants in the field—who should be marked as national culinary treasures, and to whom we are most indebted—are Carl Sontheimer, Chuck Williams, and Fred Bridge. The latter, proprietor of the Bridge Company, first made us aware that we should use good, serviceable kitchenware in our homes, and he and Chuck Williams, of Williams-Sonoma, above all have dedicated time and effort to bringing the best of Europe, and the United States, into the average American kitchen. Carl Sontheimer's Cuisinart machines have created a revolution in food preparation. I cannot think of anyone else who has single-handedly adapted a machine, constantly updating and modifying it, to fulfill the needs of the present-day cook. Let's take our hats off to them.

Although I live a great part of the year in rustic surroundings, with an erratic electric supply and where primitive volcanic-rock *molcajetes* and metates are my constant kitchen companions, I love new and shiny machines that work well. My first prize for design, shared with Cuisinart, would go unquestionably to Hobart for their KitchenAid mixers of whatever model. No other industrialized country has anything to touch them—England, France, and Germany to boot; only too often, other mixers are of light weight and the fancy bowl has such a broad bottom that the beaters never touch the mixture around the bottom.

A coffee/spice grinder is an absolute must. I keep one for coffee and a second for spices, sugar, *pepitas* (pumpkin seeds), sesame seeds, and the like. Forget those with an oval shape—design, not function, was the overruling factor, and the blades can't work as efficiently.

A Moulinex food mill is a must, with three different-gauged disks, but get one made entirely of metal and not colored plastic, which is not as strong.

You'll need a good, heavy blender with a glass jar—eschew those countertop devices and plastic jars—but the bottom of the jar must be detachable for easy cleaning. I'll take a Waring or Osterizer anytime.

I like heavy cast-iron frying pans of all sizes.

For heavy casseroles or Dutch ovens, I would choose Le Creuset's enameled heavy metal. The most useful sizes for my cooking needs are an oval casserole, 11½ inches long, which will take one large chicken, and a large round one, 11¼ inches in diameter.

Of course I have Mexican *cazuelas* and bean pots galore of different shapes and sizes.

No metal griddle can compare with a soapstone griddle—I have a 14½-inch circular one—for English muffins, crumpets, oatcakes, and potato scones.

When you can't find whole wheat flour of the right consistency, then grind it yourself. I have a heavy electric wheat mill that grinds with stones—alas, an unmarked brand.

The new culinary toy, an ice cream machine, is the latest comer to the kitchen, and now I wouldn't be without one. A Simac-Il Gelataio 800 fell into my hands and I love it.

A 4-quart pressure cooker, while not for everything, is indispensable for some recipes here. I have had a Presto for twenty-four years and it's still going strong.

I like lots of spatulas with wooden handles and plastic dough scrapers (I first saw one in Mexico at the baker's and they were later made available in New York by Isabelle Marique), along with a couple of paint scrapers, which serve their culinary purpose.

I like a hundred wooden spoons and stirrers with broad bases and differing lengths of handles.

Palette knives are useful in three sizes, the most useful of all being the large 10-inch blade, 1½ inches wide.

A Europiccola Pavoni 800 ml espresso machine has brought joy to my breakfast table, providing the electric current is on—and froths up the milk invitingly to go with my homegrown coffee. *(See page 202 for how to froth milk without a machine.)*

A small diet or postal scale is needed for weighing small amounts of yeast or whole spices, etc.

A good workmanlike pair of scales that gives both pounds and kilograms is essential. Do not choose one where the container keeps falling off, or one that hangs on the wall. The Mexican-made Ade Oken is minutely accurate.

If you don't have an elaborate flour mill equipped for corn, then you can very easily obtain a Mexican corn grinder that is operated by hand—it is tough work, mind you, but it does the job. This type of corn grinder is sold in leading Mexican or Latin-American grocery stores.

Apart from a normal-sized rolling pin, I often use a dowel about 12 inches long and ¾ inch in diameter for rolling out crackers, crispbreads, or cookies.

A regular household air-temperature thermometer is very useful when you are raising dough.

A large stainless-steel preserving pan is a must if you are going to cook many jams, jellies, and *ates*. In Mexico I have a series of different-sized unlined copper *cazos,* which apart from being practical are very decorative in the kitchen.

INGREDIENTS

Time, place, quality, and good company (if any) are ingredients that can add up to an eating experience equal to none.

Bread crumbs   When you want fresh or slightly stale bread crumbs for bread sauce, stuffings, or Christmas puddings, be sure to buy good, chewy bread with a thick crust and avoid the so-called French and Italian breads that disintegrate when they are the slightest bit dry. Buy a baguette from a reputable baker, a sourdough—which has still remained pretty honest bread—or even a light Russian rye with a thick crust that does not have the slightest trace of sweetness. Cut the bread open and let it get stale for a day or two in a dry place. Take out all the crumb, reserving the crust *(see below),* put the crumb into the food processor, and process until you have a fairly rough texture. One cup, loosely packed, equals approximately 2 ounces.

Toasted bread crumbs   If you need toasted bread crumbs for coating meat or fish for frying, or for sprinking over the top of a dish like Tian a la Mexicana, never buy the packaged ones, as they are far too sweet and have an unpleasant sandy texture. Use the reserved crusts of bread and bake in a slow oven—about 300° F—until a pale golden color and very crisp. You will get a much more interesting texture, and therefore flavor, if you do not grind them too fine or evenly. You can do a little at a time for a few seconds in the blender or food processor, but better still, if you have the patience, take a heavy rolling pin and crush them by hand. I usually make a larger quantity than necessary and keep them stored in an airtight container in a cool place.

Chilies   The Mexican chilies used in recipes here are:

> fresh   ***serranos, poblanos, habaneros***
> dried   ***anchos***
> canned   ***jalapeños en escabeche*** *(pickled jalapeños)*
> ***serranos en escabeche*** *(pickled serranos)*

The *chile serrano* is a small, slender, bright green chili. An average size would be about 1½ inches long and about ½ inch wide. It is used unpeeled with all its seeds.

The *chile poblano* is a large triangular chili with a shiny, undulating surface and a dark to mid-green skin. The size varies considerably depending on the season and where the peppers come from, but an average one would be about 4 inches long and 3 inches wide at the top, tapering to a pointed tip. These chilies are almost always used after they have been flame-peeled. Place the chilies straight on the flame of a gas burner (no fork-roasting nonsense, or you will be peeling chilies all day) and char them slightly all the way round—they should be blistered and browned. Immediately place them in a plastic bag and let them "sweat" for about 15 minutes. The skin should then come easily away from the flesh. Be careful not to char them too much or you will burn right through the flesh. For those of you who have electric burners, rub a little oil over the surface of the chilies and place them under a preheated broiler—about 1 inch from the heat—and keep turning them as they blister and brown. *Do not put them in the*

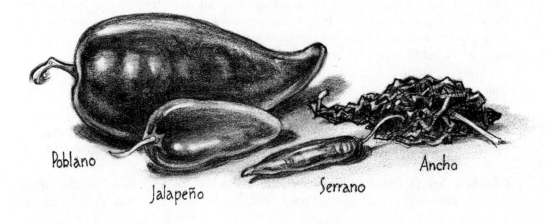

Poblano   Jalapeño   Serrano   Ancho

---

oven, as this will cook the flesh too much. If you have a charcoal fire, then put them on a grill just a couple of inches from the glowing charcoal.

The *chile habanero* is a fresh chili used in the Yucatán region of Mexico. It is reputed to be the hottest of the lot and has an unequaled fragrance. It is bright, light green when freshly picked and ripening to yellow and then orange. It is very difficult to find and in fact can only be found where there are people from Yucatán around. In the New York area the *chile congo* can be substituted, as it is substantially the same chili—the same flavor but with a more wrinkled surface. The latter is used in some parts of the Caribbean: Haiti, Jamaica, Trinidad, and possibly other islands. If not available, substitute *chile serrano* or any other fresh green chili. This is a small chili, about 1 inch in length and about ¾ inch wide.

The *chile ancho* is the *chile poblano* ripened and dried. It has a wrinkled skin and is reddish brown in color. This color darkens as the chili becomes more and more dried out. There is no satisfactory substitute for this chili.

Canned *chiles jalapeños en escabeche* are called for in the Cactus Salad and Chicken Salad II. They are canned in a light acidic brine and give a sharp, vinegary taste to the dishes in which they are used.

The *chile serrano en escabeche* is the *chile serrano* canned in a pickling brine. This is not a substitute for the fresh *chile serrano* but is specifically called for in Salpicon de Res, Estilo Zitácuaro. At a pinch, *chiles jalapeños en escabeche* could be substituted.

Cooking fats   Unless olive oil is called for, I use safflower oil as a rule, but in many cases, pie pastry, for instance, it is necessary to use some good pork lard, for which there is no real substitute if you want good results. Since I find most commercial brands inferior or filled with preservatives, I usually make my own:

2 pounds sheet lard (leaf fat)   1½ POUNDS LARD
1 cup cold water

I find it easier to cut the fat into small cubes (you can put it through a meat grinder or in a food processor, but you still have to chop it first). Cover with the cold water, mix well, and set aside overnight in the refrigerator.

Put the fat and water into 2 thick frying pans and place in the oven. Set the oven at 300° F and leave for about 1 hour. Stir well. If the fat is changing to a pale gold, then start draining off the lard. Do not drain before this because the fat will still contain some water. Continue cooking until the pieces of fat are a deep golden brown. Drain off the fat for the last time and put the pieces of fat out for the birds. The process will take about 2 hours in all.

Store in sterilized jars with tightly fitting lids in a cool place, or in the refrigerator. This lard should keep for months *if* all the water has been absorbed during the cooking time.

NOTE Your processor or meat grinder will become very messy with all that fat. Process or grind some stale bread, and most of the grease will be absorbed.

Chicken fat (schmaltz)   It seems an awful waste to throw all that good chicken fat away after all the hard work and food that has gone into the chicken—which you are paying for. Chicken fat, or schmaltz, is delicious for frying potatoes, chicken livers, bulgur, and rice, among other things.

Remove all the fat from the chicken, chop roughly and put into a bowl with water. Leave overnight in the refrigerator. The following day, drain off the water and put the fat into a small, heavy frying pan with a very little finely chopped onion. Cook over low heat until all the fat has rendered out and the fatty skin is a deep golden brown. Strain the fat and store in the refrigerator until ready to use.

Couverture chocolate   This is that fine dark chocolate used for dipping. If it is unavailable, simply use the best-quality bitter or semisweet chocolate from a reliable manufacturer.

Dates   When buying dates for the recipes in this book, try to find loose or compressed dates in a rectangular block. Do not fall for those in a fancy package where you cannot see what you are buying. I actually bought some like that out of necessity and had to throw them away, since they were overly sweet, covered with dextrose.

It may be difficult to find the compressed dates, as I discovered recently in California. If the "fluffed up" dates are used—they have to be pitted—you will need to increase the quantity, using half as much again, as in the recipe for Matrimony Cake, where 8 ounces is increased to 12.

Dried fruit   The British are inordinately fond of cakes, puddings, and breads crammed with dried fruits: raisins, sultanas (white raisins), currants, and, for special occasions, large seeded muscats, which are added for extra flavor. I happen to prefer the flavor of the lighter-colored Australian muscats, which have a more distinct flavor than the darker Californian variety.

Flour   For all the bread recipes I stipulate *high-gluten flour, or bread flour,* which is much more readily available now in almost all parts of the United States. If however, like me, you find supplies difficult to get, then you may find it easier to buy *gluten flour,* which is a gluten concentrate. Although the manufacturer advises that for each pound of flour ¼ cup should be replaced by ¼ cup gluten flour, I increase this amount to ⅓ cup when I am making Crumpets and English Muffins. This method also has the advantage that you can control the amount you use, which is particularly useful when you are working with whole wheat flour, which has a low gluten content.

A whole treatise could be written—and indeed has been written, by Elizabeth David in her *English Bread and Yeast Cookery*—about *whole wheat flour.* It varies so enormously that you will need to experiment with those available—unless you can grind your own—until you get satisfactory results. The recipes given here will serve as a guide. I steer clear of whole wheat "pastry flour" simply because I do not like pastry made with it. It is very finely ground and therefore unsuitable for bread making. I have found two excellent brands of unbolted (unsifted or coarse), stone-ground whole wheat flour in my travels around the country. They are:

Old Stone Mill, put out by Balanced Foods, Inc., North Bergen, N.J. 07047, and Harrington's Hodgson Mill Enterprises, Gainesville, Mo. 65650.

Herbs If you do not have fresh herbs available, then always look for the best whole-leaf dried herbs, never powdered. Throw out of the kitchen dried coriander, basil, or chervil because they have lost the essential oils that make them so aromatic. *Epazote,* too, should be used only fresh.

Mushrooms During the rainy season in Mexico I can get a plentiful supply of many types of fresh wild mushrooms. I always dry a quantity of *cèpes* and *morilles*—thin slices of cepes and whole morels. When I want to use them I barely cover them with water—⅓ cup mushrooms to ⅓ cup water—and simmer for 5 minutes, then let them soak for a further 10 minutes or so, not too long or they will lose their flavor in the water. Drain them, reserving the water in which they were soaked, which has a lot of concentrated flavor. Strain the water through a paper filter or two layers of fine cheesecloth, to catch any tiny particle of dirt that was adhering to the mushrooms, and use it for sauces, or in the same dish in which the mushrooms are included.

Nuts Anytime I am cooking with nuts, I always toast them first, lightly, to bring out the flavor.

Onions For any Mexican or Mexican-type recipes, I always use the large white onions from California, which are sharper than the brown ones. The latter are too sweet for Mexican dishes.

Salt I always use sea salt in cooking at home or in my classes. I usually like to buy the large or medium crystals and grind them finer, when necessary, in the coffee/spice grinder.

Seville oranges Seville oranges can be bought in small quantities the year round in Latin-American groceries, where they are called *naranjas agrias.* At the height of their season, in January and February, Seville oranges can be ordered for making marmalade, etc., from leading fruit stores, such as Balducci's in New York.

I have come across the odd tree, virtually neglected, in Florida and southern Texas, while in California they are to be found in the park of the state capital, Sacramento, and lining the streets and campuses of Claremont and Pomona. In Arizona there is a sour orange tree, that is used as root stock for grafting, but while the fruit is sour, it does not have the wonderfully complex flavor of the true Seville orange.

Spices   Wherever possible, buy whole spices and grind them yourself as needed. Or grind a larger quantity and keep in airtight bottles in a cool, dark place.

Sugar   For some English recipes I like to use *Demerara,* fine brown sugar crystals, which gives a slight texture to cookies, etc. The nearest equivalent to this sugar is labeled *turbinado* and is sold in health food stores. Failing that, use light or dark brown soft sugar, but on no account get Brownulated, which always seems to me to be so unappetizing and unreal. One cup of tightly packed brown sugar equals about 6½ ounces.

  Confectioners' sugar, or icing sugar, as it is called in England, varies according to the different proportions of cornstarch added. This has caused some trouble in translating a recipe such as Viennese Fingers, in both the United States and Mexico. I now prefer to grind my own confectioners' sugar. Granulated sugar can quickly be ground down to a powder in the coffee/spice grinder.

Tortillas   I like to garnish soups with small squares of fried tortillas, as is customary in Mexico. For this you need corn tortillas of very good quality— mealy, whitish in color, and not tasting of an overdose of the lime with which the corn is softened. Cut the tortillas into small squares and allow them to dry off overnight. Fry in hot safflower oil until a deep golden brown and drain on paper towels. Or, if you are on a diet, after drying them, toast them until crisp on a lightly greased baking sheet in the oven at 350° F for about 20 minutes, depending on thickness. (Beware of a tortilla that is too thin; it will have a certain amount of wheat flour in it and is not the real thing.)

Yeast   I much prefer to use cake rather than dried yeast; it is now readily available in the "cold" case in supermarkets. If you can obtain only the granular, or dried, yeast, then substitute ½ ounce dried yeast for 1 ounce fresh.

APPETIZERS

How often have you been faced with a complicated menu when eating out and wished you could just make a meal of several delectable appetizers and forget about the main course? I often do just that, as long as the maître d' will let me get away with it. I feel the same when I am planning a special menu. I can think of lots of tantalizing appetizers and soups that I love to prepare, but the main course is another matter entirely. There are some people, of course, who still expect appetizers to be those silly canapés and dips, which have been all but abolished from my simplified repertoire of entertaining food.

Of course, I could eat smoked salmon and caviar every day for quite a long time, or the delicate flesh of the Adriatic spider crab, which I tried for the first time this summer. It was simply dressed with a fruity olive oil and lemon juice. When in England I like to feast on large prawns, or little brown shrimps, crab, and scallops, and when I am in New York I like to start a meal with those unequaled littleneck or cherrystone clams as well as crisp, metallic-tasting oysters—the fat baggy ones I find unpalatable—with just a touch of lemon and black pepper. None of that unspeakable cocktail sauce or horseradish, thank you! It was in Peru that I had the best scallops on the half shell that I have ever eaten—the coral-colored roe was still attached—and they had been broiled very briefly with a little butter and Sardo, a Parmesan-like cheese.

Give me a good fish terrine, a warm *boudin blanc,* a plate of well-made charcuterie, or quenelles, and my meal is made. But those represent the more exotic side of my life and tastes. Much of the year I live in rural Mexico, and apart from a few delicacies—you probably consider them staples—that I hoard for special occasions (good fruity olive oil, Parmesan cheese, canned truffles, and wrinkled black olives) I make satisfying *antojitos* with the finest corn masa prepared by Elisorio's wife and fill them with seasonal foods: quesadillas filled with stewed squash blossoms, corn fungus, wild mushrooms cooked with chili and *epazote,* or *sopes* and *cazuelitas* topped with the superb spicy local chorizo. When the avocados are ripe in the orchard I make a guacamole and serve it with hot, flabby blue or deep red corn tortillas. On the rare occasions that I can find fresh enough seafood, I mix shrimps, crabs, or clams with fresh tomatoes, chilies, coriander, and lime juice, *a la marinera.* I can get *charalitos* (very small fish) from nearby lakes and fry them crisp or make a "caviar" from carp roe. But many of these recipes have already appeared in my earlier books.

In my town, pork is killed locally and very fresh, so I can make headcheese, pickled pigs' feet, and pork and liver terrine for the colder days.

Cazuelitas (Little Cazuelas⋆)

This is a popular "snack" that is prepared in the northeastern part of Mexico but little known elsewhere. The recipe was given to me by a dear friend and wonderful cook, Berta G. de Morales Doria, who is a native of Nuevo León. *Cazuelitas* are served hot from the pan along with Mexican rice (which is traditionally served alone as a pasta course in Mexico). They are fattening, I must admit, not so much because of what goes into them but because you cannot stop at one or two—after four you might consider it.

I prefer *cazuelitas* that are filled with chorizo, but they can also be filled with beans, or zucchini squash cooked with tomato. For the Chihuahua cheese you could substitute a good-quality medium Cheddar, but the chorizo presents a problem. Good Mexican-type chorizo is hard to come by, and only in Chicago have I found some that is authentic. Shun like the plague that ultra-red chorizo in a plastic casing: it dissolves like a meat stew that has been overseasoned with the wrong condiments. The *cazuelitas* will certainly be more delicious if made with real tortilla masa from the tortilla factory (providing it isn't too yellow), but if not, you will have to use ordinary *masa harina,* adding water to make the dough in the usual way.

filling

    ½ pound chorizos
    ⅓ cup finely grated cheese, for garnish

dough

    1 cup (about 10 ounces) tortilla dough
    2 small potatoes cooked with their skins on (about 4 ounces)
    ¼ cup grated cheese (Chihuahua in Mexico, medium Cheddar in the U.S.)
    Sea salt to taste
    Lard for frying

Strip the skin off the chorizos, crumble, and fry until well cooked. Do not have the flame too high, as the ground dried chilies in them burn very easily.

Put the tortilla dough in a bowl. Crush the potatoes roughly—I personally do not peel them—and add them with the ¼ cup cheese and the salt to the tortilla dough. Mix the ingredients together well and do not knead too much, as the dough should be lumpy. If it seems dry and crumbly, then add a little water. The dough should be pliable, as if you were making tortillas. Take a piece of the dough and roll it into a ball about 1¼ inches across. Press the center in with the thumbs to form a well and continue to press, thinning the dough out around the sides to form a small cup shape that is slightly flared at the top.

Heat the lard in a frying pan—it should be about ½ inch deep—and fry the *cazuelitas* well over high heat, flipping a little of the hot lard into the center well. They should be slightly golden on the outside and doughy inside. Fill each one with some of the crumbled chorizo, sprinkle them with the ⅓ cup cheese, and serve immediately. *Cazuelitas* do not take kindly to sitting around or reheating—this is pan-to-mouth food.

⋆Cazuelas *are round, glazed earthenware cooking pots.*

Mushrooms in Oil

For about four months of the year, during the rainy season, wild mushrooms of many different types abound in the markets of central Mexico. But when there are only the blander, cultivated ones around, this is one of my favorite ways of preparing them. The recipe was given to me by Lola Thiel. I met Olof and Lola on a cargo ship between Antwerp and Veracruz when I was going to Mexico to rejoin Paul in 1957, and they became close friends of ours. Lola had a wonderful touch with food, and I shall always remember the superb meals we ate in the blue-and-white Swedish dining room of their house in Cuernavaca.

    1 pound mushrooms
    ⅓ cup oil, half olive and half safflower
    1 teaspoon sweet paprika
    2 cloves garlic, peeled and sliced
    2 scallions, finely chopped, with the tender green parts of the leaves
        Sea salt and freshly ground black pepper to taste
        Pinch of sugar
    3 tablespoons finely chopped parsley
    2 teaspoons roughly chopped fresh basil or dill

Wipe the mushrooms with a damp cloth—put into water only if they are sandy. Trim off the tough ends of the stems. If the mushrooms are small, cut them into quarters; if not, then into thick slices. Heat the oils in a wide, heavy pan. Add all the ingredients except the parsley and basil. Cover the pan and cook over medium heat for about 35 minutes. Remove the lid, adjust the seasoning, add the fresh herbs, and cook for a further 10 minutes over a slightly higher flame. Serve hot or cold as an appetizer.

Chinese Chicken Liver and Gizzard Hors d'Oeuvre

If you cook chicken regularly, you may suddenly find you have a freezer full of messy little bags with livers and gizzards in them. No? Well, if you are a Chinese cook and have the right spices, go out and buy a package of livers and gizzards and make this unusual, tasty, and economical snack.

When I first went to Mexico and married Paul, I began to take cooking very seriously—we both put on quite a lot of weight. I began collecting recipes from anyone who would give me a new and interesting one. Among our acquaintances were a couple who were friendly with the former Nationalist China air force general Peter Mao, who was alleged to have absconded with several million dollars earmarked to buy airplanes for Nationalist China. He was imprisoned in Mexico City's notorious Lecumberri penitentiary for several months. He told us that most of all he missed the sort of good food he remembers his mother used to prepare when he was young. He became so hungry for it that he decided to teach himself how to cook and had a small kitchen set up in his prison quarters. There he started to re-create the flavors and textures of the dishes he remembered so vividly.

After he was released he would often cook Chinese food for his friends. Paul and I were invited to one of these parties, and our host let me go into the kitchen while he was preparing the dishes. I wrote the recipes down at the time in a sort of kitchen shorthand. I remember I often used to cook them, but with the lapse of time my notes were not that clear. My friend Jerrie Strom, who is a most accomplished Chinese cook and teacher, reconstructed them for me.

Political discussions on those evenings were long and heated, but when I heard Paul's booming voice from the far end of the room saying, "Come on now, Peter, tell us, just what did happen to those millions?" I knew it was time to leave.

½ **pound chicken gizzards**
½ **pound chicken livers**
 1 **tablespoon light soy sauce**
 1 **tablespoon dry sherry**
 1 **teaspoon sugar**
 2 **slices peeled fresh ginger, the size of a quarter**
⅛ **teaspoon five-fragrance powder**
 1 **small whole scallion, cut into 3 pieces**
   Cornstarch for coating
 2 **cups vegetable oil**
   Roasted pepper-salt *(see note at end of recipe)*

Remove the fatty tissue from the outside of the gizzards and the tough inner skin; rinse well. Score the rounded sides of the gizzards in a diamond pattern, cutting half through the flesh.

Remove any connective tissue and patches of bile from the chicken livers; rinse, and cut into halves.

Put the chicken livers and gizzards in a small saucepan, add the seasonings (next 6 ingredients) and cover with boiling water. Bring the water up to a boil again, lower the flame, cover the pan, and simmer for 5 minutes.

Remove the pan from the heat and set aside until the water cools to room temperature. Drain and roll each piece in the cornstarch.

Heat a wok or deep frying pan; when hot, add the oil and bring it up to a temperature of 375° F (when a scallion thrown into the oil foams immediately, the oil is the right temperature).

Shake off any excess cornstarch from the livers and gizzards and deep-fry them for about 2 minutes, or until crisp, stirring constantly. Remove from the oil with a slotted spoon or strainer and drain on paper towels. Sprinkle with the pepper-salt and serve either hot or at room temperature.

NOTE *To make your own roasted pepper-salt* For every 3 tablespoons table salt use 1 teaspoon Szechwan peppercorns. Heat a small skillet. Add the peppercorns and cover with the salt. Keep the heat very low for about 5 minutes and stir until the salt begins to brown. Turn off the heat, cool, and crush or grind the salt and pepper together. Store in an airtight jar.

Romanian Eggplant Spread

1½ CUPS

When I first came to live with Paul in Mexico City in 1957, we moved into a simple, bright apartment a stone's throw from Chapultepec Park. "It had something of a Mediterranean feel about it," remarked one of his colleagues at *The New York Times*. It was barely furnished because neither of us had much money in those days, but the park made up for it. The abundant ash trees were always glossy in the sun—in presmog days—and they brought a constant breeze in through the door and windows of the terrace. It was in that apartment that I started to cook seriously in Mexico. Luz, our part-time maid, helped me with the Mexican part of it, Elizabeth David's books were my bibles for French and Italian food; while Inge Lotwin, my neighbor across the hall, taught me all I know about corning beef, dill pickles, and, among other things, this Romanian eggplant dip or spread.

I welcome this recipe, plain as it is, because there is nothing to disguise the delicious smoky eggplant flavor. Inge insists that a vegetable oil, not olive oil, was used in Romania.

1 **large eggplant (about 1½ pounds)**
2 **tablespoons vegetable oil**
1 **tablespoon finely chopped onion**
   Sea salt to taste

Place the whole eggplant over the open flame of a gas burner or a charcoal fire. When it is well charred on one side, turn it over and continue charring until it is mushy right through. Make 3 vertical slashes in the skin and cut through to the center from stalk to tip. Set the eggplant in a sloping position for about 15 minutes so that the bitter brown juice seeps out.

Scrape the flesh from the charred skin and discard about half of the seeds attached to the fleshy center of the eggplant. Discard the skin. Chop the flesh fine until it is almost reduced to a pulp—but it must have texture and not be too smooth—and stir in the rest of the ingredients. Set aside to season for about ½ hour and serve at room temperature with melba toast or crackers. May be served also as part of a mixed hors d'oeuvre.

Serbian Vegetable Caviar (Srpski Ajvar)

A few years after my arrival in Mexico, Morris Rosenberg was transferred there as bureau chief for the Associated Press, and he and Lucie became my closest friends. Lucie Rosenberg was born in Yugoslavia of wealthy parents and, apart from having an innate understanding of it, she has an encyclopedic knowledge of European food. She and her Yugoslav friends, Leah and Sofia in particular, taught me a lot about food and cooking and I have always been grateful to them. They would laughingly remind Lucie of their school days when she would carry in her lunch box thick slices of bread stuffed with foie gras, which she lost no time in exchanging· for a peanut butter sandwich.

This is a recipe from Lucie, or rather her father, who was a fastidious eater. When I made it for him to critique, he told me that it was very important that the peppers and eggplant should have a charred or smoky flavor—this is an interesting quality that is required in some Mexican regional food.

>   2 green peppers
>   1 red pepper
>   1 eggplant (about 1 pound)
>   2 cloves garlic, peeled and mashed
>   2–4 tablespoons vegetable oil
>   Sea salt to taste
>   15 turns of the pepper mill

Place the peppers straight on the flame of a gas burner or a charcoal fire. When they are well charred, turn and continue charring until they are blistered and brown all over. Place in a plastic bag and set aside for about 15 minutes. The skin can then be easily slipped off the flesh. Cut away the stalk end, slit the peppers open vertically, and remove the seeds. Set aside.

Place the unpeeled eggplant straight on the flame of the gas burner (or charcoal), and when it is lightly charred, turn and continue charring all around, by which time the flesh should be cooked and soft. Make 3 vertical slashes from stalk to tip, and leave the eggplant in a sloping position for about 15 minutes so that the brown, acrid juice can drain out. At the end of this period, remove the stalk and calyx and scrape the flesh and seeds away from the skin. Discard the skin.

Chop or mash all the vegetables together and stir in the rest of the ingredients. (If you use the food processor, which is not advisable, take care not to make a puree out of the mixture; there should be some texture to it.) I prefer to leave it to season overnight in the refrigerator; in fact, it improves daily. Serve at room temperature with melba toast or crackers. May be served also as part of a mixed hors d'oeuvre.

Taramasalata, English Style

I much prefer taramasalata made with the very English smoked cod's roe. The English may be scorned for many aspects of their gastronomy, but it would be hard to find fault with the superbly smoked haddock, herring (for kippers and bloaters), salmon, and cod's roe that used to be a part of our everyday diet when we were growing up. Mind you, there are now lots of bad imitations. For instance, purist that I am (over some things, not all, I beg to add), I was shocked to see on a recent visit to London a reddish-colored—instead of deep orange—so-called smoked cod's roe that had nothing to do with the real thing either in flavor or in texture. . . . "Off with their heads!" said the Queen.

Smoked cod's roe was a winter treat, and we would spread it on very thin toast or make very buttery sandwiches with it. This recipe comes from my sister, Jean Southwood, who for many years was catering officer at the Royal College of Art and distinguished herself not only for her excellent dinner parties, but for keeping a very personal touch in her institutional food.

> ½ pound cod's roe*
> 1 clove garlic, peeled
> ¼–⅓ cup good fruity olive oil
> Lemon juice to taste
> Freshly ground black pepper

Remove the skin from the cod's roe and scrape any remaining scraps from it. Discard the skin. Pound the roe in a mortar together with the garlic, gradually working in the olive oil (as if you were making mayonnaise). When the oil has all been incorporated, add the lemon juice and plenty of freshly ground black pepper. Serve at room temperature.

If you do not use it all up at once, then seal with melted butter and keep in the freezer compartment.

NOTE You could use the food processor for this, but the texture would not be the same; it would be too smooth, while the mortar-made version has a certain interesting graininess to the roe.

Petrossian makes a particularly good product, which is widely available in gourmet shops.

Terrine de Campagne

There are perhaps a handful of books that I have used constantly over the years, and one of them is Elizabeth David's *French Provincial Cooking*. It was she, unwittingly, who really started my serious cooking, and I know of no other writer who, in a few eloquent words, can so conjure up the taste, texture, and aroma of an unknown dish.

While this recipe is from *French Provincial Cooking,* I have, rather presumptuously, made a few minor changes.

Any terrine or pâté is far better if left to ripen for several days, so I suggest you start putting this together at least 5 days before you want to serve it.

¾ pound unsalted sheet lard (leaf fat) or other pork fat
½ pound pork liver
1 pound pork belly (unsalted)
1 pound lean stewing veal
15 black peppercorns, roughly crushed
10 juniper berries, crushed
1 clove garlic, peeled and crushed
A rounded ¼ teaspoon powdered mace
½ cup dry white wine
3 tablespoons brandy
2½ teaspoons ground sea salt, or to taste
Pork lard as necessary for sealing

Cut up one third of the pork fat into small, irregular pieces. Blanch in boiling water for 2 minutes and set aside to drain. Cut the remaining fat into thin strips to cover the top of the terrine, and set aside.

Cut up the pork liver, belly, and veal roughly and pass through the medium disk of the meat grinder. (I prefer not to use the food processor for this. The KitchenAid attachment has a disk with ³⁄₁₆-inch holes that is perfect for this recipe.) Mix together all the ingredients except the thinly sliced pork fat and the lard for sealing. Cover the bowl and refrigerate overnight.

Preheat the oven to 325° F. Place a water bath on the middle rack of the oven with enough hot water to come halfway up the sides of a 2-quart mold or terrine. (A roasting pan makes a good water bath.)

Stir the meat mixture well and transfer to the mold. Cover the top completely with the reserved strips of fat and bake until the meat shrinks away from the sides of the mold and the juices are a pinkish brown, about 1½ hours in a gas oven. If you have an electric oven with heating elements at the top, then reduce the heat slightly after the first ½ hour of cooking time.

Remove the terrine from oven and allow to cool. When the fat that has collected around the edges and on top of the meat has just congealed but is still soft, cover the top with foil; place a heavy object on top and allow the terrine to cool off completely. Before storing in the refrigerator, smear the extra lard thickly over the top so that no air can penetrate and store for at least 4 days before using.

If you are not using the entire terrine at once, smear the exposed part with more lard so that it will retain its pink hue and not turn grey. It should keep safely for at least 2 weeks and even longer in cold weather.

Be sure to serve the terrine at room temperature—the common mistake is to serve it too cold—with toast points or crusty French bread and cornichons.

NOTE Do not attempt to cook the terrine in a convection oven. Anything that has such a dense texture, or cooks in a water bath, does not cook through to the center—or if it does, then the outside is overdone and dry.

Chicken Liver Pâté

Whichever way you slice it, this *is* fancy; it is fussy to make but well worthwhile—it is by far the best chicken liver pâté I have ever eaten. Of course, it is better still if you are lucky enough to find some goose or even duck livers. If you have to settle for chicken livers, try and find those that are a golden brown, rather than a dark reddish brown color. If you do not want to splurge on a whole truffle, then try and get a minute can of truffle shavings—one of the things I always bring back from France.

This is my interpretation of a recipe I have cooked over the years from a delicious little English cookbook called *Definitely Different*. It was published by the *Daily Telegraph*—no date on it, but given to me by my mother in 1956.

START FIVE DAYS AHEAD

1¼ pounds goose, duck, or light-colored chicken livers
1 small can truffle shavings or 1 small whole truffle, thinly sliced
⅓ cup Madeira
½ teaspoon sea salt
Freshly ground black pepper
A very scant ¼ teaspoon freshly ground nutmeg
A very scant ¼ teaspoon powdered ginger
2 tablespoons brandy
1¾ pounds pork belly, unsalted
3 egg yolks
8 ounces sheet lard (leaf fat), cut into very thin strips
Chicken fat or lard (for sealing)

Put aside 3 of the largest pieces of liver. Make several small incisions in each of them and insert about half of the truffle shavings or slices. Set aside.

Put the Madeira, salt, pepper, nutmeg, and ginger in a small saucepan and simmer for about 10 seconds. Stir in the brandy and set aside.

Chop the remaining livers and the pork belly roughly and put into the container of the food processor. Grind as fine as possible. Press this mixture through a fairly fine sieve. (It is terribly hard work, so I compromise by using the colander attachment of the KitchenAid mixer, which works perfectly for this recipe. However, you will have to do a little at a time, and keep stopping the machine and scraping the debris from the sides of the container.) However hard you work at it, you will get equal amounts of debris and puree, so don't shoot for the moon. Don't throw the debris out, either: season and cook it in the oven like a meat loaf; it is delicious, and slightly chewy.

Remove any white cord adhering to the egg yolks and beat them until smooth. Stir them into the meat puree. Add the spiced Madeira and the rest of the truffle shavings and stir well. Set the mixture aside to season overnight in the refrigerator.

Preheat the oven to 350° F. Place a roasting pan on the middle rack of the oven. Have ready a 1-quart glass, china, or earthenware mold. Fill the roasting pan with enough hot water to come halfway up the sides of the mold.

Line the mold with overlapping strips of the sheet lard, reserving some for the top, and put half of the mixture into it. Place the large pieces of liver on top and cover with the remaining mixture. Cover the top with the remaining strips of lard and then with foil. Bake until the meat shrinks away from the sides of the mold but the juice is still pinkish in color, about 2 hours. Remove the mold from the water bath and set aside to cool. When the liquid fat around the edges and on top has started to congeal but not completely set, cover the top with foil and weigh down with a heavy object, leaving the pâté to cool off completely. Seal the top with chicken fat or extra lard so that no air can get in, cover with foil, and set aside in the bottom of the refrigerator for about 4 days. If you are not going to use the pâté all at once, after cutting a piece reseal the exposed surfaces with fat to retain the pink color and good flavor.

Serve with melba toast—only homemade; the commercial variety is too sweet—toast points, or crusty French bread.

NOTE Do not try to cook this in a convection oven because by the time the inside is done—it takes hours and hours—the outside will be inedible.

Chile Ancho con Queso
(Chile Ancho with Melted Cheese) 4 SERVINGS

Chile con queso, a popular dish from the northern Mexican state of Chihuahua, is usually made with a milder green fresh chili called Anaheim, which is charred and peeled before cooking. But since I am very partial to the rich flavor of the *chile ancho*—ripened and dried *poblano*—I thought I would try to use that instead and leave out the tomato called for in the original recipe.

Chile con queso should always be served as soon as the cheese has melted and preferably accompanied by a pile of hot, flabby tortillas—either corn or flour—so that each person makes his own taco.

For this recipe it is important to have fleshy, flexible chilies, in other words the latest crop to be dried. If you cannot buy loose chilies where you can select them yourself, then always feel them well through the packaging. The really dried, almost brittle ones are all right for sauces where they have to be soaked and blended but not suitable for this recipe.

If possible, choose a shallow pan or *cazuela* in which the *chile con queso* can be both cooked and served.

The best melting cheese I know—especially for the price—is a block domestic Muenster from Wisconsin that is slightly soft to the touch.

        4 large *chiles anchos*
        2 tablespoons safflower oil
        4 rounded tablespoons finely chopped white onion
   ⅔ cup milk (full cream, not low-fat)
        Sea salt to taste
        8 ounces melting cheese, cut into thin slices *(see note above)*

Remove any stalks from the chilies, slit them open, and remove seeds and veins, which should be discarded. Rinse them briefly in cold water, wiping off any dirt adhering to the outer skin. Cut into very narrow strips—about less than ¼ inch—with a pair of scissors. Set aside.

Heat the oil in a shallow pan *(see note above),* add the onion, and fry gently without browning until translucent, about 3 minutes. Add the milk and chili strips, cover the pan, and cook gently for about 5 minutes, or until the chilies are soft. Add salt to taste, taking into consideration the salt content of the cheese. Spread the cheese evenly over the chili strips and cook again, covered, over the lowest heat until the cheese has melted. See serving instructions above.

Headcheese

I never think headcheese is as appreciated as it should be. When well made, it is tangy and has all sorts of interesting textures running through it. The pork butchers make a lot of it around where I live in Michoacán. Unlike the French, they use vinegar in place of wine, and then the headcheese is molded into shape by a tightly woven soft basket that is drawn into a circular shape with drawstrings at the top and bottom.

This is Jacques Pépin's recipe. He made it for dinner one crazy weekend when he, Pierre Franey, and I happened to be spending the weekend in Craig Claiborne's house. Craig had invited me to make muffins, crumpets, and, of all things, *pozole* (pork and hominy soup) for a column he was doing for *The New York Times*. It turned out to be the hottest weekend in the history of Long Island. Jacques was just finishing a series of cooking classes in Craig's kitchen when the air-conditioning unit gave up the ghost, along with the filter mechanism on the swimming pool. I remember vividly being kept awake not only by the unbearable heat but by a neighbor's cat yowling all night. "I wonder why that cat stopped so suddenly last night?" said Craig, for he had also been kept awake by it. "Because in desperation I got up and threw a bucket of water over it," I said.

The heat continued, but the cooking had to go on—the batter for the crumpets bubbled over uncontrollably, and the muffins ballooned up. It was then time for the *pozole*. We cut the pig's head in two and I put one half of it and the corn on to cook separately. "What on earth shall we do with the other half?" someone asked. "It won't keep in this weather." "Make headcheese," I shouted, and no sooner said than done: Jacques had the other half bubbling away in the pot.

That column turned out to be one of the funniest ever, and it was only when I read it that I found out that to get that half head for the *pozole,* Craig had had to order six whole heads, and to get one tablespoon of lime for the corn, he had a sixty-pound bag sitting outside the kitchen door. To this day I don't know whatever happened to the other five heads!

> ½ **pig's head, weighing 5–6 pounds, cut into 4 pieces**
> 1½ **tablespoons sea salt, or to taste**
>   **Water to cover**
> ½ **medium onion, finely chopped**
> 2 **cloves garlic, peeled and finely chopped**
> 1 **cup dry white wine**
> 2 **tablespoons good Dijon mustard**
> 2 **heaped tablespoons roughly chopped mixed fresh herbs: basil, marjoram,**
>   **thyme, tarragon, parsley; or as a substitute if fresh not available, ½ teaspoon**
>   **dried herbs and 1 tablespoon each chopped parsley and chives**
>   **A lot of freshly ground black pepper to taste**
> 1 **rounded tablespoon green peppercorns, drained★**

Rinse the pig's head well, changing the water 3 times. Singe off any remaining coarse hairs on the pig's head. Put the pieces of head in a large saucepan, add the salt, cover with water, and cook until tender but not too soft—the meat should come away fairly easily from the bone—about 2 to 2½ hours. Drain the pieces, reserving the broth, and set aside to cool. Strain the broth, return to the saucepan, and reduce to 3 cups.

As soon as the meat is cool enough to handle, remove the eye and discard. Take all the meat (rind, tongue, brains, and ear, etc.) off the bones and chop roughly. Put the chopped meat into the reduced stock, add the onion, garlic, wine, and mustard, and cook over a fairly high flame for about 15 minutes. Add the herbs and pepper and cook for a further 5 minutes. Adjust the seasoning. Stir in the peppercorns. Pour the mixture into a 7-cup mold, cover, and refrigerate until set into a thick jellied texture.

You can eat it right away, but it is even better if allowed to ripen for another day before cutting.

Serve with cornichons and hot mustard.

★*Jacques used ⅓ cup finely chopped cornichons.*

Ensalada Trompa de Res, Estilo Chalet Suizo 6 SERVINGS

One of my favorite haunts for a well-cooked, reasonably priced meal in Mexico City is the Chalet Suizo in Calle Niza. Although it does not appear on the menu, one of their specialty dishes and my favorite light dish is *ensalada trompa de res*—beef muzzle salad. It is attractive to look at: very thinly sliced gelatinous meat in a sharp dressing with marinated onion rings. (I am sure that by this point I have lost some squeamish readers.)

Test-cooking this recipe in Zitácuaro, Michoacán, where tacos of barbecued head are a popular midmorning snack, presented quite a problem. Nobody would sell me the muzzle alone. I made two trips to the abattoir, talked to everyone who would talk to me, including Don Rogelio, who sells the barbecued-head tacos in the market: "If we cut off the muzzle the meat will fall off the rest of the head," he explained. "But you take it off anyway," I said, but saw that he was not going to give way. Don José León, a well-known gastronome around town, said he would try; Arturo at the long-distance phone booth, whose brother is a butcher, said he would try; and everyone pitched in to no avail—my search became the *cause célèbre* in the town.

When I was trying to sleep one night, the solution came to me. Our vet, Everardo, had told me that he inspected slaughterhouses in the city twice a week, and I had never seen a barbecued head in Mexico City. I spoke to his wife in their shop the next day. She looked surprised and doubtful in quick succession but said she would ask him. Two days later Mrs. Vet hailed me as I drove by: "We have your *encargo*," she said, and dragged out of the refrigerator reserved for vaccines and such a very messy-looking plastic bag. I ignored it until I got home and then held it out at arms' length to Elisorio—I could now see that it contained five little grey furry muzzles, and they were very bloody. "Do you like *trompas?*" I asked him. Hardly waiting for his answer, I proposed that if his wife cleaned them I would give him three of them. I couldn't help thinking of the sweet little Cebus (humped Indian cattle) that they had come off. . . . I didn't have to wait an hour before Elisorio came back with the usual broad grin on his face, whistling happily at the thought of a good free lunch.

Now, you can't sit in front of a plate of food and think about what it was when it was alive. That is morbid and takes the joy out of eating. I am sure if more people would remember that and just allow all their gluttonous instincts to take over, they would be able to eat and enjoy things like muzzles, or even tongues and ears (the crunch in headcheese).

You will have to find a butcher who actually goes to the slaughterhouse and will bring you the muzzle, and it will still have the fur on it. I asked Elisorio's wife how she got the fur and outer skin off, and she told me she put the muzzle into the hot ashes of a wood fire for a minute or so. But if you don't have the wood ashes, then plunge it into boiling water for a minute or two—not longer, or the cooking process will start and the skin will toughen up like leather—and shave off the fur and some of the outer skin. Then follow the recipe.

As ridiculous as it may seem, a small beef muzzle—about 1¼ pounds—cooked and thinly sliced, almost shaved, will make 6 small servings for a first course or appetizer.

START FOUR DAYS AHEAD

brine

- **4 cups cold water**
- **3 tablespoons sea salt**
- **2 tablespoons granulated sugar**
- **1 tablespoon saltpeter**
- **1 beef muzzle (about 1½ pounds), skinned** *(see note above)*

salad dressing

- **2 cloves garlic, peeled and crushed**
- **Sea salt to taste**
- **1½ tablespoons olive oil**
- **5 tablespoons mild white wine vinegar**
- **2 medium purple onions, thinly sliced**
- **Freshly ground black pepper to taste**
- **Lettuce leaves to garnish the plates**

Put the water in a china or glass bowl, add the salt, sugar, and saltpeter, and mix together well. Pierce the muzzle all over lightly with the point of a sharp knife and set in the brine. Cover the bowl and store at the bottom of the refrigerator or in a cool larder for 3 days, turning the muzzle every day in the brine.

Remove the muzzle from the brine and rinse well. Put in a saucepan and cover with water. Cover the pan and simmer until cooked, about 3 hours. The muzzle should be tender (it is gelatinous but not bony)—but not too soft or you will not be able to slice it thin. It should not be too firm either, as, like pigs' feet, the muzzle tends to stiffen up when cold. Remove the muzzle from the cooking liquid and, while still warm, scrape off any remaining outside skin. Cool the meat in the refrigerator for about 2 hours, then slice wafer-thin with a ham slicer. (If you do not have an efficient slicer, then it will help to freeze the muzzle slightly before attempting to slice.) Put the slices in a glass or china bowl.

Crush together the garlic and salt and mix in the olive oil. Gradually beat in the vinegar, and when it is well incorporated, pour the dressing—it must be very vinegary—over the meat. Add the onion slices and freshly ground pepper and mix well. Set aside to marinate in a cool place—not in the refrigerator—for about 2 hours. Serve on a bed of lettuce with French bread to accompany the salad.

SOUPS

It happened not long ago that I had traveled from the hot, dry altiplano of central Mexico into a bone-chillingly damp Detroit spring. All I wanted to eat was a bowl of hot homemade soup, and I thought longingly of all those satisfying Mexican soups I had left behind. I tried to swallow some of the predictably oversalted and glutinous concoctions that passed for soup in my hotel restaurant and a neighboring soup and salad bar but found them horrible—when a friend came to my rescue and took me to a small, family-run Greek restaurant. It happened to be a few days before their Easter celebrations and on the menu was a meatless lentil soup. It came hot, unblended, textured, and honest from the kitchen—where somebody obviously knew and cared. I gloated over it between mouthfuls and knew that at that moment I wouldn't have exchanged it for the most elegant champagne and caviar.

I never particularly liked soups when I was growing up. At home they were always thick and strongly flavored: the usual post-Christmas turkey soup, almost like diluted gravy; oxtail soup (I preferred oxtail stewed) or celery, with a thick white base; and, as a special treat, mulligatawny, which I suspect came right out of one of Crosse & Blackwell's fancier tins. My favorite at that time was a lighter Scotch broth—lamb broth with barley and carrots. But now, after I've lived in Mexico off and on for so many years, my tastes have changed. The Mexicans know how to make the most delicious soups. They are mostly made with an unthickened base of stock, with vegetables and meat providing the crunch and body, and they change in content and color as the seasons progress: fresh corn kernels with green chilies, full-opened squash blossoms with their tender vegetables attached, a host of wild mushrooms and pungent herbs.

Even the most mundane chicken *consomé* (one *m* in Mexico) is made more nutritious and crunchy with the addition of finely chopped onion, sharp green chilies, diced avocado, or crisped tortillas, while the heavier *menudo* of tripe and chilies or *pozole* of pork and hominy or a simple *caldo de res*—broth with beef and vegetables—is a satisfying meal in itself. And these are soups made in the marketplaces or the humblest restaurants in Mexico. What do you find in the average American eating place but smooth tomato sauce/soup, too sweet by far and with a metallic aftertaste, glutinous chicken and rice cornstarched and MSG'd to the limits, and mushroom cream with some of those slimy little canned mushrooms on top? In England one hardly fares better. The soups are still too strong in the main—and I am talking about the average-priced restaurant—resembling overliquidized stews often redolent of stock that has been stewing in the pan too long.

I love some, but not all, of the great soups of the world: bouillabaisses, bisques, a classic consommé rose, Tuscan bean soup, a Canadian *paysanne* of green split peas, green turtle consommé, or a good borscht; not to mention Chinese and Thai soups with their surprising fresh flavors and crisp textures. Japanese soups are too salty and fishy for my taste, and the cloying, gluey creaminess of vichyssoise is my bête noire.

There are a lot of soups made at home today that seem pleasant enough at the first few spoonfuls, but after that they begin to pall. You know the type I mean. The base ingredients, whatever they might be, have been pureed until quite smooth. They have been thickened with far too much cream, often egg yolks as well, and then flavored with things like curry powder—God forbid— or an overpowering dose of not-quite-good-enough sherry. (I must confess I was probably guilty of those thick, rich soups in the heyday of my entertaining many years ago.) Who wants to start a meal with a bowl of sauce, for that is what many of them resemble? Soup, in my opinion, unless like bouillabaisse or *pozole,* it constitutes a whole meal, should be served in small, tempting quantities that open the appetite and intrigue the palate. I exclude from these remarks anybody who has been doing hard chores in near-zero temperatures.

It would be superfluous for me to give recipes for all my favorite soups, for they can be found elsewhere, so I have just included here those which have been given to me by friends down through the years, or which I have invented, or which just happened because of the feast-or-famine situation of my vegetable patch.

Chicken Broth   ABOUT 4 QUARTS

Consomé de pollo, chicken broth, is not only a popular soup in itself in Mexico but is used as a base for many other types of soup. It is usually excellent— although heavily oversalted—especially where chicken tacos are served, because all of those simmering chickens have made a contribution. For the recipes in this book, canned chicken broth will not do, nor will a cube of that overseasoned gritty stuff. Make a really good chicken broth from scratch, one that jells thickly when cold and has some authority. And when you can't use it all at once, reduce and freeze it in ice cube trays.

To begin with, so much depends on the quality of the chickens. You will get very poor results if you use those skinny little chickens with a lot of slimy stuff in the joints when you cut them open. Try to find a hen—generally called fowl in supermarkets—and stew it slowly, being careful not to put in too much carrot, which makes the broth sweet, or herbs that are too strong. And don't brown the bones first; you want a whitish broth, not one that resembles a beef broth. In Mexico, I use a lot of chicken feet—that lends a good, gelatinous quality to the broth—along with the head, back, intestines, giblets, et al. Be generous with the amount of chicken parts you use and cook very slowly for a very long time. Then let it all sit in a cool place overnight before you reheat, strain, and skim.

    5–6 pounds chicken parts, giblets, etc. *(see note above)* **or 1 fowl, cut up,**
       plus 2 pounds parts
    1 medium white onion, roughly chopped
    3 small cloves garlic, peeled and crushed
    1 medium carrot, rinsed (no need to scrape) and cut into rounds
    1 small rib celery, roughly chopped *(optional)*
      Sea salt to taste
    5 whole peppercorns

Put all the ingredients (including a little salt—you can always adjust later) in a stockpot and add cold water until it comes to about 3 inches over the top of the bones. Cook over a very slow flame for about 6 to 7 hours. Set aside in a cool place overnight.

The next day, skim off any fat that has congealed on the surface. Bring to a boil, strain, and skim a second time. Adjust the salt.

The broth may be kept in the refrigerator for up to 3 days, but it should be reboiled each day. Or it may be frozen as is, or reduced and frozen.

Asparagus Soup

4 CUPS OR 6 SERVINGS

Whoever thought of putting orange flavor into asparagus soup? Well, you eat asparagus with *sauce maltaise,* so why not? Sherry Migdail said it was probably her invention; she and her journalist husband, Carl, lived in Mexico City at the same time we did. It is a nice change, because asparagus soup tends to be rather dull—that is, if you can bear to make fresh asparagus into soup. You could in a pinch use frozen asparagus, but put it into the water while still frozen.

    6 scallions
  1½ pounds fresh asparagus
    2 tablespoons unsalted butter
  1½ cups boiling water (1 cup, if using frozen asparagus)
      Sea salt and freshly ground black pepper to taste
  1½ cups strong chicken broth
   ¼ cup freshly squeezed orange juice
      Finely grated rind of 1 orange (about 1 heaped teaspoon)
   ½ cup cream or *crème fraîche*
      Croutons *(optional)*

Discard only the tops or spoiled leaves of the scallions, and chop the rest roughly.

Snap the tough ends off the asparagus stalks. Scrape the lower part of the stalks with a potato peeler or sharp knife. Cut off the tips and chop roughly, then tie them up in a square of cheesecloth, using a piece of fine string, and set aside. Heat the butter in a saucepan and fry the scallions gently, without browning, until soft. Add the asparagus stalks and cook for a few seconds in the butter. Pour the boiling water into the pan, add the bag of asparagus tips, season, and cook over a high flame until tender—about 4 minutes, depending very much on the thickness of the asparagus. Do not overcook; it should still be a little crunchy. Remove the bag of tips, untie, and set aside.

Transfer the contents of the pan (not the tips) to the blender jar and blend until smooth. Return the puree to the pan, add the broth, orange juice, and rind, and when the soup begins to simmer continue cooking for about 10 minutes. Add the cream, adjust the seasoning, and heat through gently. Serve the soup garnished with the asparagus tips and with the croutons, if you wish.

Carrot and Coriander Soup
4 TO 5 SERVINGS

I was never too thrilled at the prospect of carrot soup; it always seemed to be too sweet and innocuous and required an awful lot of salt. However, it seemed that overnight we had an abundance of carrots in the lower garden—as Elisorio explained it, among other explanations, "The packet slipped in my hand." I found myself eating carrots in many different ways almost ad nauseam; then the idea hit me for this soup. The final garnish is crunchy and pure Mexican. No nouvelley touches for this one; stew the vegetables until they are sweet.

soup

> 2 tablespoons unsalted butter
> 3 scallions, finely chopped, with most of the green leaves
> 1 small (2-ounce) potato, peeled and finely chopped
> ¾ pound carrots, trimmed, scraped and julienned
> 2 heaped tablespoons roughly chopped fresh coriander (cilantro), leaves and tender stalks
> 4 cups well-seasoned chicken broth
> Sea salt and freshly ground black pepper to taste

garnish

> 2 tablespoons finely chopped fresh coriander (cilantro) leaves
> 2 tablespoons finely chopped white onion
> 2 tablespoons finely chopped fresh *chile serrano* or other hot fresh green chili if *serrano* is not available

Melt the butter in a saucepan, add the scallions, potato, carrots, and coriander, and sauté gently without browning for about 10 minutes, stirring from time to time. Add the broth and cook over a medium flame until the vegetables are just cooked but not too soft, about 15 minutes. With a slotted spoon, take out about ⅓ cup of the carrots and set them aside. Blend the rest of the vegetables in the broth until smooth and return to the saucepan with the unblended carrots. Adjust the seasoning and cook at a fast simmer for about 15 minutes. Season with freshly ground pepper and pass the dishes of garnish for each person to help himself *al gusto*.

Philadelphia Snapper Soup

I came across this recipe in *American Regional Cookery* by Sheila Hibben when I was researching some more unusual dishes for a "fishy" banquet. If you can go to the trouble of finding the "cooked snapping turtle," it will be well worth while. It is a wonderfully robust winter soup.

- ¾ cup chicken fat *(see recipe page 14)*
- 4 pounds veal knuckles, cut into 2-inch pieces
- 2 large onions, sliced
- 2 carrots, peeled and quartered
- 1 cup roughly chopped celery
- 1 cup flour
- 1 gallon chicken or beef stock
- ½ bay leaf
- 4 whole cloves
- 4 large tomatoes, peeled and chopped
- Meat of 1 cooked snapping turtle
- 1¾ cups Madeira
- 3 thin slices lemon
- Sea salt and freshly ground black pepper to taste
- Tabasco sauce to taste
- 2 hard-boiled eggs, chopped, for garnish

Preheat the oven to 400° F. Heat the chicken fat in an ovenproof pan until it splatters as you put the vegetables into it. Add the veal knuckles, onions, carrots, and celery and stir them well in the fat. Bake in the oven until they are nicely browned, stirring and turning them over from time to time, about 45 minutes. Remove the pan from the oven, sift in the flour, and brown over a medium flame, stirring constantly so that the flour is evenly distributed and does not go lumpy. Transfer to a large stockpot. Add the stock, bay leaf, cloves, and tomatoes and simmer for about 4 to 4½ hours.

Cut the turtle meat into small squares and add to the soup with half of the Madeira and the lemon slices; add salt to taste and a dash of Tabasco sauce. Cover the pan with a tight-fitting lid and cook over a medium flame for about 5 minutes. Strain the soup, adjust the seasoning, add the remaining Madeira, and serve garnished with the hard-boiled egg.

Sopa de Albóndigas (Meatball Soup)

Albóndiga soup had always been a favorite of mine since my early days in Mexico, but I had almost forgotten about it until last October's regional meeting of the International Association of Cooking Schools at Rancho Bernardo Inn, California, where a memorable Mexican brunch was served. Since I could never find a recipe for it in my regional cookbooks, I made up one following traditional cooking methods.

It is high time we had some changes in our brunch menus, which are heavily overladen with cholesteroly foods. Serve this light soup on a wintry morning.

meatballs

- 1 tablespoon long-grained, unconverted rice
  Boiling water to cover
- 6 ounces ground pork with some fat (medium grind)
- 6 ounces ground beef (medium grind)
- 1 small egg
- ⅛ teaspoon cumin seed
- 3 leaves fresh or dried mint
- ⅛ teaspoon dried Mexican oregano
- ⅓ cup roughly chopped white onion
  Sea salt to taste
- 4 whole black peppercorns

broth

- ½ pound ripe tomatoes
- 1 small slice white onion, roughly chopped
- 2 small cloves garlic, peeled and roughly chopped
- 1 tablespoon lard or safflower oil
- 6 ounces carrots, trimmed, scraped, and cut into ¼-inch cubes
- 6 ounces zucchini, trimmed, and cut into ¼-inch cubes
- 2 cups meat or chicken broth
- 4 cups cold water (or more)
  Sea salt to taste
- 3 fresh *chiles serranos,* or 2 fresh *jalapeños*
- 2 large sprigs fresh mint or cilantro (coriander)

Cover the rice with boiling water and leave to soak for about 30 minutes.

Mix the meats together well in a bowl. Put the egg, cumin seed, mint leaves, oregano, onion, salt, and peppercorns into a blender jar and blend until smooth. Add to the meats and mix very well with your hands. Drain the rice and add to the meat mixture. Form the meatballs about 1 inch in diameter—there should be about 24 of them—and set aside.

To prepare the broth Put the tomatoes into a saucepan, cover with boiling water, and cook for 5 minutes. Drain and cool. When they are cool enough to handle, remove the skins and cores and transfer to a blender jar. Add the onion and garlic and blend until smooth. Heat the lard or oil in a wide, heavy pan, add the tomato puree, and fry over a high flame for 2 minutes until reduced and thickened. Add the chopped carrot and zucchini, broth, and water, season lightly, and bring to a simmer. Carefully add the meatballs. Make 2 slits in the form of a cross at the points of the chilies, and add them together with the mint or coriander sprigs. Continue cooking over a very low flame for about 50 minutes. When the soup is cooked, the broth will be cloudy and slightly thickened with the juices of the meat; it will have a rich gleam on the surface. Add a little more water if necessary.

This recipe can be prepared a day ahead. Adjust the salt just before serving.

My Mushroom Soup

This soup is my own invention. Cultivated mushrooms, briefly cooked, strike me as too slimy and tasteless, so I prefer this slow-cooking method inspired by Elizabeth David. While the flavor of the mushrooms is greatly enhanced, it is not as overpowering as that of dried mushrooms.

        1 pound mushrooms (wild ones are best if available)
        1 tablespoon lemon juice
        4 small cloves garlic, peeled and chopped
        2 tablespoons unsalted butter
        1 tablespoon safflower oil
          Sea salt and freshly ground black pepper to taste
     2½ cups well-seasoned chicken broth
   ⅓–½ cup *crème fraîche* or heavy cream

to serve

        1 tablespoon Madeira for each cup
          Croutons and chopped chives, for garnish

Preheat the oven to 300° F.

Wipe the mushrooms with a damp cloth, rinsing in water only if they appear to be very sandy or have a lot of earth under the gills. Slice the mushrooms thin. Choose a shallow dish in which the mushrooms can be spread out in a double layer. Add the lemon juice, garlic, butter, and oil to the mushrooms, season lightly, and bake slowly in the preheated oven until they are cooked through, very brown, and the juice quite thick and dark—about 1 hour *(see note below)*. Set aside a few of the mushrooms for a garnish, and transfer the rest to the blender jar. Add the broth and blend until smooth. Transfer the mushroom puree to a thick saucepan and heat through for about 5 minutes. Add the cream, adjust the seasoning, and heat through again for about 5 minutes, but do not allow the soup to boil.

Put 1 tablespoon Madeira in each soup cup, fill with soup, and garnish with croutons, chopped chives, and a few of the whole mushrooms.

NOTE This step can also be done in a *sauteur* or frying pan, but the mushrooms would have to be covered and stirred frequently during the cooking time.

Epazote and Potato Soup (Sopa Diana Kennedy)

Anybody who has read my books must surely know of my passion for that most Mexican of herbs, *epazote (Chenopodium ambrosioides)*, so I won't be repetitive here and describe all its wonderful properties, culinary and medicinal. One evening I was going to have supper with a dear friend of many years' standing, María Dolores Torres Izábal, who is an excellent and inventive cook. When I arrived at her house, she said, "I know you don't like to eat much at night, so I have prepared a very light supper." My supper turned out to be this soup, and on the table by my plate was the printed recipe: *"Sopa Diana Kennedy, con todo cariño para Diana de María Dolores."*

It has become one of my favorites.

> 3 rounded tablespoons unsalted butter
> ½ small white onion (1½ ounces), thinly sliced
> ½ pound waxy potatoes (preferably red bliss), peeled and cut into thin rounds
> 4 cups well-seasoned chicken broth
> 1 fresh *chile serrano*, roughly chopped
> 5 heaped tablespoons roughly chopped *epazote*
> Sea salt and freshly ground black pepper to taste

garnish

> 2 *chiles serranos* (or more), finely chopped *(optional)*
> ½ cup fried tortilla squares or croutons

Melt the butter in a saucepan, add the onion and potato, and cook gently, without browning, for about 5 minutes. Add the broth and cook over a medium flame until the potatoes are just soft but not mushy, about 15 minutes. Blend, in the blender, a little at a time together with the chili and the *epazote*. If you want an appetizing green-speckled effect, then do not overblend. Return the blended mixture to the pan and simmer for about 8 to 10 minutes. The soup should not be too thick, but it will thicken as it stands and may be diluted with a little more chicken broth to taste. Adjust the salt and add the pepper.

Serve garnished with more chopped chili—if you like it—and the fried tortilla squares or croutons.

Swiss Chard and Zucchini Soup

Once it has taken root, Swiss chard is indestructible, surviving the drought and inundations of my vegetable garden. It is not one of my favorite vegetables because it always has a slightly muddy taste, but since it is always around, I thought I would invent a soup in which I could use it. It is a strong-flavored soup but addictive. Of course, it is always better with a couple of spoonfuls of unsalted butter or thick cream stirred in seconds before serving, or with a crispy topping of croutons or tortilla pieces (as in the recipe for Epazote and Potato Soup), which satisfy my penchant for different textures.

Try not to serve this soup immediately. If you let it sit, covered, for about 15 minutes, it develops a better flavor.

  ¾ pound Swiss chard
  ½ pound zucchini
  2 tablespoons unsalted butter
  3 tablespoons finely chopped white onion
  2 cloves garlic, peeled and chopped
  3 cups well-flavored chicken broth
    Sea salt and freshly ground black pepper to taste

optional

  2 tablespoons unsalted butter or 4 tablespoons heavy cream *(see note above)*
    Finely chopped *chile serrano* to taste
    Croutons or fried tortilla squares

Rinse the Swiss chard well in cold water, making sure that no sandy soil adheres to the ribs of the stems. Remove the thick stems and chop fine. Spin the leaves for a few seconds in a salad spinner to remove excess water and roughly chop. Set aside. Trim the zucchini and cut into very small cubes. Set aside.

Melt the butter in a heavy saucepan, add the onion, chopped chard stems, and garlic, and cook, stirring constantly, over a high flame for about 5 minutes. Add the zucchini and chard leaves, with 1 cup of the broth, cover, and cook over a medium flame until the vegetables are just cooked—about 10 minutes. Transfer the vegetables with 1 cup of the broth to a blender jar—you may want to do this in two batches—and blend until almost smooth. Return the puree to the saucepan with the remaining broth, adjust the salt, add the pepper, heat to a simmer, and cook over a low flame for about 5 minutes more.

Add the butter or cream, chili, and/or croutons or tortilla squares if desired.

Gazpacho

Or rather Antonio Olazcoaga's gazpacho recipe, which is textured and pungent. He was "a fine old Basque glutton, now dead, who was a good friend of Paul's and mine," wrote Sam Brewer at the top of the recipe. Sam and Paul were both working journalists in Spain in the early fifties. Sam adds: "If one has servants (as in Spain) who will do the necessary pounding in a mortar as Antonio instructs it is much better." Much as I agree, I take the short cut and use the processor.

I make gazpacho only when tomatoes are really ripe and of good flavor. I personally don't like extra tomatoes and chopped onion added; Sam mentions them as optional. I use brown bread crumbs, as he suggests, and I also like to have whole wheat bread croutons to garnish.

  3 cloves garlic, peeled and roughly chopped
  ½ large green pepper, top and seeds removed, and roughly chopped
  1 teaspoon sea salt, or to taste
1½ pounds very ripe tomatoes, unskinned and roughly chopped
  ½ cup red wine vinegar
  ¼ cup water
  ½ cup whole wheat bread crumbs *(see page 12)*
  ½ cup fruity olive oil

garnish

  1 cup finely diced cucumber
  1 cup diced green pepper
  2 cups browned croutons (preferably whole wheat)

optional

  1 cup diced tomatoes
  ½ cup finely chopped onion

Put the garlic, green pepper, and salt into the container of the food processor and process until smooth. Gradually add the tomatoes and continue processing until almost smooth. Add the vinegar and water and mix well. Add the bread crumbs, and while you continue to process, gradually add the olive oil through the special dripper as though you were making mayonnaise. (Adding the oil gradually also ensures that it does not separate from the rest of the ingredients while standing.)

Refrigerate the gazpacho, and when ready to serve put a cube of ice into each plate (actually I don't add ice, as I don't like things too cold). Pass the bowls of garnish separately so that each guest can help himself.

VEGETABLES
AND SALADS

The vegetable garden of my ecological house in San Pancho is a hit-or-miss affair. I should perhaps explain that the garden is planted over a triangular piece of land that demarcates the filter bed for all the drainage from the house. In theory the vegetables should receive sufficient nutrients and irrigation from this source, while in practice it doesn't quite work like that. But that is another story. In fact, we now have two vegetable gardens. Elisorio, the man who looks after my ranch, became impatient with the light, loamy soil brought in by the contractors for the filter bed garden—although he seems to have forgotten completely that the first year we had a magnificent crop of corn, beans, and tomatoes—so in disgust he started another of his own right between the cow shed and the goat's pen. Since it receives the effluence from both, it has done rather well from the start. But it is still a case of feast or famine. Sometimes we have four types of lettuce, wonderful crisp little cucumbers, fava beans and peas galore, while at other times we have a sparse crop of radishes so peppery that they resemble misshapen chilies, little groups of Florence fennel appearing where they were not planted, and a few onions here and there in between odd clumps of coriander, but nothing growing in a straight line, or even the semblance of one.

Now, I can never be accused of being orderly—except while giving a cooking class—but I do like to see orderly-growing vegetables, so I went out one day and planted some *mâche* in a very straight row. Although I watered it regularly and gave it special attention, it was puny and very soon wilted and died. One morning Elisorio appeared at the door with a small bunch of magnificent *mâche* and a triumphant look on his face. "I told you your garden was no good, señora," he said. "Come and look at my plants." I went down there and couldn't see a sign of them. "Look," he said and reached down to brush aside a tall fava bean stalk and some bushy carrot tops. There indeed were two magnificent *mâche* plants—but only two.

One day I gave Elisorio a package of yellow crookneck squash seeds to plant. A few weeks later I saw that some healthy plants had grown up and small yellow squash were forming nicely. The next day I looked again and they were gone. "Do you suppose that squirrel ate them?" I asked him innocently. Elisorio's face was a sight to be seen. He pushed back my discarded old sombrero that he had adopted to a rakish angle on the back of his head and laughed heartily, showing off the big gap where three teeth had been the week before. Once he recovered from his mirth he confessed that he had thought they were all sick and cut them off for the goat.

A month or so ago, I noticed that we were beginning to get a solid line of carrots. They were growing so close together that the roots were intertwined like Siamese quadruplets. "Why did you sow the seeds so thickly?" I asked. "Well, it's like this, señora: if I plant a few they don't come up, and if I plant a lot they all come up. But," he added, "I have to admit that my hand surpassed itself this time."

Of course, we have our problems with aphids, one hundred types—or so it seems—of beetles, caterpillars from the white cabbage butterfly, and, worst of all, the *gallina ciega,* the fat white grub of the June bug that lives on roots of plants. We take care of most of the insects with a spray of wild tobacco and soap, but the *gallina ciega* has to be dug out by hand. One day I saw Elisorio with a huge, succulent grub in his hand. "Kill it," I shouted, as it had been eating my favorite asparagus plant. "No, señora, this is Maximilian's midmorning snack." Maximilian is our large white turkey-cock, and while I had to admit he deserved it because the fertility rate of the female turkeys is awe-inspiring, I was even more impressed that my lessons in recycling had not gone unheeded.

Feast or famine, I live on salads and vegetables either gathered from my two vegetable patches or bought from the peasants in the marketplace.

VEGETABLES

Although I am not, nor ever could be, a complete vegetarian, I live on vegetarian meals most of the week when I am at home.

I shudder when I think of how vegetables were cooked when I was young. You could smell the cabbage or brussels sprouts boiling before you got to the kitchen, and the smell lingered there until the next day. There were rather stringy runner beans, soft cauliflower always blanketed with a layer of white sauce—albeit well made—with cheese, and watery marrow, that ridiculously overgrown squash so beloved in the British Isles. Thank goodness times have changed. We owe an enormous debt of gratitude to the Chinese and the disciples of nouvelle cuisine, all of whom have given us vegetables that are crisp and colorful. Of course, there are some delicious stews with vegetables reduced almost to a mush: ratatouille, for instance, was like that when I first had it in Saint-Tropez so many years ago—I do not like ratatouille with crunchy lumps of bitter vegetables.

Though it may sound sacrilegious, I don't really like steamed vegetables either. A lot of goodness goes into the water, and they are never seasoned properly. Purees remind me of Gerber's, but I love vegetables that have been blanched and sautéed or stir-fried with a little chicken broth. Vegetables done this way have a sweetness that is lost when they are steamed. I remember I was cooking dinner once for a friend who was in the middle of moving house. The vegetables in an uptown New York fruit store in those days were not very promising in a cold January, but I julienned kohlrabi, turnip, and parsnip, then cooked them in a little chicken broth and butter—the children, who would normally not be caught dead eating those vegetables, came back for seconds.

I don't like anything swimming in butter and, worse still, with almonds—a sort of cop-out, I feel. Carrots are superb cooked as I mentioned in the previous paragraph, with lots of chopped parsley and a touch of butter to finish, and lots of freshly ground black pepper and nutmeg or turmeric. One minute is enough for freshly picked peas—I don't like the brilliantly colored frozen ones—or fava beans, with a little chopped fresh summer savory. Yes, they are wonderful raw, but that slight cooking brings out another dimension. So you can imagine my reaction when confronted with a plate of raw cauliflower, broccoli, etc., around a dip—one has to have the digestive system of a cow.

I remember Mother's braised vegetables, so good on a winter's day: celery, parsnips, and carrots. I have added to them Belgian endive and the bulb of Florence fennel, which does very well in my Mexican garden. It is unfortunate in a way that Elisorio has also taken a liking to it—I see him chomping away on that and the tenderest cucumbers as he goes about his chores.

Sautéed Spinach

4 SERVINGS

This is the way I like to cook spinach—chilies with everything? Just about, or you could substitute a little fresh grated ginger root. I cook it like this if I am going to stuff an omelette, or make a soufflé. The amount of broth and the cooking time have to be reduced a little if it is very fresh leaf spinach. However, most of the spinach we get today is the tougher beet spinach.

- 1 **pound spinach**
- 1 **tablespoon oil**
- 2 **tablespoons unsalted butter**
- 5 **tablespoons finely chopped onion**
- 2–3 **cloves garlic, peeled and chopped**
- 2 *chiles serranos,* **or any hot fresh green chili, finely chopped**
- ¼ **cup chicken broth**
  Finely ground sea salt to taste

Pick over the spinach and remove any tough stalks. Spin for a few seconds in a lettuce spinner to remove excess water. Chop roughly. Heat the oil and butter together in a heavy pan or wok. Add the onion, garlic, and chilies and cook over a lively flame until the onion is translucent, about 3 minutes. Add the chopped spinach to the pan and stir briefly. Add the broth and cook over a high flame, turning the spinach over until wilted, about 5 minutes—but see the note above for tender leaf spinach, which would take about 3 minutes. Adjust the seasoning. Cover the pan and let it sit off the flame for a further 5 minutes before serving.

Corn Soufflé

This recipe is one that I evolved for one of the series of little books The Great Cooks' Library. It is a moist soufflé that is cooked in a water bath and does not rise as spectacularly as the lighter and more traditional cheese soufflé.

corn mixture

        1½ tablespoons unsalted butter, plus extra for buttering the dish
         2 tablespoons finely chopped onion
         1 small clove garlic, peeled and finely chopped
        1½ cups corn kernals (if corn is not the freshest possible, use frozen and measure
            before defrosting)
         2 fresh green chilies, finely chopped *(optional)*
           Sea salt and freshly ground black pepper to taste
           A scraping of nutmeg

roux

         2 tablespoons unsalted butter
         1 heaped tablespoon flour
        ½ cup warm whole milk
         4 eggs, separated, at room temperature

Preheat the oven to 375° F. Place a water bath inside, on the middle rack; a roasting pan is suitable with water to the depth of 1 inch in it. Butter well a 1½-quart soufflé dish.

To prepare the corn mixture Melt the 1½ tablespoons butter. Add the onion and garlic and fry briefly without browning until the onion is translucent. Add the corn kernels, and the chilies, if desired, season, and cook until tender but still crisp, about 5 minutes. Set aside.

To prepare the roux Melt the 2 tablespoons butter and add the flour, stirring constantly as it froths up for about 2 minutes. Gradually stir in the warm milk and cook the mixture over a low flame, stirring all the time until it thickens, about 5 minutes. Add the corn mixture. Beat the egg yolks briefly just to break them up and stir them into the corn mixture. Beat the egg whites until they are stiff but not dry. Stir 1 large tablespoon of the beaten whites into the corn mixture and then fold in the rest. Pour the mixture into the prepared dish.

    Place the dish in the water bath and bake for about 40 minutes, or until the soufflé is just firm but still moist, and nicely browned on top. Serve immediately with a tomato *coulis* or some salted sour cream and chili strips.

POTATOES

I must confess to having a passion for potatoes—among other things, of course. Every time I return to the United States I rush off and buy some of those wonderful red bliss potatoes. I steam or boil them in their skins and then eat them with lots of chopped parsley, chives, and melted butter. For baking I prefer the potatoes of England because they have a tougher skin than that of the Idaho, and they are very mealy. I am fascinated by the little wild potato from Zacatecas in north-central Mexico, and by the wizened, frozen potato of the Andes, *chuño*. But when it comes right down to it, I would fly off any spring to England just to eat poached salmon with warm new potatoes. When you buy them they are covered with pale-brown papery flakes rather than a skin, and the flesh, when cooked, is almost transparent. We would always boil them at home with fresh mint and then toss them in butter.

I love all those wonderful fattening French ways of cooking potatoes— *pommes de terre Anna, gratin à la dauphinoise* or *savoyarde*—but two recipes in particular that I find myself using over and over again are *pommes de terre à l'ardennaise* with garlic and juniper berries, and *pommes de terre, Sauce Bouillade,* with red peppers and garlic.

TIP So often when you cook potatoes for a potato salad they fall apart, or when you cut them they look unappetizingly ragged around the edges. To avoid this, a good way to cook them is: slice the unpeeled red bliss or other waxy potatoes to just less than ¼ inch thick. Put them in a heavy pan in which they are no more than 3 layers deep. Barely cover with water and put the lid halfway over the pan. Cook the potatoes—they should barely simmer—over a low flame for 5 minutes. Turn off the heat, cover the pan completely, and allow them to finish cooking in their own steam. By now they should be *just* past the *al dente* stage. (Time of cooking will, of course, vary with quality and thickness of pan, type of heat used, etc.)

Potato Scones   ABOUT 10 SCONES

These doughy potato scones, a specialty of Scotland and Ireland, can become addictive, especially if you love potatoes as I do. They are generally made with white flour or rough oatmeal mixed with peeled mashed potatoes, and are eaten hot spread with butter. When I lived in Scotland, I used to eat them for breakfast with a fried egg on top, but they are also good with bacon, with melted cheese on top . . . what you will. Sometimes I add coarsely ground whole wheat flour (2 ounces) instead of the oatmeal.

    1½ ounces (rounded ½ cup) quick oats
    ½ pound unpeeled potatoes (I prefer cooked and roughly mashed with their skins)
    ¼ teaspoon finely ground sea salt
    1 tablespoon unbleached, all-purpose flour, plus flour for kneading and rolling
    1½ tablespoons unsalted butter, melted

Put the oats into the blender jar and blend for about 3 seconds. They should be broken up rather than ground. Add them to the potatoes, together with the salt, flour, and melted butter. Knead well. Sprinkle the pastry board lightly with flour and roll out the dough to approximately ⅛ inch thick. Heat a griddle and brush with butter. Cut the scones with a round 3-inch cutter, prick them well, and cook for about 3 minutes—by this time the underside should be lightly browned—turn the scones over, and cook for a further 3 minutes on the second side. As soon as they are cooked, cover with a napkin and keep warm until ready to eat. You can freeze them and then reheat on a well-buttered griddle.

NOTE It is easier to work the dough if the potatoes are still slightly warm.

Pommes de Terre au Grain de Sel, Sauce Bouillade   4 SERVINGS

This recipe is adaped from one in Elizabeth David's *French Country Cooking*.

> **1 pound red bliss potatoes, or other waxy potatoes, peeled and cut into**
> **   1-inch cubes**
> **Boiling water to cover**
> **Coarse sea salt to taste**

Cover the potatoes with boiling water, add salt to taste, and cook until still a little *al dente,* about 8 to 10 minutes. Drain and dry off in the hot pan.

sauce bouillade

> **1 tablespoon rich olive oil**
> **1 tablespoon pork lard**
> **3 small sweet red peppers, seeded and cut into small squares**
> **4 cloves garlic, peeled and smashed**
> **½ cup dry white wine**
> **   About 2 tablespoons water**
> **½ tablespoon flour**

To prepare the sauce   Heat the oil and lard together and sauté the red peppers until soft, about 3 minutes. Add the garlic and sauté for 2 minutes more. Stir in the wine and reduce over a high flame for 1 minute. Add the water to the flour and mix to a smooth paste, add the flour mixture to the pan, and cook the peppers over a low flame for about 8 minutes. The sauce should be fairly thick and coat the back of a wooden spoon well. However, if it is too thick, then add more water and continue cooking a minute or so longer.

Transfer the potatoes to a warm serving dish and pour the hot sauce over them. Serve immediately.

British-Style Roast Potatoes

Roast potatoes should have a good, rich crust outside and be floury and soft inside. Mother always cooked them to perfection and there is a simple trick to it: Parboil them first and while still hot roast them in splattering fat. Of course, we always used the fat part of the drippings from the Sunday roast, but you could use good lard instead. You don't want a waxy potato for this, so Idaho or yellow would be good.

    1 pound medium-sized potatoes, peeled
       Cold water to cover
       Sea salt to taste
  ½ cup fat skimmed from pan drippings *(see note above)*

Cut the potatoes in half lengthwise so you have a lot of flat surface—they shouldn't be too large either; about 2 to 2½ inches long and about 1 inch thick is ideal. Put the potatoes in water to cover, add salt, and bring to a boil, lower the flame, and cook over medium heat for about 12 minutes. Drain well and set aside.

While the potatoes are cooking, **preheat the oven to 375° F.** Have ready a shallow baking dish, metal preferably, into which the potatoes will fit in one layer with plenty of space in between them. Put the fat into the pan and place on the top shelf of the oven to heat through as the oven heats. When you can hear the fat sputtering, put the potatoes into the pan, turning each so that it is coated with the hot fat. Turn them once more to make sure. Roast the potatoes on the top shelf, turning them as soon as they are well browned on one side, and continue turning and basting until they are crisp and brown all over, about 40 to 45 minutes.

Pommes de Terre à l'Ardennaise (Grated Potatoes with Juniper Berries and Garlic)

I had made this recipe a number of times and given some to my maids Sylvie and Ephy to taste . . . they rolled their eyes in approval. Potatoes were cheap at that time, but my neighbors would certainly not think of buying olive oil or butter, so I showed them how to prepare the recipe with the locally pressed sesame oil and strips of *chile poblano* fried with sliced onions *(rajas)*. It was a great success. Socorro was helping me with the cleaning one day and I offered her some of these potatoes with her lunch. She ate silently but with relish and then settled back in her chair to talk. "You know, I have great faith in potatoes," she said. "For months I had such swollen feet and ankles that I could hardly walk, and one day Juan [her husband, who scorned potatoes and never ate them] was reading a book of herbal cures when he came across a remedy for my condition—potatoes. I ate at least one kilo a day and in a week I was cured."

"Seven kilos of potatoes in one week!" I exclaimed. "Didn't you get very fat?" "No," she said, "on the contrary, and now Juan swears by them too and eats them all the time." This is my version of an Elizabeth David recipe.

  2 **pounds red bliss or other waxy potatoes, unpeeled**
  5 **tablespoons unsalted butter and 2 tablespoons olive oil**
  1 **rounded teaspoon sea salt and a lot of freshly ground black pepper**
12 **juniper berries, crushed**
  8 **cloves garlic, peeled and crushed**

Grate the unskinned potatoes in the food processor or by hand grater. Cover them with cold water and leave them for about 1 minute. Strain and squeeze as dry as possible in cheesecloth.

Heat a very heavy 10-inch frying pan and melt the butter in the oil. Mix the potatoes with the salt, juniper berries, garlic, and pepper. When the oil is hot, add the potatoes, press down, and cover. Cook over a high flame for about 10 minutes—test from time to time to see if the bottom is browning and not burning. Lift the potatoes with a spatula and turn them over, half at a time. Continue cooking a further 10 minutes, covered, and repeat the turning process. After 30 minutes they should be forming a coagulated mass. Remove the lid, turn for the last time, and brown the bottom of the potatoes well. Total cooking time should be about 40 minutes. Serve directly from the pan.

Just cook up to the last 10 minutes and hold uncovered. When ready to serve, brown over a high flame on both sides.

Pommes Soufflées, without frustrations

I discovered I was not alone in failing miserably to get my *pommes* to *soufflé* despite adhering to the most careful of instructions. A good friend, Jean-Yves Ferrer, Director of Maxim's in Mexico City, came to my rescue. He took me into the kitchen to see how easy it really is; but like all easy things there are some twists.

First choose flattish, longish potatoes. Cut a vertical slice off one end of the potato and check for a water marking or "vein." If there is one, use the potato for something else. If not then proceed by peeling rather thickly into an even oval shape. Cut into horizontal slices almost exactly ³⁄₁₆-inch thick. Do not wash.

Have ready 2 deep skillets with oil to the depth of ½ inch in each one. Heat the first one to 250° F. Add a few of the potato slices—do not crowd the pan—and shake the pan, gently turning the slices over until they begin to blister or puff but remain a very pale gold color. Remove and drain. Meanwhile heat the second pan until very hot—375–400° F, add the potatoes, which should immediately puff up. Cook until they are a deep golden color—about 3–4 minutes. Drain and serve.

Cooking may be delayed for several hours in between the two frying stages.

SALADS

Salads, glorious salads! Can you imagine being condemned to live in a country—and there are plenty—where you can't eat fresh salad every day, or nearly every day? But I should qualify that—not *any* salad, the type, for instance, that you find when you are on the road in the average motel restaurant: a huge plateful of iceberg lettuce, enough for twenty-five rabbits, with all those thick glutinous dressings. Mind you, I didn't like salads when I was growing up. It was Father's job to make them at home, and he prided himself on it. He would cut up lots of greens, beets, tomatoes, etc., very fine and then douse it all with lots of mayonnaise, Heinz mayonnaise, until it wept and died. And by the way, never let the most vigorous person at the table toss the salad—he will toss it to death; you want to toss lightly and briefly.

The serving of salad has its pretensions, too, now, starting with the menu: salad is always "garden fresh" while you know very well that it has been perked up with some chemical to make it look greener or stand up longer. "Your choice of our delicious dressings"—i.e., French and Italian dressing that no Frenchmen or Italian would recognize, and that terrible oil and vinegar! Then there is the cold plate, a plate so cold that the oil congeals on it and all the flavor disappears. But surely the ultimate pretension is the frozen fork. I think it first happened to me in Arizona, when I was confronted by a young waiter inclining almost ceremoniously and holding out to me, meticulously wrapped in the whitest of napkins, a frozen fork. He looked amazed when I refused. "My inlays," I explained, "are jangling at the thought." Enough of gripes. When traveling I think longingly of a salad at Chez Panisse, or Green's in San Francisco, a winter salad in France, in Northern Italy . . .

Anchovy and Walnut Winter Salad

After my annual winter visit to my mother in England, I used to go to stay with friends in Paris. They were wonderfully generous hosts, and we would visit their favorite bistros and some outstanding North Vietnamese restaurants in our quest for good food. One year, on the spur of the moment, we decided to go on a quick trip to Lyons. Unfortunately, we had chosen the very fortnight in which most of the big-name restaurants were on vacation. All were closed except Pyramide, in nearby Vienne. I am afraid that dinner was not a success. The moment we walked in, we were told in no uncertain terms that we could have only the prix fixe dinner, and after rich but delicious *amuse-gueules* and the predictable foie gras in a brioche dough—which is not my favorite way of eating foie gras—came roast duck with two thick, overrich sauces, both of which were undistinguished and completely overshadowed the excellent cooking of the entree and desserts. However, we fared very well in another little one-star restaurant in Lyons—very typical with its businesslike air and rather tasteless French suburban decor. The food was simple and well prepared, but it was the winter salad with its hot lardons and walnuts that drew my attention. I have tried to re-create it, but without the lardons.

> About 6 cups, loosely packed, of mixed winter greens: *mâche,* chicory,
>   dandelion leaves *(pissenlit),* watercress, arugula, radicchio
> ½ cup cubed whole wheat bread, dried (for croutons)
> 1 large clove garlic, peeled
> ⅓ cup sliced fennel root
> ½ (2-ounce) can anchovy fillets
> ½ cup walnut pieces

dressing

> 1½ teaspoons Dijon mustard
> 4 tablespoons walnut oil (preferably) or a fruity olive oil
> 1½ tablespoons good red wine or sherry vinegar
>   Sea salt and freshly ground black pepper

Wash the greens, spin dry, and tear into large pieces.

Preheat the oven to 350° F. Spread the bread cubes out on a well-oiled baking sheet and let them bake until crisp, about 15 to 20 minutes, depending on how dry they are. Set aside. Crush the garlic in the salad bowl and smear it around the bottom and sides. Add the ingredients for the dressing and beat well. Adjust the seasoning and vinegar to taste—the dressing should be very sharp. Toss the croutons and fennel briefly in the dressing. Cut the anchovies into small pieces and add them with the greens and walnuts to the dressing. Toss just before serving. Do not overtoss and wilt your greens.

Ensalada de Nopal (Cactus Salad)

The idea of eating cactus is probably totally alien to those not initiated into the mysteries of Mexican food. There are even people who ask me if it is eaten raw. Well, no, you remove the prickles and cook it. In Mexico nopal cactus paddles are said to cure stomach ulcers, and its medicinal properties for heart ailments are at present being explored by the Japanese. Certainly cactus provide fiber in a diet, but anything is possible with these natural foods, which kept a large pre-Hispanic population alive and strong.

Cactus paddles for cooking—the slimmest and tenderest—are available the year round, but they are at their best in the spring when the cactus plant throws out its new shoots. If you wander through a Mexican market at that time, the most spectacular of the prepared foods will be a large, circular tray of cactus salad covered with slices of intensely red tomatoes, lots of coriander, and white onion. The nopal cactus gives a crunchy texture and slight acidy flavor to the salad, which is one of my favorites.

Nopals, like okra, give off a slimy substance when cooked, and the best method of cooking them to retain their nutrients and yet make them acceptable is the one that I wrote about in *Recipes from the Regional Cooks of Mexico, al vapor,* which I am repeating here.

There are a surprising number of markets now carrying fresh cactus paddles during their season in the United States, and I am afraid I cannot recommend either the bottled or canned commercial ones as a substitute.

> 1½ **pounds fresh nopal cactus paddles**
> 2 **tablespoons vegetable oil**
> 2 **scallions, chopped, with the green leaves**
> 2 **cloves garlic, peeled and chopped**
> **Sea salt to taste**

With a sharp knife, scrape the prickles off the cactus, taking care not to remove all the outer green layer that gives it color. Rinse the paddles well in cold water to make sure that none of the almost invisible prickles are still adhering to them. (In the Southwest I came across a method of removing prickles more easily by plunging them into boiling water. I do not advise it, because it affects the final color and texture.) Cut into narrow strips about ¼ inch wide and 2½ inches long.

Heat the oil and fry the scallions and garlic in it gently, without browning, for 2 minutes. Add the nopals and salt, cover the pan, and cook over a fairly high flame until all the slimy substance comes out—it helps to stir from time to time—about 8 minutes. Remove the cover and continue cooking and stirring over a high flame until that substance has been absorbed—about 15 to 20 minutes. Set aside to cool off.

for assembling salad

    The cooked nopals
1½ tablespoons fruity olive oil
2 tablespoons vinegar
    Heaped ¼ teaspoon Mexican oregano
1 heaped tablespoon finely chopped white onion
3 tablespoons crumbled *queso fresco,* or white crumbly mild cheese
1 heaped tablespoon roughly chopped fresh cilantro (coriander)
1 tablespoon liquid from chili can *(see below)*
    Sea salt to taste

garnish

2 medium tomatoes, unskinned and cut into thin slices
1 tablespoon crumbled *queso fresco*
1 scant tablespoon roughly chopped cilantro (coriander)
1 medium purple onion cut into thin rings
    Strips of canned *chiles jalapeños en escabeche* to taste

While still slightly warm, mix the nopals with the rest of the ingredients and set aside to season—not in the refrigerator—for about 1 hour. Test for additional salt.

    Garnish the salad and serve at room temperature, never cold.

    This salad can also be served as a first course with hot tortillas.

Oriental Watercress Salad

4 SERVINGS

This recipe was suggested to me some years ago by a young Korean who owned a vegetable stand on Manhattan's Upper West Side. This is my version of it, authentic or not.

2 cups firmly packed watercress, thick stems removed
2 tablespoons roughly chopped fresh coriander (cilantro)
½ teaspoon finely chopped fresh ginger root
3 small scallions, trimmed and finely chopped, with the green leaves
1½ tablespoons Chinese sesame oil
3 tablespoons rice vinegar, preferable Japanese
3 teaspoons soy sauce
1½ tablespoons sesame seeds, lightly toasted

Wash the watercress well and spin dry. Put in a bowl with the chopped coriander. Set aside. Beat together the ginger root, scallions, oil, vinegar, and soy sauce until well amalgamated, and toss the salad with this dressing and the toasted sesame seeds. Serve at room temperature.

Jicama in Lime Juice

I never thought much of jicama served as it is generally in Mexico—sliced and sprinkled with chili powder, lime juice, and salt—until my friend Roberta Schneiderman was visiting me in Mexico. She told me that some Mexican friends of hers had served this on a recent visit. It is delicious. Serve it either plain, eaten with a toothpick as an appetizer; mix it in with a salad; or use it as an accompaniment to broiled meats.

1 medium jicama (about 1¼ pounds), peeled and cut into ¾-inch squares
2 tablespoons finely chopped white onion or scallions
½ cup freshly squeezed lime juice
3 tablespoons grated cheese (*añejo* in Mexico, Sardo or Romano in the United States)
1 canned *chile jalapeño en escabeche,* roughly chopped, or to taste
1 heaped tablespoon finely chopped cilantro (coriander) leaves and tender stalks
Sea salt to taste if necessary

Put the jicama and onion in a china or glass bowl and stir in the lime juice. Set aside to marinate for about 2 hours. Stir in the rest of the ingredients and serve at room temperature. Salt should not be necessary with the rather salty cheese.

This dish doesn't keep beyond the day it's made.

Brown and Wild Rice Salad

The idea of rice salads in summer always appeals to me, and then as I bite into the rice I realize I don't particularly care for its texture when it's cold. This is a variation that gives plenty of texture and flavor. You can mix your salad depending on your mood: Italian, Greek, Mexican, substituting spices and ingredients accordingly.

1 cup long-grained, unconverted brown rice
½ cup wild rice
2¼ cups cold water
1 rounded teaspoon sea salt, or to taste

Rinse the rice and wild rice briefly in cold water and drain. Put into a pressure cooker with the water, cover, and bring up to pressure. Lower the flame and cook for 30 minutes on the lowest pressure *(but see note on page 74 on rice of different properties).* Remove from the flame and allow the pressure to reduce normally—but not under cold water. Remove the lid and stir the rice quickly with a fork, sprinkling the salt over it. Place a tea towel over the rice, replace the lid, and allow the rice to finish cooking in its own steam for 20 minutes. Every grain should be slightly *al dente* and standing apart from its neighbor.

NOTE If you do not have a pressure cooker, cook the brown and wild rice together, using the normal cooking method for brown rice.

seasoning

> 5 tablespoons good olive oil
> 3 tablespoons white or red wine vinegar
> Sea salt to taste
> Freshly ground black pepper
> ¼ teaspoon freshly ground nutmeg, turmeric, or paprika *(optional)*, depending on the type of ingredients you want to mix in the salad

Stir the oil, vinegar, and seasonings into the rice while still warm and then add the rest of the ingredients to taste.

Suggestions for rice salads of different types:

MEDITERRANEAN

grated lemon rind/cured black olives/chopped anchovies/very finely chopped garlic/roughly chopped fresh basil

MEXICAN

chopped green chilies/chopped fresh cilantro (coriander)/cubed jicama/cubed avocado/cubed cooked nopals

AMERICAN

chopped celery/green or red peppers in strips/diced cucumber/tuna fish in chunks

LIGHT DISHES

I think it must have been about 1950 when I went with a friend to Provence for the first time. I went with my head full of dreams about living there, having just read *Perfume from Provence* by Lady Fortescue and for years having reread *Lettres de Mon Moulin* by Daudet. Although we didn't go in springtime and see the flowers of Grasse or the sheep going up the mountainside to their summer pasture, I was not disappointed. We had very little money to spend, so had to take the cheapest part of the train, which we shared with Algerian migrant workers on their way to Marseilles from Paris. As they lined the corridor, we couldn't make a move in the night without eyes peering at us through the window of the compartment. And we had the smell of mutton, which they were constantly eating, or so it seemed, and the heavy smell of their Gauloise cigarettes. We were glad to get there and finally board a bus that whisked us along the Corniche.

It was there just as Cézanne had painted it: the land rising steeply on one side covered with rugged little pines that were permanently bent against the wind, and to the right the unforgettable azure mirror of the Mediterranean. Everyone who was anyone had gone back to Paris, and the houses of the little resorts that we passed were shuttered and deserted. I was clutching in my hand, fearful of losing it, a letter from the owner of a little apartment, assuring us that we could occupy it: an old wine *cave* that looked right over the Vieux Port of Saint-Tropez. It was one of those memorable vacations for the sounds, tastes, and colors that we encountered.

I can't now remember why, but in the afternoons we were allowed to go through the back door of the local bakery and choose our bread straight from the oven, and we ate that with omelettes and aromatic Camembert—gloriously unpasteurized—every day for three weeks, saving our pennies for the big event of the day, dinner at the local bistro. I can still savor those meals today and see the faces of the owners as they welcomed us like very special guests. Although it was a prix fixe meal, something extra was sent to the table every night: an extra half bottle of local wine, a liqueur, or a second dessert. How I loved those earthy meals redolent with fruity olive oil and herbs. Several times in the week we would start with a rich, mushy ratatouille. I remember fresh sardines broiled on a bed of savory spinach, and the smallest little crabs mixed up with sea-flavored rice, *riz aux crabes*—it was a revelation to someone with rather a proper English upbringing to be sitting in a restaurant in which everyone was noisily and happily sucking the insides and juice from those little crabs.

It was altogether an enchanted holiday.

Many years later I went back along the Corniche—it had grown, become busy, it wasn't the same. All those memories came flooding back, things I hadn't thought of for years, as I made my *tian* the other day with vegetables from my garden in Mexico.

I have adapted this wonderfully satisfying dish to vegetables grown here in Mexico. If I serve it hot as a main dish for meatless days, I add three beaten eggs and a lot of crumbled *queso fresco* (the Mexican fresh cheese). Onion is a matter of taste; I happen to use very little because it doesn't agree with me, but you can add a lot more, thinly sliced. I serve *tian* either hot or cold and like to drink a chilled, dry rosé with it.

TIAN

One of the national dishes of Provence, but a family dish; one that the tourist will search for in vain on the menus of restaurants.

It is the container which indicates the contents, and the *tian* owes its name to the vast and heavy terrine of the earthenware of Vallauris, where it is sent to cook on a wood fire in the baker's oven. The dish consists of a gratin of green vegetables, spinach, and chard *(blettes)*, sometimes mixed with marrows, all finely chopped, and first melted in—this is essential—olive oil.　　　　—H. Heyraud, *La Cuisine à Nice*

    3 tablespoons rich olive oil
    ½ small white onion, finely chopped
    3 cloves garlic, peeled and finely chopped
    3 *chiles poblanos,* charred, peeled, and cut into strips *(see page 13)*
    1 pound zucchini, trimmed and cut into small squares (about ⅜ inch)
    1½ cups fresh or frozen (do not defrost) corn kernels
    ⅓ cup roughly chopped *epazote* leaves *(optional)*
    20 zucchini or pumpkin flowers *(optional)*
       Sea salt to taste
    3 tablespoons Parmesan cheese
    1 cup cooked rice, preferably brown or long-grained white

topping

    1½ tablespoons olive oil
    5 tablespoons roughly ground bread crumbs
    1 tablespoon Parmesan cheese

You will need a round casserole at least 2 inches deep and of 4-cup capacity.

Heat the 3 tablespoons olive oil in a large frying pan, add the onion and garlic, and fry gently, without browning, until translucent. Add the chili strips and cook for a moment longer. Add the zucchini, corn, zucchini flowers (if using), *epazote,* and salt to taste (remembering that the Parmesan has to go in), cover the pan, and cook over a medium flame, stirring from time to time, until the squash is tender but not soft, about 15 minutes. Set the vegetables aside to cool a little before adding the 3 tablespoons Parmesan cheese and rice.

Heat the oven to 375° F. Lightly oil the baking dish and transfer the vegetables to the dish—they should be about 2 inches deep in the dish, to keep moist.

Heat the 1½ tablespoons olive oil for the topping, add the crumbs, and stir them for a second or two over a high flame. Sprinkle the 1 tablespoon Parmesan cheese over the top of the *tian.* Bake until it is very hot all the way through and you can hear it bubbling, about 20 to 25 minutes.

NOTE If you are using the beaten eggs and *queso fresco,* add them with the Parmesan cheese and rice.

Pancakes (Crepes)

Shrove Tuesday was the day for making pancakes when I was growing up. Everybody's mother made pancakes, and we and our friends all learned to toss pancakes (or, more elegantly, crepes) at a very early age. We did this while listening to the commentary over the radio on the traditional Shrove Tuesday pancake race held at Olney in Buckinghamshire.

Mother's pancakes were very thin and had a particularly nice lacy brown pattern on the first side; the surface was a little more solid but still etched with a golden brown on the second. You could see through them and they didn't taste the least bit eggy. I remember that we consumed an awful lot of them because they were such fun to make. As they came out of the pan they were sprinkled with lemon juice and castor (fine granulated) sugar, rolled, and sprinkled on top with more lemon juice and sugar, then eaten immediately. I still love them that way and abhor those solid, pallid disks that look as though they have been cooked on one of those ridiculous upside-down pans . . . off with their heads!

½ **cup milk**
¾ **cup water**
1 **large egg**
4 **ounces unbleached, all-purpose flour** (*please weigh*)
  Large pinch of sea salt
2 **tablespoons melted and cooled unsalted butter, plus about 2 ounces unsalted butter for the pan**

Put the milk, water, and egg in the blender jar and blend until the egg is beaten well; gradually beat in the flour and salt. Blend until smooth. Add the 2 tablespoons melted butter, blend briefly again, and set aside in a cool place or in the refrigerator for about 2 hours—I sometimes leave it overnight. When I am ready to make the pancakes, I blend once again briefly to make sure that the batter isn't lumpy.

Heat a crepe pan, frying pan, or nonstick skillet, put a small piece of butter in the pan, swirl it around, then pour into a receptacle that should be kept at hand for melted butter. Now try your batter for thickness (not only do flours vary, but if you haven't weighed it, your measurements won't be accurate): pour a little of the batter into the pan, swirl it around rapidly, and it should form a very thin transparent skin. If it is too thick, add more milk or water, blend, and test again. I use a 5-inch crepe pan and find that 3 tablespoons of the batter—for convenience, I use a ¼-cup measure as a scoop and don't fill it—is sufficient to make one crepe. After each crepe, rebutter your pan; this will keep the crepes nice and golden. The first side that is cooked has the prettiest appearance, so that should go outside when you serve the crepes. Pancakes really are durable; you can freeze them or store them in the refrigerator for several days and they always come up smiling. However, they are at their best eaten right away, especially if you are using them for dessert.

See the introductory note and the following recipes for some serving suggestions.

Crepas de Cuitlacoche

This, an elegant dish by any standard, was invented by the distinguished Mexican gastronome the late Jaime Saldivar. *Cuitlacoche* is the Nahuatl name given to the fungus that grows on corn. It resembles large, deformed kernels and its soft black flesh is encased in a silvery grey skin. In Mexico it is available in small quantities the year round—it is even canned—but it is at its best, juicy and crunchy, during the summer rainy season. This is my interpretation of Jaime's creation.

You will never find *cuitlacoche,* or corn fungus, in American markets.★ Although it is not supposed to, it does occasionally occur on hybrid strains of corn. No doubt most farmers would throw it out in disgust, but if you do come across it, growing by accident, cook it and eat it—it is perfectly delicious. Even if you can never find it, make this recipe anyway with ordinary mushrooms. It is well worth while.

filling

8 *chiles poblanos,* charred and peeled *(see page 13)*
2 pounds *cuitlacoche*
2 tablespoons safflower oil
2 tablespoons unsalted butter
¼ medium white onion, finely chopped
2 cloves garlic, peeled and finely chopped
1 teaspoon sea salt, or to taste
2 heaped tablespoons roughly chopped *epazote* leaves *(optional—there is no substitute)*

sauce

1½ cups *crème fraîche* or homemade sour cream
2 reserved chilies and the reserved tops
¼ teaspoon sea salt, or to taste

crepes

Butter for greasing the dish
12 (5-inch) crepes *(see recipe for Pancakes on page 66)*
Filling and Sauce
4 ounces medium, slightly acidy Cheddar cheese
2 of the *chiles poblanos,* cut into strips

Remove the stalks of the chilies and discard. Cut off the thick tops and set aside for the sauce. Slit the chilies open lengthwise and remove the seeds and veins. Reserve 2 chilies for the sauce. Cut the flesh of 6 of them into ¼-inch strips—4 will go into the filling, and 2 are reserved for decorating the dish.

★*With the exception of Chino's wonderful vegetable gardens in Rancho Santa Fe.*

Remove any leaves and tassels that remain on the *cuitlacoche* and shave off the fungus and any remaining corn kernels as near to the core as possible. Chop roughly. Put the oil and butter into a large frying pan, add the onion and garlic, and cook without browning for about 2 minutes. Add the chili strips from 4 of the chilies and cook for a further 3 minutes over a medium flame, stirring them from time to time to prevent sticking.

Add the corn fungus and salt, cover the pan, and cook over a medium flame, stirring from time to time until it is tender but still crunchy and moist—do not allow it to become mushy—about 15 minutes. Add the *epazote,* if you are using, and cook 5 minutes longer. If the mixture is too juicy, then reduce over a high flame quickly; if it's too dry, during the cooking period add a little water.

To make the sauce Put the chilies and cream into the blender jar and blend until smooth. To prevent curdling, stir in the salt just before using.

To assemble the crepes **Preheat the oven to 350° F** and place the rack in the top half of the oven. Grease well a shallow ovenproof dish into which the crepes will just fit in one layer. Fill the crepes, roll, and set side by side in the dish. Pour the sauce over the crepes. Cover the dish loosely with foil and bake until heated through and bubbling. Sprinkle the top with the cheese, decorate with the chili strips from the remaining 2 chilies, and return to the oven just until the cheese melts. Do not brown.

Crepes Filled with Mushrooms and Fennel with Corn–Sour Cream Sauce
4 TO 6 SERVINGS

This is a recipe that I dreamed up for a little book edited by Beard, Glaser, and Wolf in the Great Cook's Library series. It can, of course, be made with corn tortillas, but the quality of tortillas, except on the West Coast, is so abysmal that I advise crepes. You do not need an expensive cheese for a composite dish like this one. If you buy the domestic block Muenster, which is soft and creamy and melts well (beware the more rubbery products, especially those in a round package), it is more than adequate for this recipe.

filling

- 1 pound mushrooms
- ½ fennel bulb, with some of the leaves
- 2 tablespoons unsalted butter
- 3 tablespoons finely chopped white onion
- 1 clove garlic, peeled and chopped

sauce

> 3 cups very fresh or frozen (do not thaw) corn
> 1½ cups whole milk
> 2 tablespoons butter
> ⅔ cup sour cream, preferably *crème fraîche* or homemade
> Sea salt to taste
> Freshly ground black pepper

crepes

> Unsalted butter to grease the dish
> 8 ounces domestic Muenster *(see note above)*
> 12 thin 5-inch crepes *(see recipe for Pancakes on page 66)*

Cut off the tips from the stalks of the mushrooms—that's where the dirt is. Put the mushrooms into a colander and dunk them in cold water several times to release any sand or dirt. Drain and cut into thin slices. Trim the tough outside layers from the fennel bulb and chop the leaves fine—you will need about 1 heaped tablespoon for final decoration of the crepes; set aside. Julienne the fennel root and set aside.

Melt the butter in a frying pan and cook the onion and garlic until soft but not browned. Add the mushrooms and fennel root to the pan and cook uncovered for about 15 minutes—the vegetables should be tender but still a little crisp. Set aside.

To prepare the sauce Put the corn and milk—one third at a time—into the blender jar and blend until smooth. Pass the puree through the fine disk of the food mill. Heat the butter in a heavy pan, add the corn puree, and cook—stirring almost all the time, for it sticks easily—until it begins to simmer and thicken, about 15 minutes. Allow the mixture to cool off a little and then stir in the sour cream and add the salt and pepper to taste. Set aside.

To assemble the crepes Preheat the oven to 400° F. Set the oven rack in the center part of the oven. Butter well an ovenproof dish in which the crepes will just fit in one layer—not too large, or the sauce will dry out at the edges.

Cut three quarters of the cheese into 24 thin strips. Grate the remaining cheese. Put 2 strips of the cheese into one of the crepes and then some of the filling—the crepe should be nice and fat. Place on prepared dish. Repeat with the rest of the crepes.

Pour the sauce over the crepes and bake until they are well heated through and the sauce begins to bubble. Sprinkle the top with the grated cheese and chopped fennel leaves and return to the oven until the cheese melts but does not brown.

Chicken Salad I

Chicken salad with all that mayonnaise is a bore—and fattening to boot. As you well know by now, I love the sharp *serrano* chilies when they are fresh (canned are all right in certain things) and cilantro (fresh coriander), so I came up with this crisp, refreshing salad to be served on small lettuce leaves—Bibb is ideal, but avoid strong greens that will fight with these flavors.

> 1 **whole chicken breast with bone (about 1 pound)**
> **About 2½ cups well-seasoned chicken broth**
> 3 **tablespoons dark Chinese sesame oil**
> 1½ **tablespoons lime juice plus 1½ tablespoons freshly squeezed orange juice; or 3 tablespoons lemon juice**
> 2 **tablespoons roughly chopped fresh cilantro (coriander), or to taste**
> 1 **scallion, finely chopped, with the green leaves**
> 1 **heaped cup diced cucumber (about ¼-inch squares)**
> 1 **fresh *chile serrano* or any fresh green chili, finely chopped**
> ¼ **teaspoon finely grated ginger root**
> **Sea salt to taste**
> 1 **tablespoon toasted sesame seeds**
> **Lettuce leaves**

Put the whole chicken breast—bone, skin, everything—into a pan with the chicken broth and cook over a slow flame until just tender, about 15 to 25 minutes, depending on the size. Do not let the breast become too soft. Allow the breast to cool off in the broth. While still lukewarm, remove the bones and skin and discard. Cut the meat into ½-inch squares and season with the sesame oil and fruit juices. Toss in the rest of the ingredients except for the sesame seeds, and season. Set aside in a cool but not cold place to macerate for about 1 hour. When you are about to eat, toss in the sesame seeds, stir well, and serve on delicate lettuce leaves at room temperature.

Chicken Salad II

Fonda San Francisco in Mexico City is one of the most versatile restaurants I know. In the daytime it is a *cocina popular* where office workers can eat a simple, home-cooked meal at a very reasonable cost, while in the evening there is a change of scene. With colorful tablecloths, cushions, flowers, and the like, it is transformed into an intimate little dining place that has a most innovative menu, while the food itself is presented with imagination. For example: the *sopa de flor de calabaza* is served up in a hollowed-out green squash (the round *criollo,* as opposed to the long zucchini). Their *ensalada de pollo* caught my attention as being very interesting in flavor and texture. It is no doubt a recipe from Huatusco in the state of Veracruz, the birthplace of owner/gourmet Paco García Muñoz. I didn't ask Paco for his recipe because I can never find him; he moves around the world like quicksilver. I have instead re-created it, and I hope he will approve.

This recipe is called a "salad" and it can be served on a bed of lettuce, but I almost prefer it as a topping for a *tostada*—the tortilla toasted crisp and not fried—or stuffed in avocado halves. If you leave out the oil, it is perfect for dieters.

1 **whole chicken breast with bone (about 1 pound)**
  About 2½ cups well-seasoned chicken broth
⅓ **cup finely chopped white onion (not minced)**
3 **tablespoons lime juice**
  Sea salt to taste
½ **teaspoon Mexican oregano**
2 **canned** *chiles jalapeños en escabeche,* **or to taste, roughly chopped**
2 **tablespoons fruity olive oil** *(optional)*
  Lettuce leaves
  Thickly sliced avocado

Put the whole chicken breast—bone, skin, everything—into a pan with the chicken broth and cook over a low flame until just tender, about 15 to 25 minutes, depending on the size; do not let the meat become too soft. Allow to cool off in the broth. While the breast is still lukewarm, remove the bones and skin and discard. Shred the chicken.

In the meantime, put the onion into the lime juice with salt to taste and set aside to macerate for about 1 hour.

Mix all the ingredients except the avocado and lettuce together, adjusting the salt, and serve at room temperature—not cold—on a bed of lettuce topped with slices of avocado.

Every once in a while I get a craving for a good plateful of bulgur to go along with a roast chicken or pot roast. It also makes a very good stuffing, and it's delicious alone with a large amount of plain yogurt and chopped coriander on top. You will need a coarse bulgur for this recipe. If you are not familiar with the three types: coarse is for cooking as a cereal, medium for tabbouleh, and fine is for kibbe. I suggest you go along to a store that specializes in Middle Eastern foods and sells them in bulk—never trust a package unless you can see what is inside. I say this from an experience I had recently on the West Coast that was repeated in New York City—when I didn't have time to go down to the East Twenties or Atlantic Avenue in Brooklyn. I wanted to prepare some tabbouleh, and my quest took me to a number of specialty food and health food stores. I was offered a package of preflavored tabbouleh mix—what on earth happened to all that fresh mint, parsley, and lemon juice?—and I was also offered cracked wheat. I stood amazed in silence as the shop assistant held up some broken reddish grains. "This is what everybody uses for tabbouleh," she assured me. It was cracked wheat all right, but not precooked and prepared in the way that any Lebanese cook would demand. I couldn't help thinking on my way home of all those horribly chewy tabboulehs being made around town that one would have to have the stomach of a horse to digest.

How to prepare it at home After that experience in trying to buy bulgur for tabbouleh, I decided that I would try and make it myself—or at least understand the process, as I found out later. It took a little time to find someone who actually made it from scratch, but I was finally introduced to an energetic Lebanese lady who works in a Zitácuaro school in the mornings, tends her yard-goods shop in the afternoons, and also caters the occasional banquet. She makes bulgur for the whole Lebanese community in the town and usually prepares upward of 22 pounds at once. I experimented with 1½ pounds.

First you need whole-grain wheat—light-colored, not the deep brownish red, which tends to be softer. You put it to boil in cold water, and a lot of it because the wheat absorbs the water and expands. For my small quantity, after one hour it was breaking open—"flowering," as the Mexican expression goes—just like the hominy for *pozole*. You then drain the wheat and spread it out on perforated trays to dry in the sun—or in a very warm, dry place with plenty of air circulating. This process should take four days, during which time you turn it over and make sure that all the grains get exposed to the air. (Señora Divi doesn't make the bulgur in very damp weather.) At the end of this time you rub the grains against each other with your hands or against a fine wire tray to loosen more of the husks, and then pour the grains from one hand or one bowl to another in front of an electric fan so that the loose chaff flies away. After that the wheat is stone-ground and again poured in front of the fan to get rid of all the remaining chaff. At this stage you need three sieves with different-sized perforations so that you can divide the ground wheat into fine, medium, and coarse.

I took along the wheat that I had prepared at home for her inspection. Part of the family was there—including the brother-in-law, who had installed all the glass in my house—and all offered their advice. In the first place, I had bought the wrong wheat—the red, which was the only one available here in Zitácuaro. "You only let it dry for two days instead of four," declared Señora Divi; and of course it was full of chaff because I do not possess an electric fan and there was no wind during those stormy days. By then I decided that it was quite enough for me to understand its preparation, as I simply do not have the patience to do my own.

To cook the bulgur

> 2 tablespoons chicken fat *(see page 14)*, butter, or oil
> 3 scallions, trimmed and roughly chopped, with all but the tougher tops of the leaves
> 1 large clove garlic, peeled and chopped
> 1 cup coarse bulgur
> 1¼–1½ cups well-seasoned chicken broth, very hot
> Vegetables *(optional; see note below)*
> Sea salt and freshly ground pepper

Heat the fat or oil in a heavy pot about 8 inches in diameter and at least 3 inches deep. Add the scallions and garlic and fry gently without browning for about 2 minutes. Add the bulgur and stir well so that the fat or oil covers the grains evenly. Continue frying and stirring for about 5 minutes. Add 1¼ cups hot broth and the vegetables, if using *(see below)*, stir well, cover the pan, and cook over a low flame for about 15 minutes, or until all the liquid has been absorbed and the grains are tender but not mushy. Test for seasoning and adjust. If the grains are still very chewy, sprinkle on another ¼ cup broth and continue cooking. When the bulgur has reached the right consistency, remove from the flame and leave, covered, in a warm place to continue expanding in its own steam.

NOTE I often add cubed or sliced vegetables to the bulgur, depending what I have around. They should be added at the same time as the broth. I can suggest one or more of the following: ⅓ cup roughly chopped fennel root/¼ cup thinly sliced carrot/⅓ cup raw peas (or unthawed frozen peas)/⅓ cup dried mushrooms, loosely packed *(see below)*.

If using dried mushrooms, I prefer to soak and sauté them first with a little onion. Then add the water in which they were soaked to the pan after straining it through a double layer of cheesecloth.

Brown Rice

I love sticky Japanese rice, moist but chewy risottos, pilafs, Mexican and Chinese rice—but what has happened to American rice? It is the dullest of the lot, fallen to a new low with the advent of converted, precooked, what-you-will rice—and even preflavored, God forbid!

I have always believed in eating healthy foods prepared with whole grains because I like the flavor and texture as well as the nutritional value. And that goes for brown rice. I began experimenting with brown rice some years ago, trying to make it work for traditional, ethnic recipes with some, if not total, success: for instance, I don't particularly like it cooked in traditional Mexican style. But I did find that it makes an excellent partner for wild rice.

Brown rice takes much longer to cook than ordinary rice and I always feel so much is lost in the cooking water—unless you bake it, of course—so I came up with some rice recipes cooked in the pressure cooker, which gives great results.

Brown rice—on its own or mixed with wild rice—makes excellent rice, salad, rice stuffing for a chicken (see the recipe for Stuffed, Braised Chicken), a variation on risotto, as plain or as fancy as you care to make it.

I find it is better not to put the salt in until after the rice is cooked, to prevent burning with the heat of the pressure cooker.

> 1½ tablespoons unsalted butter or oil
> 1 heaped tablespoon finely chopped onion
> 1⅓ cups long-grained brown rice
> 2½ cups cold water or light chicken broth
> Heaped ½ teaspoon sea salt, or to taste

Heat the butter or oil in the pressure cooker, add the onion, and fry gently until translucent. Add the rice; stir well but do not cook in the butter. Add the water or broth—but no salt—put the lid on the pressure cooker, and bring up to full pressure. Lower the flame and cook at low pressure for 35 minutes. Allow the pressure to reduce naturally, not under cold water. Remove the lid, stir in the salt, and loosen the grains quickly with a fork. Cover with a tea towel, replace the lid firmly, and set aside to steam for a further 20 minutes.

VARIATION Suggested addition after cooking brown rice: ⅔ cup roughly chopped parsley and 2 cloves garlic, peeled and finely chopped.

Brown Rice "Risotto" in a Pressure Cooker 3 TO 4 SERVINGS

Now that brown rice has "caught on," there are some softened and refined brands appearing on the market—although the label does not indicate this. Choose those that are real, earthy brown rice, with a slight greenish hue, and avoid the pale golden variety. You will have to experiment, as the cooking time needs to be adjusted.

> 1 cup long-grained brown rice *(see page 74)*
> 2 tablespoons unsalted butter
> 1 tablespoon safflower oil
> ¼ small onion, finely chopped
> Rounded ⅓ cup dried mushrooms *(optional; see note below)*
> 2½ cups well-seasoned chicken broth
> Sea salt to taste, depending on broth
> ⅓ cup roughly chopped parsley
> ⅓ cup finely grated Parmesan cheese

Rinse the rice briefly and drain. Heat the butter and oil in a pressure cooker, add the onion, and cook, stirring, until translucent. Give the rice a final shake to get rid of excess water and stir it into the fat, together with the soaked mushrooms, if used. Add the broth and the salt if necessary, cover, and bring up to pressure, lower the flame, and cook over low heat for about 25 minutes. Remove the cooker from the flame and allow the pressure to reduce naturally and slowly. The rice should still be textured and have the moisture of a well-made risotto. Toss with the parsley and Parmesan.

NOTE Dried mushrooms have to be soaked before using or they will have a very strong flavor. Cover the mushrooms with water, bring to a simmer, and cook for about 3 minutes. Set aside to soak for 5 or 10 minutes. Strain the mushrooms and add to the rice, then strain the broth through 2 layers of cheesecloth and add that to the rice.

WHOLE-GRAIN PASTA

I can do without meat anytime if I have a good plate of pasta. I am afraid I do use the food processor and, although I was chided by my friend Marcella Hazan, I do use a machine to roll it out, at least these whole-grain pastas.

I like to "mix and match" my cuisines and often use, for instance, Mexican vegetables with Italian pasta. Last year, when friends arrived unexpectedly, they were surprised to be eating whole wheat tagliarini *(tallarines)* with brilliant blue mushrooms and yellow corn. A fascinating combination is linguine with chopped *cuitlacoche* (corn fungus) and chili strips. I quite often julienne zucchini, chayote, or fennel root, or blend the dark-green *chilaca* (substitute *poblano* in the United States) with thick cream and serve that along with a *picante* tomato sauce over the pasta. Anything goes so long as we don't call it authentic.

The following two recipes are based on one for white flour that Jerrie Strom and Fran Jenkins use in their Italian cooking classes in Rancho Santa Fe.

Triticale Pasta
5 SERVINGS*

I like the texture that triticale flour gives to breads, crackers, and pasta. As with whole wheat flour, pasta made of triticale is more suited to tagliarini and linguine—stringy pastas, as I call them—than the more solid ravioli, lasagna, etc.

  1½ cups triticale flour
  ¼ teaspoon sea salt
  2 small eggs, at room temperature, slightly beaten
  2–3 tablespoons water
  2 tablespoons light olive oil

Place the flour and salt in the bowl of the food processor and, using the steel blade, turn on for 1 second. Gradually pour the eggs into the flour and process for about 12 seconds, or until the mixture resembles coarse meal. You may need to scrape the bottom of the container with a spatula in the middle of processing, as this flour tends to stick more easily. Add the water and oil and continue processing until the dough forms a ball around the blade, about 1 minute. (Flours vary so much that you may need a little more liquid—or a little less—to reach the correct texture.) Remove the dough from the container and follow the instructions for rolling whole wheat pasta on page 77.

Can anybody but the Italians really agree on how far this will go round?

Whole Wheat Pasta

Whole wheat pasta will probably become more popular in these days of high-fiber diets. The commercial whole wheat pasta does not appeal to me, but I do like the homemade, which has more texture and is not such a somber color. The most important thing is to find the right flour. In the East, Heckers puts out a consistently good whole wheat flour, but it is not distributed throughout the country. You will have to experiment with locally distributed brands or loose flour, providing it is not pastry flour. (I don't happen to think that pastry should *ever* be made with whole wheat flour, which takes all the fun away.)

I prefer whole wheat for the "stringy" pastas rather than for ravioli and lasagna, etc.

  1½ **cups whole wheat flour** *(see note above)*
  ¼ **teaspoon sea salt**
  2 **large eggs, at room temperature, lightly beaten**
     About 1 tablespoon water
  2 **tablespoons light olive oil**

Place the flour and salt in the container of the food processor and, using the steel blade, turn on for 1 second. Gradually pour in the eggs and process for about 12 seconds, or until the mixture resembles coarse meal. Add the water and oil and continue to process until the dough forms a ball around the blade. (Flours vary a lot and you may need to experiment with your brand and increase or decrease the liquid slightly.)

Remove the dough and divide it into 3 portions. While you work with the first piece, cover the other 2 with a damp towel. If you use a pasta machine—and I am afraid I do—to roll your dough, then pass it through the widest setting of the rollers. Fold the dough into 3 and repeat the process twice. Roll and fold 3 times at each setting from 1 to 5—I can never get it up to 6, and, besides, I prefer this pasta to be a little more chewy. Cut and cook in the usual way.

TIPS For rolling pasta:
1. If your pasta breaks, go back 2 notches on the setting of the rollers and repeat the rolling twice at each setting.
2. Especially when you are using grainy flours such as whole wheat and triticale, little pieces of the pasta are apt to stick unseen underneath and at the ends of the rollers, so be sure and clean them off quite often.
3. When you get up to number 5 setting, your pasta becomes uncontrollably long and should be cut in half.

Tallarines a la Mexicana

Have ready one recipe of a whole-grain pasta (whole wheat, page 77, or triticale, page 76).

> 3 tablespoons unsalted butter
> 1 small white onion, thinly sliced
> 8 *chiles poblanos,* charred, peeled, seeds removed *(see page 13),* and cut into
> ¼-inch strips
> Sea salt to taste
> 1½ cups corn kernels (unthawed, if frozen)

Heat the butter and fry the onion gently for 2 minutes. Add the chili strips and salt, cover the pan, and cook slowly for a further 5 minutes. Add the corn kernels, stir well, and cook uncovered until just tender, about 5 minutes, depending on how tender the corn is. Adjust the seasoning.

Toss this mixture with the pasta, and add cheese or whatever else you like. Lots of chopped *epazote?* You knew I would say that!

André Claude's Omelette Verte, Ouverte

When my friend André Claude comes to visit, he gravitates quite naturally toward the kitchen. He did so on a recent surprise visit to Quinta Diana and offered to cook the brunch eggs. I asked him if he wanted some of Señorita Esperanza's special butter—which I do not share with everyone. No, he preferred the newly rendered lard sitting on the counter. It reminded him of his mother's kitchen in Vietnam. He said that one of his most vivid memories was carrying home from market a large slab of pork fat to render into lard for her cooking. On this particular occasion he made his *omelette verte, ouverte* (I call it more prosaically scrambled egg omelette *aux fines herbes*) to use some of the abundant crop of chervil and parsley in my herb garden. He generally uses one strong herb—tarragon, chervil, dill, or basil—along with the parsley and chives. He used 5 eggs for 3 people and a 9-inch omelette pan.

1½ tablespoons good pork lard or butter
  3 tablespoons finely chopped white onion
  3 fresh *chiles serranos,* slit open, veins and seeds removed, and sliced into thin
     rings
  2 teaspoons freshly squeezed lime juice
  5 large eggs
    Sea salt to taste
3–4 tablespoons finely chopped herbs *(see note above)*

Melt the lard, add the onion and chilies, and as they begin to fry, sprinkle them with the lime juice. Continue to cook gently until the onion is translucent and soft but not browned. Crack open the eggs and place them over the surface of the onion as if you were going to poach them. Sprinkle with the salt and break them up quickly with a wooden spoon to resemble roughly scrambled eggs—just as they scramble eggs in Mexico. Lift up the edges of the omelette and let the uncooked mixture seep around the edges of the pan. Sprinkle the chopped herbs over the top and continue cooking until the bottom of the omelette is set firm but the top still soft and creamy, about 1½ minutes. Serve immediately.

COLD MEATS

At the first glimmer of summer sunshine, every other activity at home was dropped during the school vacation and we went off for a picnic. I never did like picnics, nor do I to this day, even if it is with champagne and all at Glyndebourne. I have visions of sitting on a damp beach in midsummer, with a bitter east wind blowing through you, and watching the waves rise and crash while hoping hard that one of the grown-ups will feel hungry and the picnic hamper will be opened up and the spirit stove lit. Or sitting in a meadow of tall grasses and wildflowers on an overhot day, sneezing like mad, with insects biting and small caterpillars hanging from the oak trees on gossamer threads dropping down your neck or into your food.

Cold meats were an important part of picnic food. Not the chic pâtés and terrines of France, or the elegant prosciuttos and country sausages of Italy, but homely, satisfying food. When we knew we were going for a picnic ahead of time, Mother would make her cold meat roll or a bacon and egg pie, or fry some thick pork sausages to eat with hot mustard and crusty bread. But if it was decided just on the spur of the moment, one of us was dispatched to the local pie shop to buy thinly sliced ham and tongue, or Scotch eggs that were still warm and crusty from the frying pan. In summer, cold meats were indispensable for high tea: a small pork pie or some rich, lardy liver sausage to spread on our bread or eat with a salad. I still get nostalgic for those tastes and love to make the recipes from time to time, and dream a little.

In Mexico the cold meats are vinegary and spicy and I love them: pigs' feet in a light pickle; the delicious *fiambre* from San Luis Potosí with pigs' feet, chicken breast, and tongue in a vinaigrette; a *salpicón* of venison soaked in the juice of Seville oranges with radishes and coriander, all of them spiced with chilies and sharp and crisp.

Scotch Eggs

4 SERVINGS

I am sure if they were promoted in the right way, Scotch eggs would rival hot dogs on any picnic. They were one of our favorite picnic foods, eaten with a salad and lots of hot mustard—Colman's, of course. Nobody ever dreamed of making them in those days—we bought them freshly fried at the local delicatessen—so this is my version of the recipe.

- ¾ **pound pork, not too lean**
- 2 **long strips lean bacon**
- ¼ **teaspoon anchovy paste**
- **Large pinch of dried thyme**
- ¼ **teaspoon roughly crushed black pepper**
- 4 **small hard-boiled eggs, shelled**
- **Lard for frying**
- 1 **raw egg, well beaten**
- **About 8 tablespoons roughly ground, toasted bread crumbs** *(see note page 12)*

COLD MEATS

Chop the pork and bacon roughly and put into the container of the food processor. Add the anchovy paste, thyme, and pepper (salt should not be necessary) and process with the steel blade until the meat is very well ground and the mixture forms a ball around the blade. Take about ⅓ cup of the meat mixture and press it out into a rough circle. Mold around one of the eggs, repeat for the other 3 eggs.

Heat the lard in the frying pan—it should be at least ¼ inch deep in the pan. Dip one of the eggs into the beaten egg, coat thickly with bread crumbs, and fry until a very deep brown, taking care that the meat is completely cooked through to the center where it touches the hard-boiled egg. Drain and serve hot or allow to cool and eat cold with a salad.

PICNICS

No matter what month of the year, at the first glimpse of sunshine at weekends our parents packed lunch and off we went to the country. Country wasn't far away in those days, as we lived on the outskirts of London—now it is all built up with row upon row of boxy little suburban houses—but we would take a bus ride that would leave us several miles from home and near the beginning of a planned footpath walk. The footpath would take us across the farmland of some grand estate, and through meadows and woods where we would always stop and picnic along the way. In springtime we would make a special pilgrimage to pick bluebells—it is one of *the* sights of England to see a carpet of mauvy-blue bluebells waving elegantly on their tall stalks under the shade of beech trees whose pale green, newly unfurled leaves dance in the breeze.

There was one picnic we always looked forward to. Father took great pride in "cutting good sandwiches"—the bread was thin, and if there was roast beef inside them it was thickly spread with drippings from the roasting pan, and there was lots of horseradish and pepper on the meat. Sometimes the sandwiches were of sliced lamb and chutney—I can still feel the crunch of the mustard seeds in that chutney (see the recipe for Green Tomato Chutney)—or a crusty roll filled with good fatty ham with a hard-boiled egg and a tomato to eat on the side—that was awkward because you had to juggle them and the tomato juice always squirted out across your lap. Occasionally Mother would make her meat roll, which was thickly sliced and eaten with our fingers. . . . I always remember that meat roll and was dismayed when my sister wrote to tell me that Mother had lost the recipe some years before she died. So I have tried to re-create it.

Mother's Poached Meat Loaf

This meat loaf has a rough texture. You could make one 12-inch roll, especially if you have a fish poacher into which it will just fit, but it is probably more convenient to make two 6-inch rolls. You will need a pan with a lid into which the rolls will just fit, and 2 rectangular pieces of thick cotton cloth or several layers of good cheesecloth (not that awful packaged nylon stuff that leaves gauzy threads all over the place) and some string to tie up the ends. I prefer to grind my own meats because I can control the texture, but I would not use a food processor for this recipe.

- 1 pound beef, with a little fat
- ½ pound pork, with a little fat
- ½ pound lean strips of bacon
- ½ cup dried bread crumbs, finely ground (not toasted bread crumbs)
- 2 tablespoons grated onion
- ¼ teaspoon dried thyme
- 10 scrapings of nutmeg
- 1½ teaspoons finely ground sea salt, or to taste
-     A lot of roughly ground black pepper
- 2 small eggs, beaten
- 3 tablespoons milk
- 4 hard-boiled eggs, shelled

poaching broth

- 5 cups beef, or veal (preferably), or chicken stock
- 2 bay leaves
- ½ onion, roughly sliced

Pass the meats and bacon through the medium disks of a meat grinder. In a deep bowl, mix thoroughly the meats, bread crumbs, onion, thyme, seasonings, beaten eggs, and milk. (Fry a little of the mixture to test the seasoning, but remember it is served cold, so you might like to exaggerate the salt and pepper a little.) Divide the meat into 2 parts and roll each into a sausage shape around 2 of the hard-boiled eggs set end to end. Wrap each roll in a cloth or layers of cheesecloth and tie securely with string at each end and loosely in the middle, just to hold the cloth in place.

   Put the broth, bay leaves, and onion into the pan and bring to a simmer, lower the rolls into the broth—it should just cover them—and *simmer* for about 1½ hours. Allow the meat rolls to cool off in the broth for 1 hour, remove, and drain—still in the cloth—and store in a cool place or refrigerate until ready to use. Must be served at room temperature with a lot of hot mustard. Strain the broth—it will now have an even better flavor—and store or freeze.

Raised Pork Pie

ONE PORK PIE

The meat pie attained its full perfection only in England and held its pride of place from the Middle Ages until the nineteenth century. Originally, no doubt, it was evolved as a splendidly convenient way of eating meat in gravy before the fork was in general use: a cold pie where the stock was jellied was, of course, particularly easy to eat with the fingers.

—Elisabeth Ayrton, *The Cookery of England*

And anyone who is as fascinated as I am in the pies of England should certainly read Mrs. Ayrton's chapter on "The Tradition of the Savoury Pie."

I'll warrant that there are few Frenchwomen who regularly make their own terrines and pâtés, and the same holds true for English housewives who buy pork pies regularly for the family but rarely make them. (Unlike many other things made commercially, raised pork pies have maintained a very good standard.)

I hadn't made my own either until a few years ago, when I began to crave one of those rich, lardy, salty pies. That craving developed into a culinary exercise of trying to re-create the same texture and flavor.

For a first attempt, don't choose the biggest, most imposing-looking mold; start with the small ones (see illustrations and sizes below).

The seasoning in a cold pie is even more important than when it is served hot, so start the day before to season the pork, and at the same time make the gelatin. It is also important to weigh the ingredients for the pastry—measuring in cups is inaccurate and can spoil the end product.

I don't see much point in making a very little quantity of stock; make enough for 2 pies and keep some frozen. Nor do I skim the broth.

stock for jelly

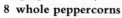

2 CUPS JELLY

- 2 pounds pork bones
- 1 pig's foot, cut up into small pieces
- 1 small onion, roughly sliced
- 1 small carrot, sliced (no need to scrape)
- 2 sprigs fresh marjoram, or a large pinch dried
- 2 sprigs fresh thyme, or a large pinch dried
- 8 whole peppercorns
- 1 bay leaf, crumbled
  Sea salt to taste

> 2 cups ordinary pork broth, skimmed of all traces of fat
> 2 teaspoons powdered unflavored gelatin

filling

> 1½ pounds lean pork without gristle or sinew for the rectangular mold and
>   2 pounds for the oval one
>   4 ounces lean bacon
>   4 ounces pork fat
>   Pinch of saltpeter
>   1 rounded teaspoon finely ground sea salt
> 25 black peppercorns, crushed or roughly ground
>   4 anchovy fillets, salt removed, or canned, drained
>   1 rounded teaspoon combined ground spices: cinnamon, cloves, mace

pastry

> 1¾ pounds unbleached all-purpose flour (not high-gluten bread flour)
>   1 tablespoon finely ground sea salt
> 12 ounces pork lard
>   1 cup plus 1 tablespoon water
>   1 large egg, well beaten

To make the stock Put all the ingredients, except the salt, into a large saucepan, cover with water, and bring to a simmer. Continue simmering—do not allow to boil fast or the broth will be cloudy—for about 4 hours. Strain the broth, discarding the bones—the pig's foot is by now too soft to eat. Skim off all traces of fat and return to the pan. Reduce over a low flame to 2 cups and add the salt. Set aside in the refrigerator to cool.

To make the stock by the quick method Heat the broth. Pour a little of it over the gelatin and stir over hot water until the gelatin has dissolved. Add the dissolved gelatin to the rest of the warm broth and stir well. Set aside in a cool place to jell.

To prepare the filling Grind together roughly ½ pound of the lean pork and the bacon. Cut the remaining pork and pork fat into small cubes between ¼ and ½ inch. Mix the meats together with the rest of the ingredients and work well with the hands so that the spices and other flavors penetrate the meat. Leave, covered, in the refrigerator overnight to season.

I usually allow for a little more pastry than absolutely necessary to give some extra to play with, for decoration and patching.

Preheat the oven to 400° F. Put a baking sheet with sides to it on the middle rack of the oven, to prevent the lard that cooks out of the pastry from dripping onto the oven floor.

In a mixing bowl, stir the flour and salt together. Heat the lard and water together in a small saucepan, and when the mixture comes to a boil, mix it in the flour with a wooden spoon. Turn the dough out onto a cold surface, such as marble, and work it with your hands lightly and quickly until almost smooth. Do not overwork or the pastry will become tough (American flour

---

generally has a higher percentage of gluten in it than British). Take about a third of the dough and roll it out to between ¼- and ½-inch thickness, about 1½ inches larger than the size of the bottom of the mold. Press this into the mold, making sure that the extra dough goes up the sides of the mold in one piece—this is to prevent leakage of juices and, later, gelatin. Continue by rolling out pieces for the sides, making them large enough to hook over the top of the mold; this will stop the pastry from slipping down the sides of the mold before you are finished, which is a frustrating business. As soon as the sides are lined with the dough, put the filling inside; this will help support the rather slippery dough against the sides of the mold. Roll out the rest of the dough lightly and cut out a piece to fit over the top. At this point, trim off the extra dough around the top of the mold and pinch the top and sides together to form a "piecrust" edge. Be sure that the edge clears the metal sides because it tends to stick and will be broken when you remove the mold at a final stage. Make 3 steam holes in the top of the pie and decorate with pastry leaves or whatever your imagination dictates.

Brush the top of the pie with the beaten egg and bake for about 35 minutes. Lower the oven temperature to 350° F and continue cooking an hour more for the rectangular mold and about 20 minutes longer for the oval mold. Depending on your oven, the top of the pie may become a little too brown during the first cooking—especially with those that have reheating elements at the top; if you see this has happened, then cover the top with several layers of brown paper. Remove carefully from the oven so as not to fracture the very short crust and set the pie to cool off for about 1 hour before removing the mold—about 30 minutes longer for the oval mold.

Preheat the oven to 400° F. Brush the pie sides well with the beaten egg and return to the oven until the pie is well browned all round, about 15 minutes. Set aside to cool off for about 2½ hours—the inside should still be slightly warm so that the liquid gelatin will still be able to find its direction through the particles of meat. (I test this by putting my finger in through the steam holes from time to time.) If the pie is too warm, then the gelatin will be soaked up by the rather soft inside of the pastry.

Warm the jellied broth slightly but do not let it become too liquid, then slide it gradually into the steam holes—with a small funnel if available. It should take about 1¼ cups. Leave the pie to cool off completely and the gelatin to set firmly. It is better if left until the following day before attacking it. This sort of pie lasts for a week or more in the refrigerator.

NOTES When I started making these pies, I found Jane Grigson's recipe to be the most helpful—in *Charcuterie and French Pork Cookery*—since many older books rather gloss over the preparations. Making a pie like this needs patience, but it is a very satisfactory culinary exercise, apart from the pie's being wonderful eating—even if it is fattening.

Ovens vary so enormously that cooking times and temperatures can only be approximate. For instance, if you have an Aga cooker or a heavy-duty restaurant oven you can cook this dish at a lower temperature, while a convection oven is not suitable for something so dense.

When I was quite young, one of my favorite cold meats was Aunt Maud's spiced, pressed beef that she used to prepare when she came home from Jamaica. I used to cook it a lot in one period of my life, and I suppose I cooked it from memory because when I looked for a recipe I couldn't find one. My sister and I searched Mother's cookery notebooks; I asked all the members of her immediate family, but no one else could remember it. This recipe is as near as I can get to the taste as I recall it, and in fond memory of Aunt Maud, who knew how to live and eat, I threw in a good cup of Jamaica rum to boot.

I prefer to cook the meat on the bone. It shrinks less and cooks more evenly. Do not let your butcher take off all the fat. A good layer of it on top is necessary for the flavor and, despite calories and cholesterol, the fat must be eaten along with the lean—just a little bit, anyway.

START NINE DAYS AHEAD

- **5–6 pounds beef brisket, bone cracked and with the fat**
- **8 cloves garlic, peeled and crushed**
- **8 whole allspice, ground**
- **8 whole cloves, ground**
- **Rounded ½ teaspoon powdered ginger**
- **Rounded ½ teaspoon ground mace**
- **Scant ¼ teaspoon saltpeter**
- **5 tablespoons coarse sea salt**
- **½ cup heavy Jamaican rum**
- **1 cup dark brown sugar**

Pierce the meat in about 20 places with the point of a sharp knife. Mix the crushed garlic with the spices, saltpeter, and salt. Moisten with the rum and rub into the meat. Let it sit, covered, in the bottom of the refrigerator for 2 days, giving it a massage twice a day. Dissolve the sugar in the liquid that has collected at the bottom of the dish and bathe the meat with it. Keep turning and bathing the meat with the liquid for 6 more days.

- **2 medium carrots, roughly sliced (no need to scrape)**
- **1 large onion, peeled and roughly chopped**
- **1 small rib celery**
- **2 Turkish or 4 California bay leaves**

Preheat the oven to 325° F. Put the meat in a heavy casserole or Dutch oven into which it will just fit. Add the juices from the dish and enough water to barely cover the meat. Add the vegetables and bay leaves to the pot and bake

*If thinly sliced, this can serve 8 to 10.

until tender but not falling apart. Turn the meat once or twice during the cooking period and top up with hot water if necessary. The cooking will take about 3 hours.

Allow the meat to cool off in the liquor for 1 hour. As soon as the meat is cool enough to handle, remove from the pot, remove the bones, and cut off a little of the excess fat, leaving a good layer. Tie the meat into an oblong shape (see diagram), put into a dish, cover, and press with a heavy weight overnight. Cut against the grain in very thin slices and serve with pickles and chutney. It is excellent for sandwiches of rye bread, with lots of hot mustard.

Cold Jellied Tongue
4 TO 6 SERVINGS

Thinly sliced jellied tongue—sliced horizontally so that you eat all the interesting textures in one slice—can compare to and even surpass many finer cuts of meat. It was always my favorite of cold meats, served with cold sliced ham and chutney. We would also have at home potted pigs' tongues, prepared in the same way; another favorite winter dish—and very cheap, too—was stewed lambs' tongues served with a caper sauce.

> 1 **cooked corned tongue** *(see page 116)*
> 2½ **cups jellied stock** *(see page 85)* **or aspic, or 1 envelope powdered unflavored gelatin** *and* **2½ cups light meat broth**

Allow the cooked tongue to cool off in its stock. When cool enough to handle, remove the skin and trim off the fat, the gristly parts of the root, and the small bones found at the base of the root. Choose a round mold or cake pan, and make sure that the tongue just fits into it, curled up. Trim some meat off the bottom if it does not. Remove the tongue and set it aside. If using gelatin, place the gelatin and ¼ cup of the broth into a water bath and stir until melted and smooth. Stir in the rest of the broth and continue stirring until the gelatin has been well amalgamated. Put into the freezer to set for about 15 to 20 minutes. The jellied stock or gelatin mixture, whichever you are using, should be at a soft jellied stage when you take it from the freezer, not firmly set. If you have used gelatin, warm it slightly before proceeding. Spoon about one third of the jellied mixture into the mold; it should cover it completely and smoothly. Place the mold in the freezer to set firmly, about 10 minutes.

Place the tongue in a curled position on top of the gelatin, and spoon the remaining gelatin around the sides and on top of the tongue—do not heat the gelatin-broth mixture too much or it will melt that at the bottom. Cover the mold and refrigerate overnight. Unmold and serve decorated with parsley or watercress. Be sure to have a very sharp knife or, better still, a ham knife to cut it.

Manitas de Puerco Guadalupe
(Guadalupe's Pigs' Feet)

SERVES 4 MEXICANS; 6 OTHERWISE

Pigs' trotters, as we used to call them at home, rate high on my list of personal soul food. I like to gnaw them off the bone and bite through all those different layers of texture. This is one of my favorite ways of preparing them. The recipe was given to me by Señora Guadalupe of Zitácuaro, who is an excellent cook.

I find it better to cook the pigs' feet in the pressure cooker, which takes less than half the time of normal cooking, but be careful not to overcook them, for they can easily lose their texture. Many people think of them as fatty; in actual fact, the amount of fat that renders out of them in the long cooking is negligible.

Start preparing both the meat and vegetables at least one day before you want to eat them, two or more if possible, as they improve with sitting. One essential for this dish is a mild, fruity vinegar. Señora Guadalupe makes hers with pineapple vinegar (see recipe in *The Cuisines of Mexico,* page 29) but alternatively use an oriental vinegar and juice from a can of *jalapeños en escabeche*. In that case, use 2½ cups oriental vinegar to 1 cup strong vinegar.

    4 **large pigs' feet (front ones, which are shorter and more meaty), about 3½
       pounds, each foot halved and cut again into 2 pieces**
    1 **tablespoon sea salt, or to taste**
    1 **tablespoon strong malt vinegar**
    2 **teaspoons dried Mexican oregano**
3½ **cups mild, fruity vinegar (*see note above*)**
    1 **small can *chiles jalapeños en escabeche* (*optional*)**

vegetables

    4 **tablespoons safflower oil**
    3 **medium carrots, scraped and cut across slantwise, about ¼ inch thick**
    6 **fresh *chiles jalapeños,* slit open slightly at the bottom**
    6 **large scallions or small boiling onions, peeled and tops removed**
 20 **cloves garlic, peeled and left whole (although I like to leave the skins on,
      especially if they are the small purple garlic)**
    3 **small zucchini, trimmed, cut in half, and then sliced lengthwise into ¼-inch
      slices**
    3 **cups mild fruity vinegar (*see note above*)**
    8 **very small waxy potatoes, almost cooked but still *al dente***
 ½ **head cauliflower, broken into flowerlets and blanched**
    2 **cooked nopal cactus paddles, cut into ¼-inch strips, or ¼ pound green beans,
      trimmed, cut into pieces, and blanched**
    2 **fresh corncobs, cut into 1-inch rounds and blanched**
    5 **California or 2 Turkish bay leaves**
    2 **large springs fresh marjoram or ¼ teaspoon dried
      Ground sea salt to taste**

Scrub the pigs' feet well and put into the pressure cooker with water to cover. Add 1 tablespoon salt and malt vinegar and bring up to pressure. Lower the flame and continue cooking under medium pressure for about 35 minutes. Allow the pressure to reduce naturally, not under cold water. If cooking in an ordinary pot, cook over a medium flame for about 2½–3 hours. Strain the pigs' feet and put them into a china, glass, or highly glazed hard-baked French earthenware dish (not into a lightly glazed Mexican *cazuela*, for instance). Reserve the broth for another use. Sprinkle with the oregano, cover with the mild vinegar, and test for salt. Add the can of chilies if you like the spicy punchiness that they give to the dish. Leave to macerate outside the refrigerator overnight or, for that matter, for several nights. Providing the temperature is cool, they will last like that for a week or more.

Put the oil in a large frying pan, heat, and add the carrots, chilies, onions, garlic, and squash and fry lightly until they are *just beginning* to change color. Meanwhile heat the vinegar, and when it comes to a boil add the fried and partially cooked vegetables, bay leaves, and marjoram and continue cooking gently for 5 minutes. Remove from the heat, adjust the salt, and leave overnight. Drain the vegetables and serve over the pigs' feet.

NOTE These vegetables will accompany the pigs' feet, but they can also be served as a *botana* (snack) with drinks, *a la mexicana*.

Mother's Meat Gelatin

Aren't there some days when you want very little to eat—but it must be just right: the purest of flavors, something homely and soothing? Well, this is it for me: a sort of unsophisticated *boeuf à la mode* that Mother used to prepare for summer suppers.

It probably doesn't need saying that different cuts of meat from the same animal—I am referring to the "muscle" meat, not to organ meat or tongue—have distinctive flavors and, of course, texture, and this applies particularly to shin and brisket.

> 1¼ pounds shin of beef, trimmed of tough outside skin and fat, and cut into 1-inch cubes
>
> About 3 cups water, or enough to cover well
>
> 1 strong bay leaf (Turkish, not California)
>
> A large pinch of freshly grated nutmeg
>
> Sea salt to taste
>
> Freshly ground black pepper to taste
>
> 1 tablespoon powdered unflavored gelatin
>
> 2 hard-boiled eggs, peeled and sliced
>
> ⅓ cup cooked peas
>
> 2 medium carrots, cooked and sliced thinly on the diagonal

Choose a heavy pan into which the meat will just fit in 2 layers. Cover the meat with the water and add the bay leaf, nutmeg, salt, and pepper. Cook over a medium flame until the water is just about to come to a simmer, lower the flame, and let the meat cook very, very slowly—the water should never come to a boil—uncovered, until tender, 2½ to 3 hours depending on the quality of the meat—the toughness varies enormously with shin. Strain the meat and reserve the broth.

Mix the gelatin with about 3 tablespoons of the warm reserved broth until smooth. Place over warm water and stir until completely dissolved. Stir in the rest of the broth.

Choose a shallow glass serving dish—about 2½ inches deep. Arrange the sliced egg, peas, and carrots, in a pattern on the bottom of the dish. Distribute the meat evenly over it and then carefully pour the broth over all. Refrigerate overnight. Unmold before serving.

FISH

Looking back now, I realize that as a family growing up in prewar England we ate an enormous amount and variety of fish. It was very cheap then, and nourishing—my mother's favorite word. In fact, we would sometimes eat it three times a day, depending on the season and what was plentiful in the market. For breakfast we often had grilled fresh herrings, bloaters (lightly smoked whole herrings), or kippers, which are herrings butterflied and heavily smoked. We always ate fish at Friday lunch (the main meal of the day); fried plaice was quite the favorite, but it might be baked whiting or hake. If we were sick it was always steamed cod or skate with an egg or anchovy sauce, which was considered light on the stomach. It was a great treat to have Dover sole, halibut, or turbot (we pronounced the final *t*). For a high tea in summer we would often have minute sweet brown shrimps—you eat everything but the head—and an occasional "dressed" crab. The large crabs from British waters were incredibly meaty and sweet. The meat, fat, and eggs are taken out, along with any stray bits of shell, and then the lobes of the shell are stuffed with the white crabmeat, while the eggs and the rest, mixed with fine bread crumbs, form a thick orange band between the two sides. That's "dressing" it. For high tea or supper there was often fried (soft) roe on toast, smoked haddock poached in milk, fried sprats (whitebait), or soused mackerel.

Every summer we would look forward to at least two very special meals of cold poached salmon, which was always served with homemade mayonnaise, delicate new potatoes that were almost transparent when cooked, and baby peas. I am always tempted to order poached salmon when I see it on a restaurant menu, remembering the pale pink curdy flesh and dark layer of succulent fat under the skin of the salmon we ate at home. Alas, I am always disappointed.

I remember that not so long ago in a fashionable Houston fish restaurant I ordered poached salmon—it was that sort of restaurant where all the "specials" are breathlessly recited by a young man who can't pronounce the French words and there is the constant chink of glasses being filled with ice—you know what I mean. Well, the fish was tough and tasteless, having been boiled in saltless water for too long at too high a temperature. I called the captain. He looked at me pityingly. "Well, if you will order such a bland dish . . ." he offered in way of explanation. When on another occasion I complained of dried-out cold salmon in what used to be my favorite New York fish restaurant, the maître d' regarded me severely. "But our customers have not complained," he said, and there was just the faintest emphasis on *our*.

I would not be true to my British heritage if I did not mention fish and chips. Occasionally Mother would let us buy some fish and chips for supper. We had to walk for about a mile to the nearest fish and chips shop and stand in line waiting hungrily as generous portions of cod were dipped into a thick batter that was transformed in seconds by the hot oil into a golden puff around the fish. In the next frying vat the chips were sizzling to a deep golden brown. We were finally served and the fish and chips wrapped in newspaper—I don't remember so much print coming off in those days—and the fat would gradually leach through as we hurried home. Of course, if you had a paper cone full of chips to eat right then and there, they were doused with strong malt vinegar first. It was our junk food—fresh, not frozen, mind you—and we loved it.

I am passionately fond of fish, and when I first arrive in London I head for Harrods food halls and gaze in wonder—and hunger—at the displays of fish. On an inclined block of ice, kept fresh with constantly running water and decorated with seaweed, trout and Dover sole cavort with shrimps and crayfish in their mouths between leaping salmon and spiny lobsters with bright red carnations in their claws. Everything is moist and shiny and emanates a fresh seaweedy smell.

I remember the meatless days of the war in South Wales that were made joyful with large salmon trout gaffed from the turbulent streams a hundred yards or so from our door; superb fish and oysters on the Brittany coast; grilled eel and dried charcoaled octopus outside the bars of Portimão; grilled swordfish steaks from Rhode Island; bluefish, shad, and Maine lobsters cooked in seawater. After long stays on my mountaintop I make pilgrimages to eat fish at the coast, and when time does not permit I drive to nearby Pátzcuaro to have a feast of that unique little white fish—which used to be large some years ago—almost transparent except for the elegant wide silver band that runs down each side from head to tail.

By this time you will realize that this slim chapter on fish recipes does not reflect a lack of interest in eating fish. It would be superfluous for me to tell you here how I like my fish broiled, poached, and the like, as there are many specialist books that deal with that most adequately. I have simply recorded some rather interesting or little-known recipes that have come my way over the years.

Fish Kibbe

ABOUT 6 SERVINGS

This recipe and the following one are two unusual fish dishes that I love. I have eaten them many times in Norma Shehadi's home in Mexico City. The kibbe is a very unusual one, made only in the area of Syria near the coasts, around Aleppo and Homs, where her parents came from. It is interesting that in Mexico pecans were substituted for the walnuts that were used "back home."

Norma's mother came to Mexico when she was still a young girl and married here but still retained the traditional Arabic way of cooking. She would prepare her kibbes by pounding the ingredients together in a marble mortar with a heavy wooden pestle.

Norma used red snapper for this recipe, but I think it is a pity to pound such an expensive fish to death. You could quite easily substitute grouper, catfish, anglerfish, etc. Although it is correct to use a fine bulgur for this recipe, I much prefer the texture of the medium.

Norma says she remembers her mother's kibbes were always swimming in oil at the end of the cooking time—we both agree that less oil is okay.

While we were making this, another friend who is well known for her excellent Arabic food came in to have lunch with us. She said that traditionally the fish kibbe is served with lemon juice squeezed over it, but we agreed that this detracted from the rather delicate flavor. Another accompaniment is tahini (see page 97) flavored with salt and crushed garlic, or onions fried in butter—to me that's gilding the lily.

1½ cups medium bulgur *(see note above and note on page 72)*
2 cups oil, light olive or a mixture of olive and safflower
1 large white onion, finely sliced
½ cup roughly chopped pecans
  Rind of 1 large orange, julienned
½ pound raw small shrimps, peeled and deveined
1 pound fish fillets, skinned and fine bones removed
1 small bunch cilantro (coriander), leaves and tender stalks
  Sea salt to taste

Cover the bulgur with cold water and leave to soak for about ½ hour.

Preheat the oven to 350° F. Have ready a Pyrex dish—the ideal size would be 9 × 9 × 2 inches.

Heat ½ cup of the oil, and fry three quarters of the onion gently, without browning, until soft. Drain and sprinkle evenly over the bottom of the dish. In the same oil, fry the pecan pieces lightly; drain and sprinkle over the onions. Add half of the orange rind and the shrimps to the onions and pecans, distributing them evenly over the dish.

Using the steel blade of the food processor, grind the fish until smooth. Remove the fish from the processor and extract any small bones, filaments of muscles, etc. (Norma showed how her mother used to do this: take a handful of fish in one hand and with the other make a scooping motion down through the mixture with a broad-bladed knife. The filaments and skin adhere to the knife and should be removed constantly. This can also be done with meat.)

Put the bulgur into a double layer of cheesecloth and squeeze to extract all the moisture. Add with the ground fish to the container of the food processor. Add the cilantro, remaining onion and orange rind, and salt, and process until you have a smooth, cohesive paste. (I stop when there is still some texture to the mixture.) Spread the mixture evenly over the onion mixture in the dish—it should be about 1 inch deep. Score the top of the kibbe diagonally to make a diamond pattern (as you would for Arabic pastries) and pour the remaining 1½ cups oil over the surface. Bake the kibbe until the top and sides are well browned and the fat sizzling on the bottom—about 45 minutes. If by this time it is cooked through but the top is not browned, then put under a hot broiler for a minute or two.

Fish with Tahini and Pecans

The fish in tahini sauce is a rich and delicious dish and certainly calls for a whole, rather spectacular fish—red snapper is ideal for this, providing you are not squeamish about leaving the head on. Otherwise, make it with very large fillets.

> 1 large onion, roughly chopped
> 4 cloves garlic, peeled and roughly chopped
> 1 teaspoon sea salt, or to taste
> 1 whole fish (about 4½ pounds) or 2¼ pounds fish fillets, cleaned for the oven but head and tail left on
> 3 tablespoons lime juice
> 2 tablespoons olive oil

tahini sauce

> 9 tablespoons tahini paste
> 2 cloves garlic, peeled and mashed
> ½ cup lime juice
> Sea salt to taste

topping

> 3 ounces (6 tablespoons) unsalted butter
> 10 ounces onions, thinly sliced
> ¾ cup roughly chopped pecans

Put the onion, garlic, and salt in the food processor and process for 3 seconds, or crush in a mortar until reduced to a paste. Spread this mixture on the inside and outside of the fish. Set the fish in an ovenproof dish into which it will just fit; you do not want a lot of space around it or the juices will tend to dry up. Cover and set aside in a cool place to season.

Preheat the oven to 350° F. Sprinkle the lime juice and olive oil over the fish. Cover loosely with foil and bake for 20 minutes. Turn the fish over and bake for a further 20 to 25 minutes, depending on the thickness. The fish will be cooked when it just comes away from the bone—if it flakes easily, it is overcooked.

While the fish is baking, prepare the topping. Melt the butter in a frying pan, add the onions, and cook gently until softened and then browned, about 20 minutes. Push the onions to one side of the pan and tilt so that the butter drains out. Fry the pecans in this butter; they will be browned in about 5 minutes.

Beat the ingredients for the tahini sauce together with the juices from the fish. Cover the fish with the sauce and warm through for 15 minutes.

When the fish is ready to serve, strew the top liberally with the fried onions and pecans.

Rougail of Salt Cod

Fascinating as it is, *rougail* is hard to define; even *Larousse Gastronomique* can only say that it is a "sort of condiment . . . served with various dishes cooked in the Creole style. This condiment, being highly spiced, stimulates the appetite."

It was André Claude who first introduced me to *rougail* made with salt cod. He served it one Christmas Day on top of plainly boiled rice that accompanied his mother's recipe for Vietnamese Pork with Orange Juice and Coriander *(see pages 116 and 117).* There are many versions, including those made with apples, eggplant, or shrimps pounded to a paste. This particular recipe, he told me, comes from the French island of Réunion in the Indian Ocean. It is often served with curried dishes there. If it is not served with curry, then curry powder may be added to flavor it. I personally like it as part of an hors d'oeuvre or on toast or rye crisp as a snack with drinks. Beware, though: it is addictive!

It is not worth while making a smaller quantity; besides, if well sealed with olive oil, it will keep for many months in the refrigerator. Don't be put off by the time it takes to cook; plan to make bread or something else that spans the three hours.

Be sure to buy a good-quality salt cod *(bacalao)*—there are many poor imitations—from a reputable supplier. Try and buy thick cuts of the dried fish, but you may have to settle for some of the tail end, too, which is much thinner and has more waste with the extra skin and bones.

Many recipes call for salt cod to be soaked for far too long a period, so that it loses all its flavor as well as all the salt. If you follow this recipe, very little extra salt will be needed in the cooking of the dish.

When André sent me the recipe he had illustrated it delightfully, and the first thing I noted was a running tap with "two hours" written by it. "Two hours, André! I live in an ecological house in a very dry climate." "Well, you can reduce it to one hour," he replied. Even one hour of running water seems antisocial when more than half of the world's people suffer a water shortage, so I have compromised. André uses ordinary cooking oil, while I like to use half olive oil—expensive extra-virgin oil is not necessary, just a good plain olive oil. I also like to leave all the seeds and veins in the chilies to make it more *picante,* but that is a matter of taste. You will need a very heavy pan to cook the *rougail* in. I find the 12-inch Le Creuset ideal for this recipe.

1 pound salt cod *(see note above),* cut into large cubes
¾ cup safflower oil
1 cup olive oil
3 pounds white onions, finely chopped (about 9 cups chopped)
½ cup lime juice
　 Sea salt to taste
4 pounds ripe tomatoes (about 7½ cups finely chopped, unskinned)
7 fresh hot green chilies, *serrano* or cayenne, finely chopped
7 fresh hot red chilies, *serrano* or cayenne, finely chopped
8 large cloves garlic, peeled and finely chopped
1 cup loosely packed fresh herbs (*not* dried), such as tarragon, mint, or basil

Have ready 4 sterilized pint jars.

Cover the salt cod with cold water and leave to soak for 2 hours, changing the water every 15 minutes. Drain. Put the pieces of fish in a saucepan, cover well with water, and bring to a simmer. Continue simmering for 10 minutes. Remove from the flame, drain, and place in cold water for a few moments. Drain again. Scrape any remaining salty residue from the surface. Remove the skin and bones and shred the meat as fine as possible—there should be about 3½ cups if fairly firmly packed.

Mix the oils together and put about ⅓ cup into a heavy pan *(see note above),* add one quarter of the onion, and as it begins to cook—slowly and uncovered—sprinkle with about 1½ tablespoons of the lime juice and a sprinkling of salt. Cook until the onion is translucent. Spread one quarter of the salt cod over the onion with one quarter of the tomatoes, chilies, garlic, and herbs. Continue cooking the mixture, uncovered, over a medium flame, shaking the pan occasionally and sliding a wooden spatula underneath to make sure it is not sticking. When the juice of the tomatoes has dried up and the surface looks shiny, but not swimming in oil—about 25 to 30 minutes—it is time to add another layer of the ingredients. Each progressive layer will take longer to cook. Keep pressing the mixture down and don't add more ingredients until the liquid of the previous ones has been absorbed and evaporated and you can hear the oil sizzling (singing, as André would say). This whole process will take just a bit under 3 hours, but don't hurry it. The mixture will resemble a shiny, textured paste—and very colorful at that—when cooked.

Store the *rougail* while still hot in sterilized jars and cover with olive oil until it comes at least ½ inch above the top of the mixture.

If the *rougail* is not going to accompany a curried dish, then mix in a good curry powder—1 tablespoon for every 2 cups of *rougail.*

Kokotxas

In the late 1950s the large Spanish restaurants in Mexico City were in their heyday. They were noisy, lively places specializing in the freshest and best— often imported—of their native food. I remember Paul and I used to eat a full seven-course *comida* (main meal eaten at two in the afternoon) for only two dollars. *Kokotxas* rarely appeared on the menu, but you could always order them. The name is Basque and refers to the lower fleshy part of the jaw of hake or cod (used in Spain), two very gelatinous fish. These parts are cooked very slowly in olive oil so that the gelatine exudes and amalgamates perfectly with the oil to form a delicate sauce. In Mexico the jaw of the red snapper is used.

When I sat conjuring up my favorite foods for this book, I remembered *kokotxas,* but I had never cooked them at home and a recipe was nowhere to be found. The person I went to to help me, Luis Marcet, has by far the best Spanish restaurant in Mexico City, El Mesón del Cid, and is an enthusiastic gourmet and writer on gastronomic subjects. By return mail I received this recipe. His recipe calls for clams or baby eels, but I prefer *kokotxas* by themselves. He wrote that *kokotxas* are considered a delicacy by the fishermen, who claim them the minute the fish is caught, cutting them out with small sharp scissors and removing the small barbs at the end of the jaw.

You will probably have to go to a rather plebeian fish market for these, or find out where Spanish restaurateurs go. Try and get them all roughly the same size, so that they cook evenly—3 inches long is ideal.

6 tablespoons fruity olive oil
3 large cloves garlic, peeled and finely chopped
1 pound *kokotxas* (fish throats)
9 clams or ⅓ cup baby eels *(optional)*
   About 6 tablespoons water
   Sea salt to taste
2 hot chilies, *piri-piri* ⋆ *(optional)*
2 tablespoons finely chopped parsley
   Roughly ground black pepper
1 tablespoon flour *(optional)*

Heat the olive oil in a heavy pan. Add the chopped garlic and sauté until a light golden color; add the *kokotxas* (and clams or baby eels if desired), stirring them constantly for 2 minutes. Add the water and salt to taste, tipping the pan from side to side. Pick up the pan and swirl it around for about 2 minutes in order to release the gelatinous juices of the *kokotxas.* Cover and cook over a low flame for 15 minutes, adding the *piri-piri* if desired. Stir in the parsley and season with freshly ground pepper. Serve immediately.

NOTE Sometimes the sauce is thickened with flour; I find this unnecessary and prefer it without.

⋆*A hot pepper used in Portuguese cooking.*

Shrimps in Pumpkin-Seed Sauce

This is a recipe from Tampico, Tamaulipas, in Mexico—or rather, my version of it. It has already been published in my earlier book, *Recipes from the Regional Cooks of Mexico*. I want to include it here because it is one of the most delicious and elegant ways of preparing shrimps. Of course, you can do as some of my friends do: substitute for the shrimps lumps of crab meat or delicate white fish, but it would be advisable to have some fish stock on hand.

This recipe will serve from 4 to 6, depending on whether it is a first or main course. Always buy small or medium-sized shrimps, which have much more flavor than the giant ones, and of course they must be fresh, with the skins on.

1½ pounds medium shrimps, unpeeled
2½ cups cold water
    Sea salt to taste
  4 ounces (about 1 cup) hulled, unroasted, unsalted pumpkin seeds
  3 fresh *chiles serranos,* or any fresh green hot chili
  ¼ medium white onion
  8 sprigs of fresh cilantro (coriander), or more to taste
  2 tablespoons unsalted butter
 ⅔ cup *crème fraîche* or homemade sour cream

Peel and devein the shrimps, reserving the shells. Put the shells in a saucepan together with the water and salt and cook over a medium flame for about 15 minutes. Strain, discard the shells, and reserve the broth. Put the cleaned shrimps into the broth and cook for about 2 minutes after they come to a simmer; they should just turn opaque, no more. Strain the shrimps, setting them aside and reserving the broth.

In an ungreased heavy pan, lightly toast the pumpkin seeds, which should puff up a little but not brown.

Put the broth, pumpkin seeds, chilies, onion, and the leaves and tender stalks of the cilantro into the blender jar and blend until smooth. (If you want an even smoother sauce, grind the seeds first in an electric nut/spice grinder.)

Melt the butter in a heavy saucepan over a low flame, stir in the sauce, and cook for about 10 minutes over a low flame, stirring it from time to time so that it does not stick to the bottom of the pan. If the sauce becomes lumpy— the starches in the seeds tend to swell rather rapidly—then simply put the sauce back in the blender and blend until smooth. Stir in the cream and the shrimps and merely heat through, adjusting the salt to taste.

Caldeirada de Belmondo 4 TO 6 SERVINGS

As I was opening a tin of sardines the other day, I caught myself humming a tune. I suddenly recalled that beautiful young man standing by the piano in an Algarve bar—he was on tiptoe, with nostrils flared romantically, singing "Mi Casa Portuguesa"—or however you say it in Portuguese. It brought back a flood of memories of when I received my first royalty check for *The Cuisines of Mexico*—nine thousand dollars—I had never before in my life had so much money all at once. I felt rich and took myself off for a holiday to Portugal.

I moved from the sedate pension to which I had been recommended and took a small apartment in a beach complex less than one mile from Albufeira. Every morning, tide permitting, I would walk along the sand and watch the fishermen unloading their catch and try to distinguish the still-gasping silvery fish. One morning I came across Belmondo there—he tended bar and cooked *caldeirada* (the Portuguese fishermen's stew) for a few early spring guests in the complex—and he invited me to join him and his brother for a lunch of fresh sardines. By the time I arrived, a charcoal brazier had been lit with dry grasses on the small terrace overlooking the sea. On the table was a flat plate of salad: crisp lettuce and sliced tomatoes seasoned with a rich olive oil, vinegar, and oregano, and beside it a dish of the ever-present boiled potatoes, which were still quite warm. Belmondo flung the sardines onto the hot grill, sprinkled them with coarse sea salt, and cooked them for a few moments on each side. Unceremoniously he picked the cooked sardines up by their tails and flung one onto the hunk of crusty peasant bread on each of our plates. He showed me how to eat them as the fishermen do. First you pull at the skin along the ridge of the back, which comes away with a minute row of bones. Then you eat one side of the sardine as if you were nibbling on a corncob and, grabbing the tail, rip off the backbone and head at one go. Then you can eat the other side, now boneless, together with the bread.

It was one of those unforgettable meals. The terrace was shaded with fig trees—the green figs were formed but not ripe—and beyond was the sea, framed by bushy, windswept pines. We drank a lot of country red wine from rough earthenware mugs and finished the meal with small, thick-skinned, but deliciously sweet oranges. Belmondo said he wasn't in form that day—he could only dispose of twenty sardines instead of his usual twenty-five.

He and his brother taught me how to clean squid and collect the ink from the sacs, and how to cook octopus. They made various types of *caldeirada,* but this is the recipe I like the best.

I am sure that there as many variations of this recipe as there are Portuguese fishermen who cook it. Rice and potatoes, for instance, are interchangeable—although I prefer it with the latter. Sometimes a bay leaf is added, sometimes it's butter instead of oil, or octopus is used instead of fish. This particular *caldeirada* was cooked with ray, sardines, shark, electric fish, and pargo, but a mixture of virtually any fish could be substituted.

⅓ cup fruity olive oil
1 pound Spanish onions, peeled and thinly sliced
15 small cloves garlic, peeled and roughly chopped
2 cups roughly chopped, unskinned tomatoes
½ cup chopped parsley, loosely packed
3 *piri-piri*,* or any hot dry red peppers
1 cup dry white wine
Sea salt to taste
1 pound potatoes, peeled and cut into thin slices
2 pounds mixed fish *(see note above)*, trimmed of skin and small bones, and cut into small rectangular pieces
½ cup water

In a deep, heavy pot heat the olive oil; add the onions, garlic, tomatoes, parsley, *piri-piri,* and wine. Add salt to taste and cook over a fairly high flame, stirring from time to time, for about 15 to 20 minutes. It should resemble a thick sauce. Put the potatoes in one layer over the sauce, cover with the fish, add the water, season again, and cook, uncovered, over a medium flame until the potatoes (and, of course, the fish) are tender, about 30 to 40 minutes.

A hot pepper used in Portuguese cooking.

Brochette of Monkfish

No visit to New York City would be complete without eating at one of my favorite restaurants, the Oyster Bar in Grand Central Terminal. I do not know of any other restaurant—at least not in the United States—that has a greater variety of superbly fresh fish and shellfish. The choice of what to eat is always a difficult one, but I invariably end up with *tournedos de lotte. Lotte* (monkfish, in the United States) is appearing in many more fish markets now and it occurred to me to try cooking them with a Chinesey sort of flavor. These *médaillons,* or thick rounds of fish, can be either broiled or cooked *en brochette* or even steamed for that matter—although I have not done so.

Monkfish is a grotesque-looking fish and, even when cleaned into two round strips, may be a little bizarre for some people. If that is the case, then get the fishmonger to trim off the pinkish flesh and tip and cut it into rounds about ¾ inch thick.

START AT LEAST 2½ HOURS AHEAD

2 pounds monkfish, preferably purchased in strips (about 1 pound each) and cut
    into slices about ¾ inch thick
1 teaspoon finely chopped fresh ginger
    Finely grated peel of 1 tangerine
1 tablespoon tangerine juice
2 teaspoons lime juice (or substitute lemon juice or wine vinegar)
1 clove garlic, peeled and finely chopped
2 tablespoons soy sauce
3 tablespoons burnt sesame or light olive oil
2 tablespoons roughly chopped fresh cilantro (coriander)
1 *chile habanero* or *congo* or substitute with 2 *chiles serranos,* or any fresh hot
    green chili *(see note page 13),* finely chopped, with the seeds

Place the pieces of fish in a glass or china bowl. Mix the rest of the ingredients together, reserving half of the oil, and pour over the fish. Stir the fish well so that it becomes evenly coated with the seasoning, cover, and set aside to season in a cool place or in the refrigerator for at least 2 hours. Turn the pieces of fish over from time to time.

Heat the broiler. Stir the fish well again and place on a broiler rack or thread onto 4 skewers about 8 inches long. Brush the fish with some of the remaining oil and broil for about 3 minutes. Turn the fish, brush with the remaining oil, and cook for a further 3 minutes, or until the fish has just become opaque—it will, of course, take longer for cuts of fish thicker than those called for.

MEATS
AND POULTRY

There are many occasions when I am just beginning to think that I could live happily without meat when, walking through a Mexican market, I see a hunk of pork, golden and crusty, being drawn from a sizzling vat of lard. Or I pass my favorite taco stand—a table set up on a spare triangle of land at the Valle de Bravo turnoff on the Morelia road—and smell the pit-barbecued lamb as it is drawn, shiny and succulent, from its bed of maguey leaves. Or I am confronted with a steaming bowl of pungent midmorning *menudo* (tripe and chili soup)—then I realize that I am probably hooked for life.

Gone, however, are those postwar days when I thrilled at the sight of a standing rib roast or the haunch of an ox, tender and rare. Now I would opt for a braised breast of veal, some *cochinita pibil* (pit-barbecued pig with achiote and orange juice from the Yucatán), or an oxtail stew. We had oxtail and a lot of other stews at home. They were cheap and "nourishing," as Mother used to say, and would keep out the cold. There was neck of lamb—scrag end to the British—cooked slowly in the oven with carrots and potatoes; the broth was the best part. There was hot pot, stewing steak layered with carrots and onions with a topping of browned potatoes, and rabbit stew—my anathema, while steamed lambs' heads and tongues were my joy. Mother used to stuff an ox heart—as it was called—with an herbed bread-crumb stuffing. It was braised slowly in the oven and served with thick brown gravy. At least once a week in the winter months there was tripe and onions—oh, that horrible white sauce!—or boiled belly of pork (we ate all the fat) with pease pudding, a mush of dried yellow peas. A favorite of mine was steak and kidney pie with its rough-puff crust, baked for hours in the slow, stout oven of the kitchen stove. There was steak and kidney pudding, too, with its steamed suet crust. There were a host of pies, with their flaky crusts: veal or chicken and ham, bacon and egg, and giblet at Christmastime. Fried rump steak and onions was then to me the epitome of luxury.

At weekends there was either a roast chicken or, more often, a "joint" or roast: perhaps a shoulder of lamb cooked to a grey color but with a wonderfully crusty fat outside; that was served with mint sauce in spring and summer and with onion sauce in winter. A roast of pork with ridges of crisp brown crackling on the top was always served with sage and onion dressing. Lambs' kidneys broiled with bacon were reserved for breakfast or high tea.

Now I realize it was heavy eating, but it was customary and suited to the climate and the active lives we led. Since then my wanderings have taken me far afield and, with the help of many friends who are great and inspired cooks, I have managed to refine my palate . . . but just enough scraps of nostalgia remain, and some of that feeling is in these recipes.

Arroz con Pollo a la Cubana

This recipe was given to me some years ago by an old friend, Vida Weaver, who grew up in Cuba.

If Seville orange juice is not available, do not buy that dreadful imitation in bottles that is sold in Caribbean stores; just mix lime and orange juice in equal parts. It is not as interesting or as delicate as the real thing, but it will do. Nor do I suggest the commercial packaged *bijol*. This typical Cuban seasoning is nothing more complicated than ground achiote (annatto) seed with cumin. I grind my own rather than use that violently red stuff—just read the label and see what I mean! I cook the rice in a large, round Le Creuset casserole; you could also use a deep earthenware dish or stainless-steel pot.

When cooked, the rice will resemble a very moist risotto, a state that is called *asopado* (soupy) in Cuba. If you prefer it drier, as some Cubans do, then reduce the liquid by about ¾ cup.

Ají dulce is a small, light green, squat chili that is mild but has a delicious flavor (the same flavor as the *chile habanero,* which is used in Yucatán, Haiti, Jamaica, etc.). It is easy to obtain in Caribbean stores. Leave it out if you can't find it; there is no real substitute.

> 1 (4-pound) chicken, cut into small serving pieces
> Sea salt and freshly ground pepper to taste
> 6 tablespoons Seville orange juice *(see note above)*
> 2 California bay leaves or 1 Turkish bay leaf
> 1 large white onion, finely sliced
> 3 cloves garlic, peeled and crushed
> ¼ cup dry white wine
> 3 tablespoons safflower or other vegetable oil
> 2¼ pounds tomatoes, unpeeled and chopped
> 1 *ají dulce (see note above)*, sliced
> 2 cups light chicken broth
> Rounded ¼ teaspoon *bijol (see note above)*
> 1 pound (2 cups) long-grained, unconverted rice
> 1 cup light beer
> ½ cup unthawed frozen peas
> ½ cup strips of red bell pepper

Place the chicken pieces in one layer in a china or glass dish. Season well with salt and pepper. Cover with the orange juice, bay leaves, onion, garlic, and wine. Leave to season for at least 8 hours, turning once during that time.

Heat the oil in a heavy pan, drain the chicken pieces, reserving the marinade, and sauté until lightly browned all over. Remove the chicken pieces. To the same oil add the marinade, tomatoes, and *ají* and cook over a fairly high flame for 10 minutes. Add the chicken pieces to the pan and cook for 5 minutes more. In a separate pan, heat the broth, stir in the *bijol,* and keep stirring until it has dissolved and the broth is a good red color. Add to the pan, bring the mixture to a boil, and stir in the rice. Cover the pot and cook over a medium flame until the liquid has all been absorbed, about 35 to 40 minutes. Stir in the beer, peas, and red pepper; adjust the seasoning and cook, uncovered, until the liquid has almost all been absorbed and the rice is perfectly tender, about 15 minutes.

Stuffed, Braised Chicken

For almost two years after moving into my house in San Pancho I had no oven, no refrigerator, and only one small burner to cook on—and no car to go for last-minute necessities. When I had company, and it wasn't going to be Mexican food, I came up with this one-pot meal: a chicken stuffed with brown and wild rice (or bulgur) and cooked very slowly on top of the stove. Of course, you could also cook it in a very slow oven at about 325° F. Try and find a very large chicken that won't cook in 40 minutes and then start falling off the bone. It is good either hot or cold. You can vary the stuffing, the vegetables, or any of the seasonings to use what you have around.

> 1 tablespoon unsalted butter, softened
> 3 small cloves garlic, peeled and crushed
>   Sea salt and freshly ground black pepper
>   Grated rind and juice of ½ lemon
> 1 (4-pound) chicken, ready for the oven

stuffing

> 2 tablespoons chicken fat *(see page 14)* or unsalted butter
> 2 tablespoons finely chopped shallots or scallions
> ¾ cup roughly chopped celery
> ⅓ cup dried mushrooms, soaked in ¾ cup water *(see page 16)*
> ⅓ cup diced ham, preferably *serrano* or prosciutto
> 1 tablespoon each chopped fresh marjoram, thyme, and basil; or ¼ teaspoon dried
>   marjoram and ¼ teaspoon dried thyme only
> 1 large egg, lightly beaten
>   Sea salt and freshly ground black pepper to taste
> 1½ cups cooked brown rice or, better still, brown and wild rice *(see pages 60 and 74)*

vegetables

> 3 tablespoons chicken fat *(see page 14)* and 1 tablespoon safflower oil
> 3 medium carrots, roughly chopped
> 3 ribs celery, roughly chopped
> 4 shallots or 2 small onions, roughly chopped
> 4 sprigs fresh thyme or ¼ teaspoon dried
> 3 California bay leaves
> 2 sprigs fresh marjoram or ¼ teaspoon dried
> 8 fresh basil leaves, only if avaiable—do not use dried
> ½ cup dry vermouth, white, wine, or white wine vinegar
>   About 2 cups chicken broth, well seasoned
>   Freshly ground pepper
>   Extra vegetables to taste: 8 small waxy potatoes; 8 medium carrots scraped; 1
>   cup peas; 2 zucchini, cut into strips

Mash the butter with the garlic, salt and pepper, and lemon juice and grated rind, and smear into the cavity of the bird. Set aside to season while you prepare the stuffing.

Heat the chicken fat or butter and fry the shallots for 1 minute. Add the celery, mushrooms, ham, and herbs and fry over a medium flame for about 4 minutes. Add this mixture, the beaten egg, and salt and pepper to taste to the rice. Stuff the cavity of the chicken with the mixture and truss securely so that the stuffing does not fall out.

If cooking in the oven, **preheat to 325° F.**

Heat the chicken fat and oil in a heavy casserole or Dutch oven into which the chicken will just fit snugly. Brown the chicken well all over. Remove and set aside. Remove all but 2 tablespoons of the fat from the pan and any spare grains of rice, which tend to burn. Add the chopped vegetables and herbs and fry, stirring from time to time, until the color just changes, about 8 minutes. Return the chicken to the pan, add the vermouth, tip the pan to one side, and reduce the vermouth over a high flame for about 3 minutes. Add 1½ cups of the chicken broth—no need to add salt if it's well seasoned—and a lot of freshly ground pepper. Cover the pan with a tightly fitting lid and bake in the center of the oven or cook over a low flame on a large burner for about 1 hour. Turn the chicken over. At this point you could add vegetables like potatoes or carrots, while peas and zucchini should come later, the zucchini 30 minutes and the peas 5 minutes before the end of the cooking time. Cook for a further 1 hour, or until the chicken is well cooked and the pan juices are a good dark brown.

Transfer the chicken and whole vegetables to a warmed platter. If the pan juices and vegetables have dried up and are sticking a little to the bottom of the casserole, add the remaining broth (hot) and scrape the pan well. Reduce for about 2 minutes over a high flame. Then you have a choice: I serve the cut-up vegetables, almost reduced to a mush, around the chicken with bay leaves, herb stalks, and all, but you may wish to remove the bay leaves, discard the stalks, and put the vegetables through a food mill, thus making a thick sauce to serve with the chicken.

Bread Sauce★

I was doing some test cooking for this book in Jerrie Strom's spectacular Rancho Santa Fe kitchen. I had just finished making the bread sauce and we stuck our fingers into it to taste. As we continued working, we kept passing the pan, for "just one more try." At last Jerrie said, "My mother used to make something almost the same as this on our farm in Minnesota. . . . You know," she said after yet another taste, "this is *pure* soul food."

A roast chicken was an occasional Sunday treat when we were growing up and the food budget was very limited. It was stuffed with a forcemeat or, for special occasions, ground pork stuffing, and was accompanied by roast potatoes *(see page 54),* overcooked brussels sprouts, and bread sauce.

Bread Sauce is very easy to make, and the first step can be done ahead—but the bread itself should be added just before serving. Don't let it sit for more than 15 minutes, or, as one British cookbook warns, ". . . it will resemble nothing more than a bread poultice."

Crumbs from a good chewy French bread should be used for the bread crumbs, since most other white bread is too soft and sweet. I have also made the sauce successfully with homemade whole wheat bread.

 1½ **cups whole milk (not low-fat)**
  1 **cup water**
  3 **whole cloves**
  3 **small boiling onions, peeled and cut into quarters**
 ½ **teaspoon sea salt**
  2 **cups dried bread crumbs** *(see note page 12)*
  3 **tablespoons unsalted butter, softened**
 ⅛ **teaspoon ground mace or nutmeg**
     Freshly ground black pepper to taste
  3 **tablespoons thick cream** *(optional)*

Put the milk and water in a heavy saucepan. Stick the cloves into three of the onion quarters and add them with the rest of the onion quarters and the salt to the pan. Half cover and cook over a gentle heat until the onions are not only soft but falling apart, about 35 to 40 minutes, depending on their size. Remove from the heat, stir in the bread crumbs, softened butter, mace, and pepper; adjust the salt, cover, and set aside for about 10 minutes. When ready to serve, stir over a gentle heat for about 3 minutes, add the cream, stir again, and serve immediately.

★*A traditional accompaniment for roast chicken or turkey in England.*

Lemon Chicken

I imagine everyone on a cooking tour gets as heartily sick as I do of the average hotel and restaurant food. Since one spends most of the day around food—either shopping, preparing, or giving a class—one longs for something fresh on the palate and very simple to prepare. This lemon chicken recipe was given to me by an Italian–American family, and while it's not as elegant as the more traditional lemon chicken recipes, you can put it in the oven and almost forget about it. When cooked, it has a nice lemony sauce, and it is good eaten either hot or cold.

1 (3-pound) chicken, split in half through the breastbone
  Sea salt and lots of freshly ground black pepper to taste
½ teaspoon oregano
2 tablespoons olive oil
2 tablespoons butter, softened
¼ cup lemon juice
  Finely grated rind of ½ lemon
1 cup water
3 cloves garlic, peeled
  Finely chopped parsley (for garnish)

Preheat the oven to 400° F.

Season the chicken halves with the salt and pepper and oregano (if using) and place skin side down in a baking dish into which they will just fit in one layer. Put the oil, butter, lemon juice, rind, water, and garlic into the blender jar and blend thoroughly. Pour this sauce over the chicken. Bake on the top shelf of the oven, turning once halfway through the cooking time and basting frequently until the skin is crisp and the meat tender, about 40 minutes. Garnish with the parsley, if you are using.

Pierre Franey's Ragoût Toulousaine

I have to include this recipe because it is sublime soul food and my favorite dish when I am in a luxurious mood. It is the ultimate in delicate understatement, but do not serve it to friends or lovers who are either ravenous or are meat-and-potato people. Don't be put off by the complexities of the recipe; it's much easier than it seems.

    4 pairs veal sweetbreads
      Sea salt to taste
    3 tablespoons butter
    1 onion, sliced
    1 carrot, scraped and sliced
    1 rib celery, sliced
    1 bay leaf, crushed
    ¼ teaspoon dried thyme
      Freshly ground black pepper
    ½ cup dry white wine
    1¼ cups chicken broth from the poached chicken *(see below)*
    ½ pound small fresh mushrooms, trimmed and cut into quarters
    1½ cups cubed breast of chicken, lightly poached *(see below)*
      About 15 poached chicken quenelles *(see below)*
    1 cup cold chicken velouté *(see below)*
    1½ cups heavy cream
    1 canned or fresh truffle, cut into strips
    ¼ teaspoon freshly grated nutmeg
    ⅛ teaspoon powdered cayenne pepper
    1 teaspoon lemon juice
    1 teaspoon Cognac

Divide the sweetbreads into their 2 natural "lobes." Cover with iced water and set aside for 1 hour to soak. Drain and discard the water. Put the sweetbreads in a saucepan into which they will just fit in 2 layers. Cover with water, add salt to taste, and bring to a simmer. Continue simmering for 10 minutes. Drain and put into cold water immediately. Trim off the gristle and membrane and press the sweetbreads onto a flat surface between 2 sheets of lightly buttered waxed paper. Leave for 2 hours, weighted down with the heaviest object you can find in the kitchen.

Preheat the oven to 400° F.

Put 2 tablespoons of the butter in a large heavy skillet or *sautoir*. Cover the bottom of the pan with the onion, carrot, celery, bay leaf, thyme. Arrange the sweetbreads on the vegetables and sprinkle with salt and pepper. Cook over a medium flame without browning for 3 minutes. Cover the pan and cook for 10 minutes more. Add the wine and ½ cup of the chicken broth, and bake for 45 minutes. Put the mushrooms into a small frying pan, barely cover with chicken broth, and simmer for 5 minutes, uncovered. Remove with a slotted spoon and add to the poached chicken cubes; set aside. Reduce the mushroom broth over a high flame until it has reduced by half.

Prepare the chicken quenelles (see below), using 1 tablespoon of the velouté, and set aside. Put the remaining velouté in a small saucepan, add the reduced mushroom liquid, and beat until smooth. Stir the cream in quickly and simmer for 5 minutes. Add the truffle strips to the pan and season the sauce with the nutmeg and cayenne. Stir in by degrees and very slowly the mushrooms and chicken. Then add the quenelles, taking care not to break them. Melt the remaining 1 tablespoon butter and stir that gently into the mixture. Just before serving, add the lemon juice and Cognac. Arrange the hot sweetbreads on a serving platter, pour the sauce over them and serve immediately.

poached chicken

> 1 large chicken breast
> 2½ cups well-seasoned chicken broth

Remove the skin and bone from the chicken breast and cut in half. Add half the breast plus the skin and bone to the pan and cover with the broth. Cook over a gentle heat until tender—about 25 minutes—and cut into small cubes. Reserve the second half of the breast for the quenelles.

chicken velouté

> 2 tablespoons unsalted butter
> 2 tablespoons flour
> 1 cup chicken broth, warmed

Melt the butter in a small saucepan and gradually stir in the flour. Add the broth little by little, stirring vigorously until the mixture is quite smooth and begins to thicken. Set aside to get quite cold in the same saucepan.

chicken quenelles

> Remaining half chicken breast *(see above)*, cubed
> 1 tablespoon chicken velouté
> Freshly grated nutmeg
> Approximately ½ egg white
> Sea salt and freshly ground pepper to taste
> ⅓ cup heavy cream
> Chicken broth as necessary

Put the chicken cubes—there should be about ½ cup—in the jar of a blender. Add the velouté, nutmeg, egg white, salt, and pepper. Blend for about 30 seconds at high speed, pushing the mixture down with a rubber spatula several times. Gradually add the cream while blending, to form a mousse-like mixture.

Butter well a small enamel-coated or stainless-steel pan and place carefully on it the small quenelles, formed by pressing a little of the mixture between 2 teaspoons that have been dipped into water before forming the quenelles. When all the mixture has been used up, carefully cover the quenelles with the remaining chicken broth to barely cover. Cover the surface with buttered waxed paper and bring the chicken broth to a simmer. Shake the pan gently while simmering for a further 3 to 5 minutes, or until the quenelles are firm.

Braised Corned Beef

My very first neighbor in Mexico City, Inge Lotwin, taught me how to corn beef. The corning is light and the meat not such a dark red color as commercially prepared corned beef. This light corning lends itself to braising the meat rather than the more usual boiling. Vegetables can be added during the last hour of the cooking time—whole unskinned potatoes, onions, carrots, parsnips, turnips, rutabagas, or cabbage that has been quartered and briefly blanched.

START FIVE DAYS AHEAD

    4 **pounds boneless brisket with some fat left on**
½ **teaspoon saltpeter**
    6 **cloves garlic, peeled and crushed**
    2 **tablespoons sea salt (not kosher salt)**
    5 **California bay leaves**
    2 **juniper berries, crushed**
    5 **peppercorns, crushed**
      Water
    1 **large onion, quartered**
      Optional vegetables (*see note above*)

Pierce the meat in about 10 places with the point of a sharp knife—the knife should reach about halfway through the meat. Take a little of the saltpeter and garlic on the point of the knife and insert it into each slit. Rub the salt well into the meat. Place the meat in a deep dish into which it will just fit; add 3 of the bay leaves, the juniper berries, peppercorns, and about ½ cup water—the amount will, of course, depend on the size of the dish, but it should come up about 1 inch from the bottom. Cover the meat (*not* the dish) with a plate and put a heavy weight on it. Cover the whole thing so that the odors do not penetrate other foods, and place in the bottom part of the refrigerator. Leave the meat in the brine for 5 days, turning it over every day. Drain the meat.

To braise **Preheat the oven to 325° F;** place the rack in the center of the oven. Drain the beef, put into a heavy baking pan or casserole with a lid, add ½ cup water, the onion, and the remaining 2 bay leaves, cover, and cook until tender but not falling apart, 2½ to 3 hours. *See note above* about additional vegetables. Slice the beef and place on a platter surrounded by the vegetables and pan juices.

To boil Cover with cold water, add the onion and remaining 2 bay leaves, bring to a boil, lower the flame, and simmer the meat until tender, about 3½ hours. Turn off the flame and allow the beef to cool off in the broth.

Salpicón de Res, Estilo Zitácuaro
(Shredded Beef, Zitácuaro)

This recipe was given to me by Señora María Alejandre de Brito in Zitácuaro, where it is a favorite meat dish. It is a simple and delicious way of cooking flank or skirt steak and makes a very good filling for tacos made with soft tortillas.

meat

> 1 pound skirt or flank steak, with some fat left on
> 1 small white onion, roughly chopped
> 2 large sprigs fresh cilantro (coriander)
> 2 cloves garlic, peeled and roughly chopped
> Sea salt to taste
> Water to cover

the seasoning

> 2 tablespoons pork lard or safflower oil
> 1 small white onion, finely chopped (about ½ cup chopped)
> 2 cloves garlic, peeled and chopped
> 1 pound ripe tomatoes, unpeeled and finely chopped
> 3 or more canned *chiles serranos en escabeche* or to taste, left whole
> 2 heaped tablespoons roughly chopped fresh cilantro (coriander)
> Sea salt to taste

Cut the steak—along the grain, not against it—into 2-inch pieces. Put the meat in a saucepan with the onion, cilantro, garlic, and salt, barely cover with water, and simmer until tender, about 25 minutes for skirt steak or 35 minutes for flank steak. Allow the meat to cool off in the broth, then strain, reserving the broth for soup. Shred the meat and set aside.

In a heavy frying pan, heat the lard or oil, add the onion and garlic, and fry gently, without browning, until they are translucent, about 3 minutes. Add the chopped tomatoes and continue cooking over a high flame until the mixture has reduced and thickened—about 8 minutes—stirring from time to time to prevent sticking. Stir in the shredded meat, chilies, and coriander. Adjust the seasoning. Cover the pan and cook over a medium flame for a further 5 minutes.

Serve alone, with hot tortillas on the side, or use as a filling for tacos.

★*Filling for 15 small tacos.*

Corned Tongue

Corned tongue is one of my favorite meats. . . . I also like to corn veal chops, veal breast, and pork tongues. I always thought one of my more elegant meals was a corned tongue served with Madeira sauce, *fleurons* of puff pastry, and pureed spinach.

START FIVE DAYS AHEAD

- 1 (2½- to 3-pound) beef tongue
- ¼ teaspoon saltpeter
- 2 small cloves garlic, peeled and crushed
- 1½ tablespoons sea salt
- 2 California bay leaves
- 4 black peppercorns, crushed
- 2 juniper berries, crushed
- Water

Pierce the tongue in about 8 places with the point of a sharp knife. Take a little of the saltpeter and garlic on the point of the knife and insert it into each slit. Rub the salt well into the tongue. Place the tongue in a deep china or glass dish into which it will just fit. Add the bay leaves, peppercorns, juniper berries, and ½ cup water. Cover the tongue (*not* the dish) with a plate and weigh it down. Cover the whole before putting it into the bottom of the refrigerator. Leave the tongue in the refrigerator for 5 days, turning it over in the brine every day. Drain the tongue, put it in a saucepan, cover with water, and simmer until tender, about 3 hours. Cool off the tongue in the cooking liquid. As soon as it is cool enough to handle, remove the skin, bones at the base, fat, and gristle. Be sure to cut the tongue horizontally so that you get all the different textures.

Vietnamese Pork with Orange Juice and Coriander

5 TO 6 SERVINGS

André Claude was born in Vietnam to a Vietnamese mother and French father. He knows everybody and turns up everywhere. He never stays in one place very long, always seeing greener pastures elsewhere. He is a whimsical man, with an enviable carefree attitude, but a great organizer, too, which must have come from his French-colonial father. He paints charming miniatures, by means of which he supports himself, but he is completely happy as long as he has enough cash in his pockets for the next meal. Luckily, rich friends seek him for his good company, savoir faire, and delicious and original food.

I met André Claude for the first time when he turned up as manager of the small motel not far from where I live in Michoacán. I would often arrive at the motel to use the telephone around ten o'clock in the morning and there he would be, sitting at the table with a broad grin on his face, beckoning me to join him in some un–San Pancho–like delicacy—one day it was an exquisite fish pâté and a good bottle of sherry. One evening at dinner he produced from some secret place a superb bottle of Blanc de Blancs to honor my guest, a visiting British ambassador. He invited me to Christmas dinner one year and served this extraordinary Vietnamese pork, with plain white rice smothered with *rougail* *(see pages 98 and 99)*.

2½ **pounds loin of pork, center cut, trimmed of most but not all the fat**
20 **small cloves garlic, peeled**
   Sea salt and freshly ground black pepper
⅓ **cup chopped coriander stalks**
1½ **cups chicken broth**
4 **California bay leaves**
4 **whole allspice**

sauce

1 **tablespoon unsalted butter**
1 **tablespoon fat skimmed from the pan juices**
3 **green onions, trimmed and finely chopped, with most of the green parts**
2½ **tablespoons lime juice**
½ **teaspoon dry mustard**
   Juice of 2 large oranges
¼ **cup finely chopped coriander stalks**

Preheat the oven to 350° F and set the rack in the middle of the oven.

Make 20 incisions all over the pork with the point of a sharp knife and insert the cloves of garlic. Season the meat with salt and pepper to taste. Set the meat on a rack in a roasting pan and sprinkle the top thickly with the ⅓ cup chopped coriander stalks. Put the broth, bay leaves, and allspice in the roasting pan, and cover the whole tightly with foil so that no steam will escape. Cook the meat until it is very tender but not falling apart, so that you can slice it easily—about 3½ to 4 hours. Set the meat aside on a warm dish for about 15 minutes. Slice the meat, cover with foil, and keep warm in the oven.

In the meantime, degrease the broth. Put the butter and 1 tablespoon of the skimmed fat in a saucepan and heat. Add the onions and 1 tablespoon of the lime juice and fry gently until soft. Add the remaining 1½ tablespoons lime juice plus the skimmed pan juices (be sure to scrape the bottom of the pan well for all the scraps adhering to it), cover the pan, and cook the sauce for about 5 minutes. Add the mustard, orange juice, and the ¼ cup chopped coriander stalks. Cook, uncovered, for about 4 minutes longer. Pour some of the sauce over the meat and pass the rest in a separate dish.

Roast Pork with Sage and Onion Stuffing 4 SERVINGS

In England, it is customary to serve roast pork with its crisp brown "crackling" on top and to cook the stuffing separately. Try to get your butcher to give you a good piece of meat with the skin on and ask him to score it for you in lengthwise ridges from ¼ to ½ inch wide. Rub a little olive oil and salt on the skin and put plenty of salt and pepper on the meat itself. Cook slowly in a 325° F oven, basting it from time to time, allowing about 30 to 40 minutes per pound, depending on the cut, of course—shoulder tends to be tougher and takes longer. About 15 minutes before the pork will be done, set the oven temperature to 425° F, to crisp the top skin. Always buy pork that has some fat on it; it will be much moister and have more flavor. The roast is done when a meat thermometer registers 160° F.

Mother used to put grated lemon rind in practically all her stuffings, but it is optional. I find that dried sage gives better results than fresh in this recipe.

sage and onion stuffing

> **7 small white onions, peeled and roughly chopped**
> **Cold water**
> **½ teaspoon sea salt, plus extra, to taste**
> **1 rounded tablespoon dried sage (not powdered)**
> **4 tablespoons (2 ounces) unsalted butter**
> **8 ounces (4 cups) dried bread crumbs, loosely packed** *(see note page 12)*
> **Grated rind of 1 lemon** *(optional)*
> **1 egg, lightly beaten**
> **Freshly ground black pepper**
> **Drippings from the baking dish**

Lightly grease a shallow baking dish about 1½ inches deep; I use a 10-inch diameter Pyrex or pottery dish.

In a saucepan, cover the onions with water and cook over a medium flame with ½ teaspoon salt until soft and falling apart, about 35 to 40 minutes. Drain, reserving the cooking liquid. Put the dried sage to soak in ¼ cup of the cooking liquid for about 5 minutes. Put the onions in a bowl and stir in the butter, the sage with the water in which it was soaked, the bread crumbs, lemon rind, and beaten egg. The stuffing should have a fairly dry consistency but not be crumbling apart. Add a little more of the onion water if necessary. Test for salt and freshly ground black pepper. Spread the stuffing over the dish evenly and pour on some of the pan drippings. Bake at the top of the oven in which the pork is roasting until a golden brown, about 40 minutes.

Djuveč (Yugoslav Pork Chops)

All my Yugoslav friends have been remarkably good cooks; one of them, Leah Mayer, gave me this recipe. It is a very hearty casserole of pork chops from Bosnia and Herzegovina with unmistakable Turkish influences—predictably, since that area of Yugoslavia was under Turkish rule from 1463 for more than four hundred years. You can easily reduce the amount of meat, since the vegetables are very satisfying in themselves. I cook this in a deep casserole, 9-quart capacity.

> 1 medium eggplant, about 1 pound
> Sea salt and freshly ground black pepper to taste
> 6–8 pork chops (or I prefer 4 pounds country-style spareribs)
> 4 zucchini
> 2 pounds green peppers
> 2 pounds onions, thinly sliced
> 1 rounded cup roughly chopped parsley
> ⅓ cup vegetable oil
> 1 cup long-grained, unconverted rice
> 2½ pounds tomatoes, thinly sliced
> 1 cup water

Peel the eggplant and cut into 1-inch cubes. Sprinkle with salt and set aside to drain for about 20 minutes.

Season the pork chops with salt and pepper and set aside. Trim the zucchini and cut into large cubes. Cut the tops off the peppers, remove the seeds, and cut into slices. Put the zucchini, peppers, and onions, in a bowl, add the drained eggplant and the parsley, stir in the oil, and salt to taste. Set aside to drain for about 15 minutes, or until the juices run out of them. Drain, reserving the juices.

Preheat the oven to 300° F.

Rinse the rice in boiling water and drain. Put half of the tomatoes over the bottom of the casserole, sprinkle over half of the rice, then half of the vegetables. Put the meat in one layer over the vegetables, cover with the rest of the vegetables, rice, and tomatoes in layers, then finally pour over the vegetable juices and the water. Cover the casserole and cook for about 4 hours, or until the vegetables and rice are thoroughly cooked through.

Alice B. Toklas's Veal and Pork Loaf

4 TO 6 SERVINGS

I am a devotee of Alice B. Toklas's cookbook. Many of the recipes are wildly extravagant, but among my favorites are Puree of Artichoke Soup, Perpignan Lobster, Brown Braised Ribs of Beef, Veal Kidneys Cooked in Gin, Fried and Roasted Breaded Chicken, and this meat loaf, which I could happily eat twice a week. I like to cook it in a round, shallow earthenware dish that can be taken to the table, a Moroccan *tagine slaouis,* for instance, or *cazuela.*

  ¾ **pound veal, finely ground**
  ¾ **pound pork, finely ground**
  1 **cup finely chopped mushrooms**
  1 **egg, well beaten**
  1 **teaspoon ground sea salt, or to taste**
    Freshly ground black pepper
  1 **clove garlic, peeled and crushed**
    A large pinch of freshly grated nutmeg
 10 **tablespoons sour cream**
  ¼ **cup fresh bread crumbs**
  ¼ **cup white wine**
  2 **hard-boiled eggs**
 1¼ **cups boiling beef consommé or strong chicken stock**

Preheat the oven to 400°F.

Put the ground meats in a mixing bowl, add the mushrooms, beaten egg, salt, pepper, garlic, nutmeg, and 4 tablespoons of the sour cream. Soak the bread crumbs in the wine, squeeze dry, and add. Mix all the ingredients together with your hands. Put 4 tablespoons of the sour cream in the bottom of the baking dish; mold the mixture around the 2 hard-boiled eggs placed tip to tip in a mound.

Pour 2 more tablespoons of the sour cream over the top of the meat loaf and smooth it out and press a crisscross pattern with the tines of a fork. Put the wine in which the bread crumbs were soaked and 4 tablespoons of the consommé in the bottom of the dish and bake, basting frequently, for about 45 to 50 minutes, or until cooked through. Pour the remaining 1 cup boiling consommé around the dish and scrape into it the little bits adhering to the sides. Serve immediately.

Iranian Broiled Lamb

Among the Sunday repertoire of roasts at home was a shoulder of New Zealand lamb cooked until crusty brown on the outside and grey inside—but the lean meat was still juicy because of a good layer of fat underneath the skin. In winter this was served with roast potatoes and a thick white onion sauce; in spring and summer, with new potatoes and either a mint sauce or red currant jelly. I still like lamb in England that way, for nostalgic reasons, I suppose. When I am in the United States, I use Julia Child's wonderful recipe for a roast leg of lamb, seasoned with mustard and rosemary, cooked to medium rare, and this broiled lamb recipe from Roberta Schneiderman. Roberta, a good friend and very talented cook, prepared this for me at one of the many delicious dinners I have eaten in her home. Her Iranian friends cut the lamb into cubes and cook it on skewers, alternating the meat with small onions. Of course, this type of marinade is intended to tenderize the tough, stringy lamb that one might expect to find in Iran, or in Mexico for that matter—but whether for tender or for tough lamb, it is delicious.

START AT LEAST ONE DAY AHEAD

- 3 pounds lamb, leg or shoulder, butterflied
- 1 cup plain yogurt
- 6 tablespoons lemon juice
- 1 large onion, thinly sliced (I prefer white onions)
- 2 teaspoons dried mint leaves (or, if preferred, 2 tablespoons roughly chopped fresh mint leaves)
- 1 scant teaspoon sea salt, or to taste
  Freshly ground black pepper
  Butter or olive oil for broiling

Pierce the meat all over with the point of a sharp knife. Mix together the yogurt, lemon juice, onion, and mint leaves, season to taste with salt and pepper, and pour over the meat. Leave the meat in the refrigerator for a minimum of 24 hours and a maximum of 72. Turn the meat over each day.

Remove the lamb from the marinade and pat dry with paper towels. Discard the marinade. Dot the lamb with butter or oil and place under a preheated broiler. Cook on one side for about 5 minutes, turn, dot with a little more butter or oil, and continue broiling until it is the color you like it—about 5 minutes on each side for medium rare.

Slice the meat downward across the grain and serve. I often sprinkle it with chopped coriander and serve with cooked bulgur *(see page 72)*.

Syrian Yogurt Sauce with Cooked Meat

Here is an interesting fresh sauce for cubes of leftover cooked meat—it's especially good with cooked lamb or chicken. If you add more meat stock and leave out the meat, it can be served as a soup. The recipe comes from a Syrian friend and fine cook, Norma Shehadi.

> 2 tablespoons unsalted butter
> 1 small white onion, finely chopped, about ½ cup
> 1 egg, very well beaten
> 2 cups plain yogurt
> ¼ cup strong meat broth *(optional)*
> 2 heaped cups cubed, cooked meat
>   Sea salt and freshly ground black pepper to taste
> ½ teaspoon dried mint

Heat the butter in a frying pan, add the onion, and cook until a deep golden brown. Set aside and keep warm. Stir the beaten egg into the yogurt, put in a saucepan, and cook over a medium-low flame, stirring all the time, until it begins to bubble and thicken slightly, about 5 minutes. Add the broth *(optional)*, meat cubes, and seasoning and continue cooking until the meat is well warmed through, about 5 minutes. Put on a warmed serving dish and sprinkle with the dried mint. I often serve this with brown rice or cooked bulgur *(see page 72)*.

YEAST BREADS

No supermarket manager need ever worry that he will catch me squeezing the Charmin—I'll be over in the bread section squeezing away in wonder that so many soft, spongy, sweetish loaves are made and consumed in the name of bread as though teeth had gone out of style.

There have been a plethora of books and articles on the subject of bread making, which in many ways is great—but so many have encouraged this "bouncy" sweet loaf (one notable exception being Julia Child's meticulous instructions for making a good French loaf). Let's get back to basics and learn to chew again.

I was brought up with lots of yeast breads, many of them doughy, but at least they had a good crust and were honest whole wheat. I remember, too, crusty, almost hollow Viennese rolls, reminiscent of the large, extraordinarily crisp "Hops" bread rolls that used to be made in Trinidad years ago. French, Italian, and Russian peasant breads are unrivaled, and in some parts of Mexico that holds true—but too many have got the message that sugar not only works the yeast faster but helps produce a more appetizing-looking crust.

Although I live near a small agricultural town where whole wheat bread is considered unpalatable and unacceptable, fortunately there is a wheat mill on the edge of town. Don Alfredo Domínguez, one of the owners, always expresses regret that his machinery doesn't produce real whole wheat flour, but he does go and hold paper bags—or lets me do so—under the tubes that eject the different parts of the grain.

I always refrigerate the most perishable parts (the germ, semolina, and bran) and then mix flour to suit my fancy: today a little more wheat germ, for my pasta some of the semolina that is quite textured, or a choice of two brans.

Bread making is fun if you are not tied to one recipe or flavor. If you don't feel like heavy rye or 100 percent whole wheat, then add some high-gluten flour, sprouted grains, or wheat berries to give it texture and make the bread more interesting. In the last century, potato was often mixed with the flour in bread making, probably as an economy; certainly a little mashed potato in rye bread or muffins, for instance, does help work the yeast, but it also gives the bread another slight dimension of taste.

I hope that some of the following recipes will give you inspiration to try something different.

TIPS Always dry the flour for yeast baking, in the sun or in a slow oven, and use while still slightly warm.

All water measurements are approximate because one may need more, depending on the weather and the type of flour.

NOTE *High-gluten flour* is already prepared principally for baking bread. *Gluten flour* (for example, as put out by El Molino) is a gluten concentrate. As a rule of thumb, ¼ cup of every pound of ordinary flour used should be replaced by ¼ cup gluten flour. See also the information on flour on page 15.

I can still hear to this day the clang of the muffin man's heavy brass bell, slightly muffled by the dense fog, on a cold winter's afternoon. He always carried in front of him a stout wooden tray, slung from his neck with thick leather straps, and on it, covered by a piece of green baize, were his wares: crumpets—I can never remember his selling muffins. We could never resist. The Benares brass toasting fork was polished and ready—my father's Sunday morning job was to make all the brass and copper pieces he loved to collect in flea markets shine until you could see your face in them. (He always said his boots had to be like that during World War I, even in the trenches, under the meticulous eye of a fearsome sergeant major.)

The largest piece of coal was pushed aside to find a glowing patch for toasting. Occasionally one of the crumpets would fall into the ashes, but no matter, it was simply brushed off and buttered along with the rest.

In those days crumpets were yeasty and chewy—certainly no raising agent other than yeast was used—and the perfectly honeycombed surface allowed the butter to trickle down right to the bottom.

After many hours, during many years of testing and having changes of mind, I have come up with this recipe, which is as near as possible to those I remember. The type of flour used is most important. You can use high-gluten flour, but it varies from place to place, so I find that by using an all-purpose flour and substituting a percentage of gluten flour *(see note on page 124)* you can control the quality better.

For this recipe I find a dough hook more efficient than beating by hand, and a lot faster, of course. Please weigh the ingredients. Measuring flour by the cup is inaccurate and can throw a recipe such as this one out of balance.

The odd size of the crumpets—3¼ inches—is dictated by the size of the standard crumpet rings available in cookware stores.

8 ounces, less 4 tablespoons, unbleached all-purpose flour
4 tablespoons gluten flour *(see note above)*
Just over ½ ounce cake yeast (4 rounded teaspoons, crumbled)
About ¾ cup warm water
1 round teaspoon finely ground sea salt, dissolved in ½ cup warm water

Put the flours in the mixer bowl and stir well. Cream the yeast with 1 tablespoon of the warm water, pressing out the lumps with the back of a wooden spoon. Add to the flour. With the dough hook, beat in the rest of the ¾ cup water and continue beating until the mixture becomes very elastic, adhering to the hook and cleaning itself from the sides of the bowl, 2 to 3 minutes.

With a rubber spatula, form the dough into a cushion shape (no need to remove the dough and grease a bowl, etc.). Cover with plastic wrap and leave in a warm place, ideally 70–75° F, for 30 minutes. At the end of this time the dough should have sponged up into a mound, with a *few* air holes in it. Beat again for 1 minute and repeat the process, leaving for another 30 minutes.

At the end of the second rising beat in the sea salt dissolved in the ½ cup warm water. Add a little at a time and beat slowly at first because the dough will slosh around in the water and go all over the place. Beat for about 2 minutes after all the water is added—the resulting batter will be very loose and grainy. Cover and set aside for another 30 minutes.

Meanwhile heat and lightly grease a heavy griddle. Place the crumpet rings, also greased, on it to heat as well. When the batter is ready, fill each ring with a good ¼ cup of the batter. If the griddle is sufficiently hot, the batter should immediately begin to bubble and form a honeycomb effect. Medium heat should be maintained so that the bottom of the crumpets do not burn, so keep adjusting the flame as necessary. Cook the crumpets until the top of the dough is completely dry—about 10 minutes—and do not make the mistake of removing the rings once the batter has set because the metal helps to convey the heat all the way round and cook the batter more evenly. Turn them over, still in the rings, and cook the top side for 1 minute—it should be just lightly golden. When well cooked, crumpets should be a deep golden brown on the bottom, the slightest hint of gold on the top, and about ½ inch thick.

Remove from the rings and cool on a wire rack. Do not use immediately. Store overnight, wrapped in a dry cloth, in the refrigerator. To use, toast on both sides lightly and put a generous amount of butter (not melted) over the top.

English Muffins

10 MUFFINS

Many years ago, when I was first starting to make muffins and crumpets, I used as a guide a late edition of Mrs. Beeton's *Household Management*. In that edition potatoes were used to activate the yeast. I thought they also greatly improved the flavor. But all the information about the use of potatoes in bread baking can be read in that wonderfully researched book by Elizabeth David, *English Bread and Yeast Cookery*.

These muffins are more chewy than and do not have that semisweet flavor of the commercial ones. They freeze well.

> **1 pound high-gluten bread flour, plus extra for kneading** *(see note page 124)*
> **½ ounce cake yeast (about 4 teaspoons, crumbled)**
> **1 ounce (2 scant tablespoons) mashed potatoes** *(optional)*
> **About 1¼ cups warm water, about 100° F**
> **1 teaspoon sea salt**
> **Butter for greasing the bowl and baking sheet**
> **Cornmeal or roughly ground whole wheat flour for the baking sheet**

Put the 1 pound flour in a mixing bowl. Cream the yeast together with the mashed potatoes and 2 tablespoons of the warm water (this is important to do before you add the salt), smoothing out the lumps with the back of a wooden spoon. Make a well in the center of the flour, add the yeast mixture, and cover with flour. Dissolve the salt in the rest of the water and gradually beat into the flour. Beat with the dough hook for about 3 minutes, or by hand for 6 minutes, until the dough is smooth and elastic and shrinks away from the sides of the bowl. It will be slightly sticky.

Scrape the dough onto a lightly floured surface and form into a round cushion shape. Wash out the bowl, grease well, and put the cushion of dough in the bowl without turning it over. Cover the bowl with plastic wrap and set in a warm place—about 70° F—until it has doubled in bulk and is spongy to the touch, about 2 hours. Carefully turn the dough onto a floured surface and knead it for 1 minute. With a special plastic cutter (far the best instrument), cut the dough into pieces of about 2 to 2½ ounces each.

Let the pieces of dough rest while you prepare a baking sheet. Butter it well and sprinkle with either coarse cornmeal or coarsely ground whole wheat flour. Roll each piece of the dough for a few seconds under the palm of your hand to form a smooth ball—this is best done on an unfloured surface to get some traction. Roll the ball lightly in the flour on the board and press down hard to flatten out until the dough is about ½ inch thick. Place on the prepared baking sheet at least 1 inch apart to allow for expansion. Cover the tray with plastic wrap and set aside in a warm place for the muffins to rise again—they should increase to about half again their original size and be light and spongy to the touch—about 1½ hours. Do not hurry the rising periods, as this gives time for a good flavor to develop.

Heat a griddle (soapstone is ideal for this) and lightly grease it if it is metal. Without turning them over, carefully transfer the muffins on a spatula to the griddle—there should be a sizzle as the dough touches the hot surface. Reduce the flame to medium low and cook the muffins for about 8 minutes on the first side, making sure that they develop a nice brown color but do not burn. Turn them over and press down if they have become unruly and risen unevenly, and cook for about 8 minutes more. Transfer the cooked muffins to a wire rack and let them cool off completely before you eat them—they tend to be a bit too soft and doughy inside if you don't allow this cooling-off time.

To serve, split the muffins open horizontally with the upturned tines of a fork, toast, and smother in butter.

NOTE All muffins can be frozen while still fresh and will keep in the freezer for a month or longer with no ill effects.

Whole Wheat Muffins

The method of making these muffins is exactly the same as for ordinary muffins except that the kneading time is much briefer and there is an addition of butter in the dough.

12 ounces whole wheat flour, roughly ground, plus extra for kneading *(see note page 124)*

4 ounces high-gluten bread flour

Just over ½ ounce cake yeast (4 rounded teaspoons, crumbled)

1 ounce (2 scant tablespoons) mashed potatoes *(optional)*

About 1 cup plus 2 tablespoons warm water, about 100°F

1 teaspoon sea salt

2 tablespoons melted butter, plus butter for greasing the bowl and baking sheet

Cornmeal or roughly ground whole wheat flour for the baking sheet

Proceed as in the recipe for English Muffins *(see page 126)*, adding the melted butter along with the salted water. Knead for 1 minute only (instead of 3) with the dough hook, or 2 minutes by hand.

NOTE All muffins can be frozen while still fresh and will keep in the freezer for a month or longer with no ill effects.

Sourdough Starter

I have long been an *aficionada* of sourdough bread but somehow never attempted it until I was given Rita Davenport's very precise *Sourdough Cookery* and then acquired *Alaska Sourdough: The Real Stuff by a Real Alaskan*. I now have a two-year-old bubbling sourdough pot in the kitchen. Actually, it is a Mexican bean pot, since I couldn't come by a wooden one, which is the correct thing. It always looks a bit disreputable, inside and out, as the dough dries and becomes encrusted to the pot, and then it has an inevitably messy plastic bag on top with a wooden spoon sticking up through it. It is rather like having a pet in the kitchen—I look at its behavior daily and know when to coax it into life with a bit of extra food when it looks sullen. When I go away I wrap it up cosily in a towel and put it into the refrigerator; when I come back, I feed it, put it in a warm place, and there it is, back to normal.

Here is my recipe for a sourdough starter.

1 pound unpeeled potatoes, cubed
1 cup unbleached, all-purpose flour
2 tablespoons granulated sugar

Put the unpeeled potatoes in a saucepan, cover with cold water, and bring to a boil. Continue boiling until soft and mushy. Drain the potatoes, reserving the cooking water. Discard the peelings and put the potatoes in the blender jar with 1½ cups of the cooking water; if there is not sufficient liquid, make up the difference with water. Blend smooth and gradually add the flour and sugar, blending all the time.

The mixture should now be like a thick batter. Store it in a china, glass, or unglazed pottery container—unless, of course, you have the correct thing, a wooden one. From now on, no metal should touch the batter, so always use a wooden spoon to stir. The ideal temperature to keep sourdough, according to the Alaskan book, is between 65° and 77° F. The mixture will begin to ferment within a day or two but will still have a sweet taste to it; that will disappear in a few more days and a more acidy taste will develop. When you want to use the starter and, say, take out about ¾ cup of it, you will need to replace it by about ⅓ cup flour, ⅛ cup sugar, and enough warm water beaten in to bring it back to its previous consistency. You mustn't swamp it; always be conservative about the amount of flour and sugar you use until it gets older and more resilient. After almost a year I don't even bother to measure what I put in.

NOTE A quick sourdough can be made by hollowing out some large, unpeeled potatoes, leaving a shell about ½ inch thick. Fill the hollows with water, cover with plastic wrap, and leave for about 36 hours in a warm place. Add this water to enough flour to make a soft dough. Cover and leave overnight in a warm place. In 24 to 36 hours the dough should be quite soured. It will not be as bubbly as the starter in the first recipe.

Sourdough English Muffins

You can make these muffins in exactly the same way as those without the sourdough, but I prefer to make the dough the night before and let it rise at a very cool temperature, thus improving the flavor.

> 10 ounces high-gluten bread flour, plus extra for kneading, or gluten flour *(see note page 124)*
> ⅓ cup sourdough starter
> ¼ ounce cake yeast (2 scant teaspoons, crumbled)
> About ⅔ cup plus 1½ tablespoons warm water, about 100° F
> 1 rounded teaspoon sea salt
> Butter for greasing the bowl

Place the 10 ounces flour in a mixing bowl and warm through in the sun or in a warm oven. Make a well in the center of the flour and add the sourdough starter; barely cover it with flour. Cream the yeast with 1½ tablespoons of the warm water (before putting salt in, because the salt would tend to kill the yeast at this stage), pressing out the lumps with the back of a wooden spoon. Put on top of the sourdough and gradually mix in the surrounding flour. Dissolve the salt in the ⅔ cup water and add to the flour mixture, beating with a dough hook or by hand, until you have a smoothish dough and the dough comes away from the sides of the bowl—about 2 minutes with dough hook, 4 minutes by hand. The dough will now be very elastic and slightly sticky.

Lightly flour your working surface—not marble; it is too cold for breads—and form into a round cushion shape. Wash out the bowl, dry it, and smear it with butter. Put the dough back into the bowl without turning it over (the seams are underneath and should remain so). Cover the bowl with plastic wrap and then a large towel. Set the dough aside in a cool place between 55° and 65° F, to prove overnight. The next morning, if the dough has not risen very much, put it in a warm place to rise to about twice its original size. Turn the dough out onto a lightly floured surface and divide into 10 pieces. Proceed exactly as for the recipe for English Muffins *(see page 126)*.

Whole Wheat Sourdough English Muffins

The method of making and cooking is exactly the same as in the recipe for English Muffins *(see page 126)*, but the kneading time should be 1 minute with the dough hook or 2 minutes by hand.

> **8** ounces whole wheat flour (not too finely ground), plus extra for kneading
> **2** ounces high-gluten bread flour
> **¼** cup sourdough starter
>   Just over **¼** ounce cake yeast (2 rounded teaspoons, crumbled)
>   About **¾** cup warm water, about 100° F
> **1** rounded teaspoon sea salt
> **1½** tablespoons melted butter, plus extra butter for greasing the bowl

Mix as in the recipe for Sourdough English Muffins *(see page 130)*; the melted butter should be added at the same time as the salted water. Knead for 1 minute with the dough hook or 2 minutes by hand.

Sourdough Breadsticks

Breadsticks, next to peanuts, are my favorite snacks, so whenever I make bread I put some of the dough aside, knead in some butter, and make breadsticks. Those made of sourdough are the most interesting in flavor—almost cheesy.

For every 4 ounces of once-risen dough, knead in 1½ tablespoons unsalted butter. It is a messy business at first, but excellent for lubricating the hands. Then follow this recipe for forming and baking breadsticks.

If you want to start from scratch, here is the recipe.

- 12 ounces high-gluten flour, plus extra for kneading, or 12 ounces less 3 tablespoons all-purpose flour (plus extra for kneading) plus 3 tablespoons gluten flour *(see note on page 124)*
- ⅓ cup sourdough starter
- ¼ ounce cake yeast (2 scant teaspoons crumbled) or ⅛ teaspoon dry
  About ⅔ cup plus 1 tablespoon warm water, about 100° F
- 1 heaped teaspoon sea salt
- 4 tablespoons unsalted butter, softened, plus extra for the bowl and baking sheets

Put the flour in the bowl of a mixer, add the sourdough starter, and sprinkle some flour over it. Cream the yeast with 1 tablespoon of the warm water, pressing out the lumps with the back of a wooden spoon, and dissolve the salt in the remaining water. Add the creamed yeast to the flour and mix briefly with the dough hook. Gradually beat in the salted water and the softened butter. Continue beating until the dough is soft and smooth and pulls away from the sides of the bowl, about 3 minutes. Turn the dough onto a lightly floured board and quickly form it into a cushion shape. Clean out the bowl, butter it well, and put the dough back into it. Cover the dough with greased plastic wrap and set aside to rise overnight in a cool temperature, about 55–65° F. (If you are in a hurry, you can raise the dough at 70° F for about 2½ hours, but the flavor will not develop as well as with the long, slow rising.) Turn the dough out onto a lightly floured surface and let it rest while you butter 2 cookie sheets and sprinkle them lightly with flour.

Break off a small piece of the dough and roll it into a ball about ¼ inch in diameter. With your outstretched hands, roll and stretch the dough to form a strip about 8 inches long and ¼ inch thick. Carefully place the strips on the prepared baking sheets one by one, leaving about 1 inch space between them for expansion. Cover the sheets with a piece of plastic wrap and set aside in a warm place—75° F—for about 45 minutes. They will expand but not double their size.

Preheat the oven to 375° F and bake the breadsticks until they are golden on the outside and crisp right through, about 25 minutes. Allow the breadsticks to cool off on a rack and then store in an airtight jar. As they get older, you can always crisp them in a hot oven for about 5 to 10 minutes. Cool before eating.

Grissini (Breadsticks)

I have always loved breadsticks, but they are always a little too sweet. In Italy this year I reveled in them and came back with a tote bag full. They all went rather fast, so I had to invent this recipe and slip it into the book.

I prefer to knead this dough by hand, but you could use a dough hook.

> 8 ounces less 2 tablespoons unbleached, all-purpose flour
> 2 tablespoons gluten flour
> ¼ ounce cake yeast (2 teaspoons, crumbled)
>   About ⅓ cup plus 1 tablespoons warm water, about 100° F
> 1 scant teaspoon finely ground sea salt, or to taste
> 2½ tablespoons light olive oil
>   Butter and flour for the baking sheets

Put the flours in a bowl. Cream the yeast with 1 tablespoon of the water, pressing out the lumps with the back of a wooden spoon. Make a shallow well in the middle of the flour and put the creamed yeast in it. Cover with a little flour. Dissolve the salt in the rest of the warm water and stir it into the flour with the oil. Knead until the dough is smooth and soft and does not stick to the board, about 3 minutes. Form into a cushion shape. Wash the bowl and grease it with buttered paper. Return the dough to the bowl, cover with greased plastic wrap, and leave in a warm place—about 75° F—for just over 1 hour to rise to double its size.

Butter 2 baking sheets and sprinkle with flour. Turn the dough out onto the board on which you are going to work. Do not put any flour on the board—if the dough is the correct texture it should not stick to begin with, and in any case the dough would then slide around on the floured surface and you couldn't form the breadsticks easily.

Take a small piece of the dough, about ½ to ¾ inch in diameter, and roll it evenly under the palm of your hand. Then, using your outstretched hands, roll and stretch the dough into the shape required: about 8½ to 9 inches long and just over ⅛ inch wide. (This is purely a guide; you can make them as thick or thin as you like.) Transfer the strips of dough to the prepared baking sheets and put them about ½ inch apart to allow for expansion. Cover the tray with greased plastic wrap and set the trays aside in a warm place (about 75° F) to prove for about 45 minutes—the *grissini* will swell but not double in size.

Preheat the oven to 375° F. Bake the *grissini* until they are golden brown and crisp right through, about 20 minutes. Cool them off on a rack and store in an airtight jar. As they get older, you can crisp them in a hot oven for about 5 to 10 minutes. Cool before eating.

*This yield is for breadsticks 9 inches long and about ¼ inch thick.

Hot Cross Buns

Hot cross buns were originally made for Good Friday but now you can get them for several weeks before Easter. The hot cross buns made by New York bakeries are very sad indeed; there are no spices in them, you have to hunt for the currants, and they are too sweet. This recipe is based on one put out by the Flour Advisory Board in London. It may seem laborious, but once you get the hang of it, like any other yeast cookery it can be fitted into the rest of the day's work. You can skip the proving of the dough before shaping, but the texture and flavor will not be the same. Some people simply cut a cross in the buns; I prefer to use crossed strips of leftover dough or pastry. Greased strips of baking parchment, ¼ inch wide, can also be used. The buns are delicious split open and buttered when they first come out of the oven, or split and toasted the next day; they freeze well. I find them addictive and can eat them every day of the week the year round.

starter dough

    4 ounces unbleached, all-purpose flour
    ½ cup whole milk
    ½ cup water
    1 ounce fresh yeast or 1 level tablespoon dry
    1 tablespoon granulated sugar

dough

    12 ounces unbleached, all-purpose flour, plus extra for kneading
    ¼ teaspoon salt
    ½ teaspoon ground cinnamon
    ¼ teaspoon grated nutmeg
    ⅛ teaspoon ground allspice
    ⅛ teaspoon ground cloves
    1½ ounces (about 2½ tablespoons) granulated sugar
    4 tablespoons unsalted butter, softened, plus butter for the bowl and baking sheets
    2 eggs, well beaten
    6 ounces (about 1¼ cups) currants
    1½ ounces citron, chopped

    30 thin strips dough, about 4 inches long (leftover bread or pastry dough will do)

glaze

    3 tablespoons milk
    3 tablespoons water
    2 ounces (¼ cup) granulated sugar

Put the 4 ounces flour in a mixing bowl. Heat the ½ cup milk and water together to about 110° F. Cream the yeast and sugar together with 2 tablespoons of the warm liquid, pressing out any lumps with the back of a wooden spoon. Add the yeast and the rest of the liquid to the flour and beat well. Cover the bowl and set in a warm place—about 75–80° F—until it has proved well and is frothy, about 15 minutes—longer for dry yeast.

Put the 12 ounces flour, the salt, spices, and 1½ ounces sugar in a mixing bowl and mix together well. Beat the butter and eggs into the risen starter and, when well incorporated, gradually add the flour mixture and the currants and citron, beating after each addition. Beat with the dough hook until the dough is soft and smooth—except for the fruit, of course—and pulls away from the sides of the bowl, about 2 minutes. It will be fairly stiff. Turn the dough onto a lightly floured surface and knead briefly into a cushion shape. Wash the bowl, butter it well, and return the dough to it with the seam at the bottom. Cover the bowl with plastic wrap and set aside in a warm place—75–80° F—until it has doubled in bulk.

Butter 2 baking sheets well. Turn the risen dough onto a very lightly floured surface and knead briefly into a cushion shape and then flatten out into a round. Cut the dough into pieces of about 2½ ounces each—about 15. Roll each piece of dough under your palm until it forms a smooth ball—if you have too much flour on the board, you cannot get enough traction. Place each ball on the baking sheet and press down well to flatten—they should be at least 1½ inches apart on the tray to allow for expansion. Cover the tray loosely with plastic wrap, allowing the dough to rise, and set aside in a warm place (75–80° F) until they have risen to about one-half again their size and are light and springy to the touch, about 30 to 40 minutes.

Meanwhile **preheat the oven to 400° F** and have the 30 strips of dough ready.

Combine the 3 tablespoons milk and water, stir in the 2 ounces sugar until dissolved, and bring to a boil; boil for about 2 minutes. Set aside.

When the buns have risen sufficiently, place 2 strips of dough on each bun in the form of a cross. Bake until the buns are well browned, about 7 to 10 minutes. Remove from oven and brush the surface between the crosses of dough with the glaze. Remove the strips of dough. Set on a rack to cool or, better still, eat them right away.

Rye Bread

One day I arrived back at my house in San Pancho to see a large hole beside the electricity post. No one had seen or heard anybody working there, and as the hole got larger and larger each day I began to wonder if someone was trying to sabotage my electricity supply. The mystery was solved one morning when the electric company's truck drew up in the lane by my entrance with a huge concrete pole—it had knocked a few hedges down on the way. Of course, it was the very day when I had made up a batch of dough for rye bread. "You will be without light for a short time, señora." The Mexican workmen are masters of understatement! I explained about the bread—I had only an electric oven in those days—and looked hopefully at the windmill, which didn't show signs of stirring. "Don't worry, we'll hurry," they promised and promptly went off for *almuerzo,* a long, midmorning breakfast. Seven hours later I had light but the time for baking had long past. I had other urgent things to do, so perforce left the partly risen dough in a cool spot overnight. Without doubt it improved the flavor of the loaf.

This is my slightly unorthodox recipe. It makes a close-textured heavy bread. I usually form the loaves into ovals and glaze with white of egg just before the end of baking time. I sometimes make muffins of this mixture, and also breadsticks.

> 8 ounces stone-ground (rough) rye flour, plus flour for the board and
>   baking sheets *(see note page 124)*
> 6 ounces high-gluten bread flour
> 2 ounces whole wheat flour
> ½ ounce cake yeast (4 teaspoons crumbled)
> 3 tablespoons mashed potatoes
> 2 tablespoons warm water
> 1½ tablespoons melted unsalted butter, plus extra for greasing
> ½ teaspoon sea salt
> 1 heaped teaspoon dillseed
> ¾ cup buttermilk
> 1 egg white, beaten until frothy

Mix flours together and dry them in the sun or in a warm oven *(see Tips on page 124)*. Mix the yeast together with the mashed potatoes and the warm water, smoothing out any lumps with the back of a wooden spoon. Make a well in the flour and pour the yeast mixture into it; cover it with some of the surrounding flour. Cover with plastic wrap and let it prove in a warm place (75° F) for about 20 minutes. When it is fermenting, stir in the surrounding flour and mix well. Add the melted butter, salt, dillseed, and buttermilk by degrees and mix well. The dough will be rather stiff and sticky. Turn the dough out onto a lightly floured board. Clean the bowl and lightly grease it. Quickly knead the dough into a round cushion shape—it shouldn't be kneaded too much—and return to the bowl. Cover with plastic wrap and leave in a cool place—55–65° F—to prove overnight.

The following day, turn the dough onto a lightly floured board and knead for about 2 minutes. Cut the dough into 2 pieces and form into oval log shapes. Grease 2 baking sheets and sprinkle with flour, put one of the "logs" on each, cover, and set aside in a warm place to rise for about 1½ hours—they will probably increase one-third more in size.

Preheat the oven to 425° F and place the racks in the center of the oven. Bake the loaves for 25 minutes, lower the temperature to 325° F, and bake for a further 20 minutes. The loaves should have a good crust and, when tapped, sound hollow—drumlike.

Brush the loaves with the egg white and return to the oven for 1 minute more. Set on a rack to cool off before cutting into the loaves.

NOTE For all the preceding bread recipes, if you like a slightly lighter, spongier bread increase the yeast by half again, or even double it.

WHOLE WHEAT BREAD

No matter how convincing the label or healthy-looking the packaging—with old-fashioned grain mills and whatnot—all commercial, wrapped whole wheat bread sold in supermarkets or health food stores is spongy and sweetish and there is not one crusty loaf among them. The bread I like is chewy and crusty. It does not rise spectacularly and is therefore rather dense, but with *lots* of texture. I like it for toasting in the mornings for breakfast; thinly cut, it makes excellent sandwiches.

The texture of the flour for whole wheat bread is most important and should be as rough as possible. I usually mill my own or take all those little bags that Don Alfredo gives me and mix to taste. If I overdo it on the wheat germ, the loaf tends to be a little sweet; then I use a little less salt. Sometimes I sprout wheat and rye and use those in my loaf, or soak wheat berries and then chop them roughly to give extra texture. There are lots of ways of making whole wheat bread both more interesting and nutritious, especially in these days of recommended high-bran diets. Why do so many people automatically throw in molasses, honey, and other sweeteners at the mention of whole wheat bread? These rough-textured, honest loaves are so much more satisfying.

Whole Wheat Bread I

This is the recipe I use when a good unbolted whole wheat flour is available *(see note on page 15)* or when I grind my own wheat. The loaf can be made with one rising only, but I find the yeasty flavor develops better with two. This makes a crusty, earthy loaf.

- ½ cup wheat berries
- ⅓ cup hot water
- 12 ounces whole wheat flour, plus flour for kneading
- 4 ounces unbleached, all-purpose flour
- ½ cup gluten flour
- ½ ounce cake yeast (4 teaspoons crumbled)
  About 1¼ cups plus 1½ tablespoons warm water, about 100° F
- 1 teaspoon sea salt, or to taste
- 2 tablespoons unsalted butter or pork lard, melted, plus extra for greasing the loaf pan

Cover the wheat berries with the hot water and leave to soak for about 15 minutes. Drain and transfer to the blender jar. Blend briefly just to break them up roughly. Set aside.

Mix the 3 flours in a bowl and add the wheat berries. Cream the yeast with 1½ tablespoons warm water, pressing out the lumps with the back of a wooden spoon. Make a well in the flour, add the creamed yeast, and cover with some of the flour. Dissolve the salt in the rest of the water and stir this together with the melted fat into the flour mixture. Mix until the dough forms a cohesive mass of rather stiff dough. Knead by hand for about 3 minutes and then form into a cushion shape.

Wash out the mixing bowl and grease lightly. Return the dough to the bowl, cover with plastic wrap, and set in a warm place—about 70° F—until it has almost doubled its size, about 2½ to 3 hours. Turn the dough onto a very lightly floured surface. Lightly grease a 1-pound loaf pan. Form the dough into a roll that will just fit into the pan. Cover with plastic wrap and set aside in a warm place (70° F) until the dough reaches the top of pan, about 2½ to 3 hours.

Preheat the oven to 400° F. Bake the bread for about 35 minutes. Lower the oven temperature to 350° F. Remove the loaf from the pan, turn it upside down, and bake for a further 20 minutes. By this time it should have a healthy crust and sound hollow when tapped. Remove and cool on a rack.

Whole Wheat Bread II

½ cup wheat berries
⅓ cup hot water
12 ounces unbleached, all-purpose flour, plus flour for kneading
¼ cup gluten flour
4 ounces (1 cup) bran
⅓ cup wheat germ
½ ounce cake yeast (about 4 teaspoons crumbled)
1 cup plus 1 tablespoon warm water, 100° F
A heaped ½ teaspoon salt
2 tablespoons unsalted butter, softened, plus extra for greasing the pan

Cover the wheat berries with the hot water and set aside for about 15 minutes. Drain and chop roughly in the blender. Put the flours, bran, and wheat germ in a mixing bowl and mix well. Add the chopped wheat berries.

Mix the yeast with 1 tablespoon of the warm water, pressing out the lumps with the back of a wooden spoon. Make a well in the flour mixture and add the yeast, covering it with a little of the flour. Dissolve the salt and melt the butter in the remaining 1 cup warm water and mix into the flour. Turn the dough out onto a lightly floured board and knead for about 5 minutes—it will be quite stiff and slightly sticky. Lightly butter a loaf tin (ideal size 9×5×3 inches) and press the dough into it. It will fill between one half and two thirds of the tin. Cover with plastic wrap and set in a warm place—about 75° F—to rise. When the dough has risen just over the top of the tin (it takes about 2 hours), it is ready to bake.

Preheat the oven to 425° F and bake the bread for 30 minutes. Lower the oven temperature to 375° F, remove the loaf from its pan, and allow to finish baking on the oven rack for about 20 minutes. Cool thoroughly on a rack before attempting to cut the loaf.

TIP To refresh stale bread, dip quickly into water and place in a very hot oven until heated through and crusty but soft inside.

DESSERTS

When the dessert trolley rolls by, my instincts are those of a *grande gourmande,* but alas, my capacity falls far short of that; but I do rather overdo it at teatime. I like a lot of little tastes of different types of sweets, and nothing pleases me more than to be dining with three other people who all agree that the order shall be four different desserts, with extra silverware and extra plates, no matter *what* the waiter thinks. I always hope that nobody will want *oeufs à la neige,* which is a great bore, or anything stuffed with pastry cream, and that there will be no glazes that turn out to be just plain Jell-O, and no soggy piecrusts—there usually are—and nothing oversweet. I love good cream but I even felt I had had enough clotted cream this summer while traveling in Somerset. It was wickedly delicious yellow stuff, but it was piled on top of all desserts, and stuffed into every bun, and enough is enough.

I suppose if I could choose the perfect dessert for half of the year I would opt for the perfect, juicy Bartlett pear and a well-ripened Boursault cheese. But that is sheer fantasy. For the other one hundred and eighty-two and a half days I would lean heavily on fruit: cherries and raspberries when they just come in, or peaches and nectarines at their peak—there are an awful lot of woolly nectarines about, I am afraid. I love the crunch of the fashionable kiwi and the wildly exotic flavor of the passion fruit. I love very tiny wild strawberries—like those I remember finding in the tall summer grass near the Maine coast, or the small, sweet Mexican ones that I will take any day before the spongy spring monsters from Southern California, which always remind me of W. C. Fields's nose. A cold lemon soufflé would not be sniffed at once in a while during the summer, while in winter I would opt for some fleshy dates along with rich Brazil nuts, or some black walnuts and a glass of Madeira . . . oh joy!

At home we were never allowed to leave the table without eating pudding— it was considered good for one, and besides one needed the bulk on those cold, damp English days . . . cold and damp winter or summer, inside the house or out. Only the Romans knew how to live comfortably in Britain. Mother was a wonderful pudding cook and produced an amazing array of baked, boiled, and steamed puddings, especially when you consider that she had no help in the house and had a full-time teaching job. I liked the steamed ones best: sponge pudding with raspberry jam at the bottom—it became the top when turned out of the basin—that turned a deep port-wine red and sank into the sponge. It was sometimes made with golden syrup, and that was a great favorite. There was guards' pudding with lots of dried fruit in it, and a ginger sponge served with a white sauce flavored with orange rind. Mother's baked apple sponge was something to be remembered, too, with its thick brown crust—sometimes made with large, juicy Victoria plums bottled from the previous year's harvest.

But perhaps the most spectacular winter's-day pudding was (don't laugh at the name) "spotted dick." It is a sausage-shaped suet dough studded with masses of raisins, sultanas, currants, or muscats, boiled in a cloth tied at the ends, and served in warm, thick slices covered with Demerara sugar (fine brown crystals), a good lump of butter, and lemon juice.

I had almost forgotten the endless variety of tarts: deep-dish fruit pies and flat tarts covered with black currant jam, mincemeat, treacle, or lemon curd. These were usually reserved to eat after the cold-meat midday meal on Mondays, which were washdays. Unfortunately, Mother also like to make those horribly wobbly blancmanges. They looked pretty enough with their fanciful shapes and pale colors, but they belied their charms with artificial flavors and insipid textures. And all that packaged custard powder—Bird's, I think it was. That custard turned up with formidable regularity to go over puddings, stewed fruit, and trifles—oh, how I love trifles when they are well made!

But to get back to today and reality. I eat very few typical Mexican desserts, which I find too sweet and cloying. Most often it will be fruit: a fruit salad of mixed tropical fruits can be delicious and intriguing, with a Manila or Hayden mango, a slice of ripe melon, some homemade guava paste or preserved peach; and when company comes—and if the electricity has not faded out—I make one of my fruit cream sorbets with lots of texture in it.

PASTRY

Making good pastry demands patience and perhaps a touch of sleight of hand. I challenge anyone to go into the kitchen and make good puff pastry first time off. My mother was an excellent pastry maker and made large batches every weekend. She was still making a delicious short crust until well into her eighties. We were, so to speak, brought up with at least five types of pastry: short crust for pies and tarts; flaky—a combination of methods of making short crust and puff, slightly firmer than rough puff—for sausage rolls and meat pies; hot-water for pork pies; puff and choux for cream buns and éclairs. Apart from seeing pastry made constantly at home, we had cooking classes at school—they were considered an important part of the curriculum, along with sewing, at the rather swanky girls' school that I attended. We learned the basics of English cookery: cakes, jams, scones, milk puddings galore—rice, semolina, sago, and my pet aversion tapioca, with its huge, chewy, glutinous lumps—roasts, puddings, and pastry. The rules for pastry making have stuck with me ever since: if it is short crust, half a pound of fat to one pound of flour, cold water, and mixed with a metal fork or spoon. And this was before we had refrigerators or even iceboxes.

Short Crust Pastry

There are an awful lot of bad piecrusts around! If you really want to learn, you must make pastry by hand and not in a machine—unless, of course, the temperature is in the high nineties and the humidity equally high. The best fats are butter and a good pork lard in equal quantities. Vegetable shortening is okay: you can get a flaky crust, but it is lifeless in both appearance and taste—I think that is why most people oversalt it. Too much water is used, as a rule. The fats in the United States are made to stay solid through thick and thin, and if you try and mix them with flour when very cold, they require more liquid, which then toughens the pastry. This sounds very unscientific, of course, but I never was scientifically minded. I am talking from experience and from having made short crust with all-purpose flours across the country. Some require more fat, others less, and the same goes for water. It is a tricky business making hard-and-fast rules for pastry. Break some rules! Don't use your fats so cold—soften them a little before using, and then you won't need as much water. The fat should be rubbed in to the flour quickly, with only the tips of your fingers, until the mixture resembles *coarse* bread crumbs. Then add the water, a very little at a time, working it with a metal spoon—I never find a fork very satisfactory. When you turn the pastry out onto your working surface it will be lumpy and not all stuck together. Gently coax it into a circle and use the rolling pin very lightly. So your piecrust won't have such an even edge to it! I have always said that the most evenly fluted piecrust is the worst to eat. If you overwork your dough it will be very smooth and certainly short, but it won't have that nice flaky texture.

Always weigh your ingredients if you want to make a really good piecrust. Don't rely on measuring cups: they are inaccurate, or, rather, the way you put the flour into them is, and all that sifting is not necessary nowadays.

1 pound unbleached, all-purpose flour
¼ teaspoon finely ground sea salt
   Scant 4 ounces unsalted butter, at room temperature, cut into small pieces
4 ounces good pork lard, cut into small pieces
   About 5–6 tablespoons cold water

Preheat the oven to 450° F. Mix the flour and salt together in a large bowl and then follow the method described above. Roll the dough out until it is about ⅟₁₆ inch thick. Cut as required and bake on the top shelf of the oven.

Mother's Fruit Slice

After making enough tarts and pies for the week, Mother always used up the leftover pastry to make jam turnovers or my favorite fruit slices. Of course, you can work with any amount of pastry, but I will give ½ pound as a convenient guide. If you want to start from scratch, make up a batch of pastry *(see recipe for Short Crust Pastry, page 144)*, using 8 ounces flour, which will make about 12 ounces of dough.

 ½ **pound Short Crust Pastry (already prepared)**
 4 **ounces (¾ cups plus 1 tablespoon) currants**
 2 **ounces (⅓ cup) sultanas or golden raisins**
  Scant ¼ teaspoon mixed ground cinnamon, nutmeg, and cloves
 2 **rounded tablespoons brown sugar—preferably Demerara, as it stays crunchy**
 2 **tablespoons lemon juice**
 2 **tablespoons granulated sugar**
  Butter to grease the baking sheet

Preheat the oven to 450° F.

Roll out the pastry to a rectangle about 9 × 12 inches and 1/16 inch thick. Mix the dried fruit with the spices, brown sugar, and lemon juice, and spread the mixture over half of the pastry, leaving a free edge of about ¼ inch. Fold the other half of the pastry over the fruit and press the edges together—the pastry is very short and should not need water for this sealing. Lightly grease a baking sheet, lay the fruit slice on it, and bake on the top shelf of the oven until golden on top, about 15 minutes. Sprinkle with the granulated sugar while it is still hot. Cut into fingers and serve either hot or cold.

Pastel Alemán *(German Cake)*

When I went to Mexico for the first time in 1957, among my friends were Mymie and David Graham. We used to go on long trips together through different parts of Mexico, and I shall always be grateful to them for this introduction to the Mexican countryside. At that time Mymie had a wonderful cook called Eva—I don't know her other name—and this is one of her recipes.

It is best to make this cake at least five days before eating it. Like the Meringue Layer Cake, it seems to last forever—you can even freeze it and it is just as delicious when thawed. To fully appreciate the contrasting textures—from the crunchy outside to the firm chocolate-cream filling—it is best to serve this cake in thin slices.

cake

    ½ pound unsalted butter, plus extra for greasing the pan and baking sheet
    ½ pound (1 cup) granulated sugar
    ½ pound unsweetened cooking chocolate
        About 6 dozen ladyfingers
    1 cup dark Jamaican rum
    4 egg whites, at room temperature

cream coating

    ½ pound unsalted butter
    ½ pound (1 cup) granulated sugar
    4 egg yolks

topping

    1 cup granulated sugar
    1 cup walnut pieces, toasted and roughly chopped

Put the butter, sugar, and chocolate for the cake in a double boiler and stir until the sugar has melted. Cook over a low flame for about 15 minutes, stirring from time to time. Set aside to cool.

While this is cooking, butter well a cake pan, 9×5×3 inches—the size is important. Line the bottom and sides of the pan with ladyfingers and crumble some of them to fill in the gaps. Sprinkle the ladyfingers well with some of the rum and set aside. Beat the egg whites until they form soft peaks. Fold into the cooled chocolate mixture. Pour half of the mixture into the pan. Cover with another layer of ladyfingers sprinkled with the rum, pour in the rest of the chocolate mixture, and top with ladyfingers and crumbs so that no chocolate is visible. Place in the refrigerator overnight.

Carefully unmold the cake onto a large platter—you may have to place it briefly in hot water, but take care not to leave it too long, as you do not want the chocolate to melt.

Put the butter and sugar for the coating in a double boiler and stir well. The sugar will melt a little, but the texture should be slightly grainy. Set aside to cool and thicken a little, but it must still be soft. Beat in the egg yolks one by one and continue beating for 1 minute more. Put the mixture in the refrigerator to cool off a little so that it can just be spread—neither too hard nor too soft. Using a palette knife, spread the mixture evenly over the top and sides of the cake in a thick layer. Return to the refrigerator for the coating to become firm.

Generously butter a small baking sheet.

To make the topping In a heavy frying pan, melt the sugar over a low flame, then raise the flame and cook until the sugar is caramelized. Stir in the walnuts and put the mixture in a thin layer over the baking sheet. Set aside to cool and harden.

Break up the brittle roughly and put in a clean tea towel. Pound with a hammer until it is broken up into small pieces. (I do not advise a machine for this, as the texture is so important and you do not want it pulverized.) Press the cracked brittle onto the top and sides of the cake. Cover well with foil and place in the refrigerator for about 3 days to ripen. When ready to serve, cut into very thin slices.

Meringue Layer Cake

This is a wickedly rich, extraordinary dessert, and if nobody eats it up at one sitting, it will keep forever, getting better all the time. In any case, it should never be eaten as soon as it is made; let it ripen for at least three days so that the layers and flavors meld. It also freezes very successfully

I personally don't like meringues that are dead white. To me they are much more appetizing when they are a pale ecru color and crisp right through. And that's how the layers should be for this cake, with the added crunchiness of roughly chopped toasted hazelnuts.

This cake looks very craggy when first assembled, but as it sits, the meringue softens very slightly, so that you can mold it into a rounded form, like the crown of a hat. You can decorate the top of it with a checkered pattern of powdered coffee and chocolate, and serve it with unsweetened whipped cream as a final flourish.

meringues

Butter, flour, and cooking parchment for the baking trays
6 egg whites, at room temperature
Pinch of sea salt
1½ cups fine granulated sugar
1 cup lightly toasted and roughly chopped hazelnuts or almonds (I do not remove the skins from hazelnuts)

filling

6 ounces semisweet chocolate
2 tablespoons milk
¾ pound unsalted butter
3 egg whites
¾ cup superfine sugar
3 tablespoons cocoa powder
3 tablespoons dark Jamaican rum
2 tablespoons coffee essence dissolved in 1 tablespoon water
⅓ cup finely chopped preserved ginger (preferably in syrup) or crystallized ginger

To make the meringues **Preheat the oven to 225° F.** Cover 2 baking sheets with a layer of cooking parchment—not waxed paper. Draw 2 circles 7 inches in diameter on each. Butter the circles well and dust with flour. Beat the 6 egg whites until frothy, add the salt, and continue beating until the whites form soft peaks—when you turn the bowl upside down, they should not fall out. Do not overbeat and let them become dry. Continue beating while you add gradually half of the granulated sugar. When this is incorporated and the mixture smooth, fold in the rest of the sugar and the hazelnuts or almonds. Divide the mixture into 4 equal parts and smear it over the 4 circles. Bake for up to 1 hour, but keep watching the color of the meringues—if they are becoming a shade too dark (this may happen with an electric oven that reheats from the top), lower the oven. When they are firm to the touch and don't collapse inside when you touch them, turn the oven off and leave them to dry out for 1 hour more. Allow to cool on a wire rack and remove the paper.

While the meringue layers are baking, make the filling.

In a double boiler, melt the chocolate with the milk and ½ tablespoon of the butter. In a second double boiler, beat the 3 egg whites until frothy, then gradually beat in the sugar, cocoa, and—1 tablespoon at a time—the butter. (Make sure that the water in the bottom part of the boiler is only simmering and not boiling.) Beat in the melted chocolate, and when it is all incorporated, continue beating over the heat for 1 minute more. Remove from the heat and set aside to cool and thicken—it should be firm enough to spread. Divide the mixture into 3 parts; add the rum to the first, the coffee essence to the second, and the ginger to the third.

Place one of the meringue layers on a large plate. Cover the meringue with one of the fillings. Cover this with another meringue layer and again cover with a filling; repeat, finishing up with the fourth meringue layer on top. Cover with foil and put in the refrigerator for 2 days. Remove the foil and mold the cake into a hat-crown shape with your hands. Cover and leave in the refrigerator another 3 days at least. Decorate as I suggest in the note above, or as your artistic soul dictates, and serve at room temperature.

This is my version of a recipe from that much-quoted little book *Definitely Different*. I love anything made of hazelnuts, but I don't think it is necessary to rub the skins off—yes, I know it sounds so easy, but it is boring and time-consuming and besides, I like the color and flavor that the skins give. I always roast my nuts before using them; it makes for a much more intense flavor. I usually serve these with ice cream or fruit salad—better still, with after-dinner coffee.

These fingers are much better if left to ripen for a day or two before eating. They keep very well in a cool, dry place and, in fact, improve in flavor as a week passes.

¼ pound blanched almonds, roughly chopped (about ⅔ cup chopped)
¼ pound hazelnuts, roughly chopped (about 1 cup chopped)
2 ounces granulated sugar, plus 2 tablespoons for rolling out dough
1 ounce unbleached, all-purpose flour
4 ounces mixed peel, chopped very fine, a mixture of the following: muscat raisins, bitter orange marmalade, prunes, candied orange peel, angelica (not dried apricots, which are too acid)
1 egg white, slightly beaten
½ teaspoon powdered cinnamon
1 tablespoon kirsch, brandy, or rum
2 tablespoons honey
Butter to grease cookie sheet

glaze

3 tablespoons granulated sugar
2 tablespoons water

Preheat the oven to 350° F. Spread the chopped almonds and hazelnuts out on ungreased cookie sheets and toast them until very slightly browned, about 15 minutes. Remove and allow to cool. Using the spice/coffee grinder, grind the nuts with a little of the sugar, and in small quantities, for 10 seconds. While they should be finely ground, they must not be reduced to a powder. Put the ground nuts in a mixing bowl, add the flour and remaining sugar and mix well. Add the peel, egg white, cinnamon, kirsch, and honey (warmed if it has crystallized) and, with your hands, mix all together to a sticky paste.

Preheat the oven to 300° F. Lightly grease a cookie sheet and place the oven rack at the top of the oven.

Sprinkle the remaining 2 tablespoons sugar on a wooden board and press the mixture out into a rough rectangular shape about ½ inch thick. Cut the dough into fingers about 2½ × ½ inches—it will help if you have a very sharp knife handy and a cloth continually dipped into very hot water to clean the knife after every cut. Transfer the fingers with a spatula to the baking sheet and bake for about 30 minutes. They should be very slightly browned but not tough around the outside. Before the fingers have a chance to cool off and stick to the baking sheet, carefully transfer them to a wire rack.

To prepare the glaze Heat the sugar and water over a low flame until the sugar melts. Bring to a boil and boil for about 1 minute, or until the syrup begins to thicken. Brush the glaze over the fingers and allow to cool before storing.

Pineapple in Honey

6 SERVINGS

Do you ever get halfway through a pineapple and get bored with it, and know that if it is left too long it will start to ferment? Apart from that, the nearer you get to the stalk base, the less sweet it is. Well, this recipe is ideal for the second half of the pineapple—or for the first, for that matter. This recipe is inspired by one given in Elizabeth David's *A Book of Mediterranean Food*. It makes a great topping for yogurt, and although it's a little too sweet for my taste for ice cream, it's a delicious sticky filling for a puff pastry slice topped with unsweetened whipped cream, or just for snacking on when you crave something very sweet.

The longer it cooks, the darker in color and more chewy it becomes, and this is how I like it. If the pineapple is very sweet, then add some lemon or lime juice.

2½ **pounds cleaned pineapple, skin and core removed, cut into ¾-inch cubes (about 6 cups)**
1 **cup honey**
2 **teaspoons lime or lemon juice** *(optional)*
 Rind of 1 lime or ½ lemon *(optional)*

Put the pineapple, honey, and juice and rind (if using) in a heavy saucepan and stir well. Cook over a fairly lively heat, stirring from time to time. It will become very juicy at first. Continue cooking rather quickly until the juice evaporates and the honey starts to thicken and caramelize, about 40 minutes. Allow to cool and serve at room temperature. When cooked, this yields about 3 cups.

Pineapple in Port Wine

I scribbled a version of this recipe down many years ago, from where I couldn't remember until just the other day, when I came across it in Dione Lucas's *The Cordon Bleu Cook Book*. It is a simple yet delicious way of using a pineapple, and of using up one that is not quite sweet enough to eat by itself. It can be eaten alone, with unsweetened whipped cream or *crème fraîche;* as a topping for vanilla ice cream, or any other ice cream; or as a fruity sherbet. A few pieces in a fruit salad add a very nice touch. Don't be stingy about the port—buy a good one. Prepare this the day before for a better flavor.

1 medium pineapple (about 2½ pounds), cleaned
Finely pared rind of 1 orange
Finely pared rind of ½ grapefruit
4 tablespoons light brown sugar, or to taste
¾ cup pineapple juice
½ cup port

Peel, slice, and core the pineapple and cut into 1-inch cubes or thin slices. Julienne the citrus rinds and put them in a pan together with the sugar and pineapple juice. Cook over a low flame until the rinds are tender but not too soft, about 5 minutes. While the liquid is still warm, add the pineapple pieces and stir in the port. Set aside to macerate overnight or for at least 8 hours.

Do not serve straight from the refrigerator; it should be allowed to reach room temperature, or the flavors will be lost.

Orange Fruit Salad

I must admit that patience is not one of my qualities, and however hard I try, I do not cut orange sections from their pithy divisions with much facility or joy. In fact, I have always cut oranges into thin rounds and enjoy the chewy texture; besides, Adelle Davis says the pith is good for us—so be it.

The wine connoisseur Gerald Asher served a most delicious orange fruit salad one evening when I had dinner with him, and I remember there was some nut brittle and mint leaves over the top. So this recipe is really his idea and my interpretation. I like the crunch and slight bitterness that fruit rind gives to this dessert and quite often I will mix oranges and tangerines—fruit, juice, and rind.

    4 large oranges
    ⅔ cup freshly squeezed orange juice
       Rind of 1 orange, thinly pared
    5 tablespoons granulated sugar
       Butter to grease cookie sheet
    2 heaped tablespoons blanched and slivered almonds
    4 sprigs fresh mint
    2 tablespoons Cointreau or Triple Sec (optional)

Peel the oranges, removing as much of the pith as possible. Cut into very thin rounds. Arrange the orange slices, no more than 3 deep, in a shallow dish. Pour the orange juice over them and set aside to macerate. Cut the orange rind into julienne strips. Put in a small saucepan with cold water to cover and bring to a boil. Drain, and add the strips to the oranges.

Put the sugar in an ungreased frying pan and dissolve over low heat.

Lightly grease a cookie sheet and set aside.

When the sugar has melted, raise the flame and cook, stirring, until the sugar turns a dark caramel color. Stir in the almonds. Pour onto the greased tray and allow to cool. As soon as it is cool and brittle, cover with an old cloth and crush roughly with a hammer—do not process or blend. Reserve until ready to serve the oranges. Then sprinkle the almond brittle over the oranges and decorate with the mint sprigs. Add Cointreau or Triple Sec to taste, if you wish.

VARIATIONS Use half tangerine juice and tangerine peel. Instead of using the almond brittle and mint, just before serving, stir in 2 tablespoons sliced preserved or crystallized ginger and 2 tablespoons slivered and roasted almonds.

FRUIT SALADS It is always a joy to make fruit salads in Mexico with all its tropical and subtropical fruits. Although many are available the year round, each has its peak season, and one succeeds another as the year progresses. In the hot spring days the cantaloupe and honeydew melons are sweet and juicy and the strawberries intense in color and flavor. They are followed closely by the first of the yellow Manila mangoes—considered by many to be the best of all— and the pineapples from the Veracruz coast. As the summer rains take hold, there are grapes, pomegranates, and small elongated papayas with intensely pink flesh, which combine and contrast with a touch of cooked quince. As fall approaches, the first apples and pears come in from the colder Sierras, to be followed later by the popular *granada china* (a type of passion fruit), *tamarillos (see page 214),* and loquats, all of which grow in my orchard. The Christmas *piñata* fruits can be made into a refreshing mixture, too: guavas, tangerines, cooked crab apples, mixed with the fragrant zest of sweet limes. The soft *sapotes* or *mameyes,* with their compact, delicately flavored, deep salmon-colored flesh, mix well with segments of grapefruit and the flesh of *chirimoyas* (custard apples)—if you have the patience to remove the numerous seeds. The choice is bewildering.

There are no hard-and-fast rules about what or how many different fruits should go into a fruit salad. Blueberries and peaches alone can be a feast, or raspberries with red currants mixed with a juicy pear and a touch of kiwi fruit for added crunch and glamour. The only rule is to use whatever is good and fresh and provides contrasts of color and texture. Here are some suggestions:

Cut each fruit in a different way and into a different size.

Use anything rather than granulated sugar syrup: honey, brown sugar, fresh orange juice, tangerine juice, grapefruit juice, separately or combined.

Don't overpower the fruit with too much liqueur, kirsch, etc.

Interesting textures and flavors can be provided by the addition of blanched, julienned orange and tangerine rinds.

About 15 minutes before serving add chopped dried apricots, pears, or pineapple; chopped dates; or whole raisins, sultanas (or golden raisins), or even currants.

As you are about to serve, stir in freshly roasted, roughly chopped nuts, chopped crystallized or sliced preserved ginger, or crystallized angelica cut into small strips.

Serve at room temperature to appreciate the full flavor of the fruits.

GINGER In Mother's house there was almost always one cake flavored with ginger among the many stashed away in large square tins—they originally came full of Cadbury's assorted biscuits (cookies) packed with precision in cushioning layers of soft corrugated paper—that were piled up in the cool larder full of teatime things. Until very recent years, one of the first things I did on entering the house was to go through those tins one by one: a gingerbread, a dripping cake with currants and sultanas, some almond tarts, scones, cookies, oatmeal-date squares—the selection seemed endless. I then and there decided just what I was going to have for tea that afternoon.

If there wasn't a gingerbread, then a parkin (made with oatmeal instead of flour), a round, soft ginger cake topped with slices of preserved ginger, or gingersnaps. Ginger marmalade was always around in that cupboard, too, though it was rather too sweet for my taste. But in prewar days the teatime treat was those luscious pieces of thick ginger root preserved in a thin syrup that came from China in enticing green-glazed stoneware jars covered with a thin bamboo strapping. (I see that Williams-Sonoma is advertising this now in its catalog.) We would cut it into slices and put it on brown bread and butter.

Gingersnaps

I have developed this recipe for very crisp, thin ginger cookies—of which I am inordinately fond—to suit my palate and to provide a substitute for the best of the commercial ones, which are not always available. They are equally good eaten alone, to accompany a dessert, or with ice cream—or roughly crumbled into an ice cream with preserved ginger. They are perfect for making Gingersnap Dessert (see index for recipe).

The dough is soft, delicate, and difficult to manage. You could, of course, put it in the freezer until very firm and slice thinly, but the cookies then won't look as nice as those made following these instructions. If you roll the dough between the plastic wrap, as I suggest, you are not picking up any unwanted flour.

I am advocating Maida Heatter's wonderful tip for delicate cookies: baking them on a sheet lined with aluminum foil.

- ¼ **cup light molasses**
- 3 **ounces (6 tablespoons) unsalted butter, cut into small pieces and softened**
- 6 **ounces unbleached, all-purpose flour**
- 2 **ounces dark brown sugar (about ⅓ cup loosely packed)**
- ¾ **teaspoon baking soda**
- ⅛ **teaspoon sea salt**
- ½ **teaspoon powdered cinnamon**
- ⅛ **teaspoon powdered cloves**
- 1 **scant tablespoon powdered ginger, or to taste**

Have ready 2 large baking sheets covered with aluminum foil, shiny side up and ungreased. **Preheat the oven to 350° F.**

Put the molasses in a small saucepan, add the softened butter, and heat very gently until the butter is just beginning to melt—but not yet transparent. Remove and stir until the butter has melted completely, and set aside to cool.

Weigh the flour in a plastic bag, add the sugar, baking soda, salt, and powdered spices, and mix all together well. Transfer to a mixing bowl and gradually stir in the cooled molasses-butter mixture. Knead the dough for about 1 minute, until very smooth—it will be rather soft. Divide the dough into 3 parts, and while you work with the first, put the rest in the refrigerator.

Place a sheet of plastic wrap on your work surface. Flatten the dough onto it, place another sheet of wrap over the dough, and roll out to between ¹⁄₁₆ and ⅛ inch, turning the wrap around as necessary and using short, gentle movements. Cut the dough with a 2½-inch cookie cutter and carefully transfer to the prepared baking sheets.

NOTE The bottom piece of plastic wrap may wrinkle as you roll. Don't try and straighten it out or the dough will crack. Just cut the dough and be extra careful when transferring the cookies to the baking tray. Then flatten out the wrinkles for the next batch of dough.

The cookies will expand about ¼ inch during cooking, so put them about ½ inch apart on the baking tray.

Bake for about 15 minutes—they should be a deep golden brown and crisp right through. If some are a little thicker than others, then turn them over and bake for a further 5 to 10 minutes with the oven turned down to 300° F.

Gingersnap Dessert

6 SERVINGS

There are lots of what I call "silly" desserts, and this is one of them—but it is so good! Thin gingersnaps are sandwiched together with layers of unsweetened whipped cream that has small pieces of preserved ginger mixed with it. You can make one large dessert but I prefer to do individual servings. It is always better to make your own gingersnaps (see the recipe for Gingersnaps on page 156), but if you don't want to go to that trouble, then I recommend the packages of Swedish ginger thins that can be found in specialty stores. Although a trifle on the sweet side, they are the best of the commercially made ones.

⅔ **cup heavy cream**
½ **cup finely chopped preserved or crystallized ginger, or to taste**
24 **thin ginger cookies, about 2½ inches in diameter**

Whip the cream until stiff and stir in the pieces of ginger. Spread one of the cookies with a thick coating of cream, top with another cookie, and repeat twice again until there are 4 layers of cookies. Decorate on top with a dab of cream and a small piece of ginger.

Have ready a shallow dish into which the 6 layered cookies can be placed side by side with at least ½ inch between them. Cover the dish with plastic wrap and place in the freezer overnight. Two hours before serving time, remove from the freezer and let the cookies come up to just below room temperature to serve. They are best left for several days in the freezer before eating.

Lemon Tart (A Franco-Spanish Family Recipe)   6 SERVINGS

No list of my favorite desserts would be complete without this wonderfully flavored lemon tart. A note at the bottom says: "Let tart stand until lukewarm before serving"—and that's how it should be served, but if you wait until the next day and serve it at room temperature, the buttery flavor of the crust comes through.

Alas, this splendid recipe is an orphan. I was quite sure I clipped it from *The New York Times,* but they disown it.

      ¾ cup unbleached, all-purpose flour
      ¼ teaspoon sea salt
      5 tablespoons unsalted butter
    2–3 tablespoons cold water
      1 cup granulated sugar
      4 ounces (about ¾ cup) whole almonds, blanched and then finely ground
      1 tart cooking apple, peeled, cored, and finely grated
      3 large lemons, peeled, and segments removed without the pith
      1 egg, lightly beaten
      1 cup heavy cream
      2 tablespoons confectioners' sugar

Preheat the oven to 425° F. Have ready an 8-inch pie or quiche pan with a removable bottom.

To make the pastry Mix the flour and salt in a bowl. Cut the butter into small pieces and work into the flour with the fingertips until the mixture resembles coarse bread crumbs. Add the water and just mix it in so that the mixture hangs together in a crumbly mass—do not handle or press it together too hard. Roll the dough out into a circle slightly larger than the bottom measurement of the pan and place in the pan so that it extends a little way up the sides. Prick the pastry all over with a fork and bake at the top of the oven for about 15 minutes, until lightly browned. Allow to cool.

In the meantime, combine the granulated sugar, ground almonds, and apple and spread over the surface of the pastry, making sure that it reaches and "seals" around the edge of the pastry. Arrange the lemon segments in a wheel over the almond mixture. Beat the egg and cream together—the egg should be well broken up but not frothy—and pour this over the surface. Bake until the tart just begins to set on the surface, sprinkle with the confectioners' sugar, and continue baking until firmly set, about 30 minutes in all. Set aside to cool until lukewarm before serving.

Blackberry Ice Cream with Hot Blackberry Sauce 6 TO 8 SERVINGS

I am not addicted to ice creams, as many people are—two spoonfuls and I have had enough; for my taste they are too sweet and cloying. Sorbets always sound nice, but they are a letdown—too thin, icy, and often too sweet—except for a sharp grapefruit sorbet with lots of crunchy globules of flesh in it. But I came across a strawberry ice cream I liked when several years ago I attended a class given by Isabelle Marique in New York, so when the wild blackberries appeared so plentifully this year I thought of making something like it.

In England, blackberries were almost always cooked with apples, which diluted their intense flavor. It was this intensity of flavor that caught my attention when I first ate *nieve de zarzamora.*

Since I love surprises of textures and tastes in food, I thought of combining this served very cold with a hot fruit sauce—and, of course, if you have the calories to spare, then put a generous amount of thick cream on top. I occasionally use a rich yogurt made of whole milk instead.

Use wild blackberries if possible, cultivated ones are sweeter but have less flavor. If you do have to use the latter, reduce the sugar.

> 1½ **pounds blackberries, wild if possible**
> 12 **ounces light brown sugar (2 cups less 2 tablespoons, firmly packed)**
> 1¾ **cups cold water**
> ½ **cup heavy cream**
> 1 **egg white, at room temperature**

Rinse the blackberries well and make sure that there are no stems still adhering to them. Put the blackberries, sugar, and water in a saucepan and cook gently until just tender but not too soft—about 7 minutes after reaching a simmer. With a slotted spoon, remove about 1 rounded cup of the whole fruit and set aside. Put the rest of the cooked blackberries and their juice into a blender or food processor and blend until reduced to a fine puree. Press this puree through a fairly fine sieve to extract most of the seeds—some will go through, but that doesn't matter—and add the whole blackberries to the puree, which should make about 4½ cups. Put half of the puree aside for the hot sauce later on, and chill the remaining half briefly—it will give your machine less work. Beat the cream and egg white together until light and stir them well into the chilled puree. Pour into the ice cream machine container and follow the manufacturer's instructions for making ice cream. (I usually remove it from the machine when it's made and store it in the freezer until I want to use it.)

To make the sauce Over a high flame reduce and thicken the puree reserved for the sauce. Add a liqueur if desired (optional) and keep it hot.

Pour the hot sauce over each serving of very cold ice cream.

Mango Ice Cream

My favorite mango is the slender yellow Manila, which comes into season toward the end of May and makes superb ice cream. Sadly, I have never seen it imported into the United States. (There is a yellowish green one from Haiti that I have seen in New York markets, but it doesn't have the same flavor.) For this recipe I used the huge Petacón mango (they can weigh up to 1¾ pounds); red-cheeked, with green and yellow markings, it comes from Colima and is imported to the West Coast and possibly other places.

The general tendency is for mango ice cream to be too sweet and rather insipid, so it is best to choose slightly underripe fruit that still has that fascinating turpentiny tang of the skin.

I like to make this ice cream on the sharp side, freeze it extra hard, and then serve mangoes flambéed with tequila over the top.

> 1½ **pounds ripe but not overripe mangoes**
> ½ **pound underripe mangoes**
> 2 **tablespoons lime juice**
> ¼ **teaspoon finely grated lime rind**
> ¼ **cup water**
> 3 **tablespoons light brown sugar**
> ⅓ **cup heavy cream or** *crème fraîche*
> 1 **egg white, at room temperature**

Pare the mangoes and cut all the flesh from the pit. Chop the flesh roughly, setting aside ½ cup for later use. Put the chopped flesh into the container of the food processor together with lime juice and rind, water, and brown sugar and process for a few seconds until you have a textured puree. Whip the cream until slightly thick, whip the egg white until frothy, and stir them both into the puree. Allow to cool in the refrigerator until ready to use.

Put the mango puree in the container of the ice cream machine and follow the manufacturer's instructions. As the ice cream begins to thicken, add the reserved chopped mango and continue until the ice cream is made. Transfer to a freezer container and freeze hard.

Serve with sliced mango flambéed with tequila (see recipe for Flambéed Mangoes).

Flambéed Mangoes

This recipe first appeared in a somewhat different form in my book *The Cuisines of Mexico*. Many years ago Howard Brown, then of the Ramada Inn in Monterrey, Nuevo León, served it to me. It was his delicious invention. I know that good mangoes are wonderful to eat raw, but this way of preparing them only enhances the flavor of the fruit.

This quantity should be enough for a topping for 3 to 4 servings of Mango Ice Cream. The best mango for this recipe is without doubt the rather slender, yellow Manila mango that ripens in Mexico in May and is available for several months. It is also available canned but tends to be overly sweet, and one has to reduce the sugar if the canned ones are used for this recipe. The large fat red-cheeked mango that is imported into the United States from the Caribbean can, of course, be used, although it is sweeter and has a more compact flesh than the Manila.

1½ tablespoons unsalted butter
1½ tablespoons granulated sugar
　　Juice and thinly pared, julienned rind of ½ orange
　　Juice and thinly pared, julienned rind of ½ lime
2 tablespoons Triple Sec or Cointreau
1 large mango, peeled, seed removed, and cut into strips
2 tablespoons tequila

Melt the butter in a chafing dish or heavy frying pan. Stir in the sugar and continue stirring until it has dissolved. Add the orange and lime rinds and the Triple Sec, and flame. When the flames have died down, add the fruit juices and boil until reduced and thickened, about 3 minutes. Add the mangoes, heat through, and when the syrup begins to bubble, add the tequila and flame again. Serve immediately.

NOTE I prefer to leave the rinds in, as they are nice and crunchy.

TEA

I am glad I was not born before tea!

—Sydney Smith (1771–1845)

"Oh, for a good cup of tea!" A truly British cry that I echo so often in my travels around four o'clock in the afternoon. Tea is my panacea, my consolation—if you will, my "fix." But it can also be horrible. Take tea at airports, for example: a thick mug, if you are lucky—it is more often a revolting Styrofoam cup that scalds your lips—two-thirds full of hot water that tastes of the kitchen and that has been reheated a hundred times in the day. There is usually a slender teabag on the saucer, put there casually as if left by accident. "Could you please put some boiling water *over* the teabag," I say timidly—and I am usually far from timid. "But the water *has* boiled" is the invariable reply, at which point I give up.

If there is one meal that I could repeat during the day—without getting too fat, of course—it would be tea. In some countries tea means a ceremonial drink, but for the British it is a social or family occasion. One can sit down comfortably without feeling that one's wasting time, take stock, and gear oneself up for the rest of the day.

Tea is such a delicate and aesthetic drink that, unless you have drunk it when it has been made properly and the full flavor extracted from it, it is practically impossible to appreciate my enthusiasm—passion, if you will.

Every afternoon at four-thirty the clock stops in my house in the Michoacán mountains, and I carry a locally made flat-bottomed strawberry basket laden with tea things up to my study. There is always homemade jam, scones, clotted cream or butter (also homemade), and milk from the morning's milking that has a layer of yellow cream on top. As I pour out my tea on a November afternoon, I watch the last brilliant rays of the sun light up the carpet of multi-colored flowers around the house and cast a golden sheen onto the forested mountains beyond. It is a magical time, and I can't help but compare it to a November teatime in England! I have perhaps the very slightest twinge of nostalgia when I think back to those prewar Sunday teas—but it quickly disperses when I think of the weather. The light would be fading fast as we walked back from Hampstead Heath and the sad, damp smell of autumn lay heavily on the air as we shuffled our feet in the matted layer of faded yellow leaves covering the sidewalk. In those days smoke curled out of the chimney pots, and as the lamplighter passed along the street deftly pulling the slender chains of the gas lamps, the mantles would suddenly explode and then glow with a bluish flame. I can even remember the clang of the muffin man's bell as he loomed out of the misty twilight.

By the time we arrived home, the tea trolley was laid ready in front of the fire. We would sit close to the flames to warm ourselves. When it was time to toast the crumpets or currant buns, the logs were pushed back to reveal the glowing coals. The brass toasting fork that Father used to polish with vigor each Sunday morning was taken down from its place by the chimney and whatever was to be toasted impaled—if there had been roast beef for lunch, then we would toast thick slices of bread and slather them with drippings from the roasting pan. We were not allowed to start with cake: watercress or fish-paste sandwiches, or bread and butter, or scones and jam had to be eaten in quantity before we were allowed to go on to the sweet things. There was always a round, layered plate rack on the table to hold the small cakes: coconut pyramids; maids of honor—tartlets of puff pastry filled with almond paste and apricot jam; Banbury cakes; Shrewsbury biscuits—all made at home. On separate plates covered with crocheted doilies were the large round cakes. There were usually three to choose from: a gingerbread, a rather dry seed cake, gritty with whole caraway seeds that I intensely disliked, and a chocolate Swiss roll (jelly roll) filled with real whipped cream or a Dundee cake with its pattern of toasted almond halves over the top. And this, mind you, was ordinary tea, not high tea. High tea takes place from five o'clock on, a sort of tea-cum-supper when something savory, hot or cold, is served.

There were special-occasion teas. Birthdays, for instance, were celebrated with parlor games and eating: orange halves hollowed out and filled, trifles with lots of whipped cream on top, little fairy cakes (very small cupcakes) covered with "hundreds and thousands" (microscopic multicolored balls like the American sprinkles), and chocolate cupcakes. All these followed sandwiches made with an extra amount of butter for the occasion, and sausage rolls with their rich pastry casing. The birthday cake itself was usually orange- or lemon-flavored—round Victoria sponge cakes sandwiched together with thick layers of buttercream and topped with an icing of the same flavor decorated with angelica and cherries. Then there were Easter teas with toasted, buttered hot cross buns, and a simnel cake, rich and buttery, with its thick almond-paste topping decorated with fluffy yellow chickens and small marzipan eggs. The ultimate test of endurance was Christmas tea (see the Christmas section) with turkey-drippings toast, Christmas cake, and shortbread.

Tea at Lyons Corner House was a special treat after shopping or going to a pantomime in the West End of London. Under the spindly palms of the immense tearoom we stuffed ourselves with cream buns and éclairs—filled with real cream—to the accompaniment of *thé dansant* music played with a coquettish lilt by a sedate and aging trio. But what rich fragrant tea they served! It never tasted quite that good at home.

If theater teas still exist, which I very much doubt, I am sure they are not as good as I remember. (At the one matinee I went to last year, only coffee was served at a bar. "The Americans have taken over" was the usher's rejoinder to my remark "No tea in the theater! What has become of England?" And he went on, "But it is very good. Like me, it is Brazilian.") At the first or second intermission a small tray laden with the paraphernalia of tea arrived miraculously unspilled at your seat—that is, if you had remembered to order it before the play began. Everything seemed to fit on it: tea for one with room for a small plate of delicate sandwiches, a measured rectangle of fruitcake, and a small dish of ice cream. There was a momentary lull in the otherwise animated conversation and the theater filled with the clink of teacups.

My favorite memory of tea is my earliest: tea at Mrs. Parker's across the road. My sister and I could hardly wait; in fact, we always arrived too early. We would walk up the immaculately manicured garden path between the immaculately pruned rosebushes set in a small lawn where not a blade of grass was out of place. A neat little maid answered our knock and showed us in. She wore her black uniform dress with starched headband and cuffs of bird's-eye lace woven with narrow black velvet ribbon and a frilly apron to match. The parrot squawked and the Pekingese dog yapped as we entered and greeted Mrs. Parker. We could hardly wait until tea was served and our favorite coffee sponge came into view. It was in fact two rounds of coffee-flavored buttery sponge cake sandwiched together with a thick layer of buttercream, also coffee-flavored. The cake was covered with a satiny-smooth layer of coffee-flavored icing and trimmed with those intriguing little silver balls or chopped hazelnuts. She always made this when we came to tea and very little of it was left by the time we said good-bye.

There have been other memorable teas and teatimes: simple but wonderfully good farmhouse teas for the asking in wartime Wales after hiking over the bracken- and bilberry-covered slopes of the Brecon Beacons, and Devonshire teas during the summer vacations with thick clotted cream and strawberry jam to smother freshly made scones.

My San Pancho teas, though much more modest, borrow a little something from all these experiences, and I bake—yes, even for myself when I don't have company—so that I have something for tea each and every day. Here are some of my favorite recipes.

A PROPERLY SET TEA TRAY, FOR ORDINARY (NOT HIGH) TEA

It doesn't have to be a silver tray—it can be a wooden one, for that matter, or the top of a tea cart—but cover it with a small cloth, embroidered or with drawn-thread work, what you will. The most important piece of equipment is, of course, the teapot, standing on its trivet. I prefer china or earthenware to metal, and I love the Japanese ones that have a nice little round strainer inside the spout. Of course, it is nice to have several sizes of teapot because it is disastrous to make tea for two in an eight-cup pot—it gets cold quickly and doesn't brew as well. There should be a small milk jug, not a great big pitcher unless you are making tea for twenty people. There should be a slop basin for the leaves left in the cups when you are about to pour seconds, with a small strainer sitting on it or on its own stand. Then a sugar basin for lump sugar and a pair of special little tongs, and a jug to hold the hot water for adjusting the strength of the cups of tea. And of course a tea cozy.

Cups and saucers are, of course, essential: china, if you can possibly manage it; please, no thick pottery mugs—you can't taste the tea—and besides, they should be reserved for hot cocoa. It is customary to place a small teaspoon in each saucer to stir the sugar in. Although "it is not done in the best of circles," I take my spoon off. I don't take sugar, and the spoon often falls off the saucer or gets in the way. There should be a small tea plate and one of those slender British tea knives for each of the guests. Dainty linen or embroidered cotton napkins are an essential; paper ones are acceptable only in an emergency. There should be a separate dish and knife for pats of butter and a small glass dish or jam pot with decorative spoon for the jam. If you are including a large, uncut cake among the tea food, then there should be a good-looking knife to cut it with.

MAKING TEA   Now for the tea itself: no teabags, no instant tea, no iced tea, and this is not the time for herbal teas—just good plain Indian or Ceylon tea leaves; I much prefer them to China tea in the afternoon, but that is a matter of taste. As a general rule, I would suggest buying tea only when it is packed in an airtight container, because it can easily become stale and musty. Buy loose tea only if you know that your specialty shop has a very quick turnover—you can waste an awful lot of money buying teas that are stale and tasteless, and the trouble is the sales clerks and, alas, even some owners, don't know the difference. I can't pretend to be an expert on teas, because I am not, but I love the flavor and strength of a flowery Darjeeling, or a pungent so-called Russian tea, or a good orange pekoe, and I vary them constantly, to compare tastes and qualities. I don't know whether it is still done, but tea in Britain used to be blended to suit the water of each region of the country. This is why some experimenting for the right teas for your area is important. New York's water makes wonderful tea, while my fresh spring water does nothing for the flavor and strength, as it lacks calcium. The very same tea that brews a delicious cup in Dallas is strident and has a chalky film over it in Paris. The only solution is to keep tasting and comparing.

You will need a hot water kettle—I think the name teakettle is misleading. A whistling one is useful, since you can hear when the water is about to come to a boil, although I personally use an electric kettle because I am always in a hurry. Well then, fill the kettle with cold water freshly drawn from the tap, and when it is close to a boil pour a little into the teapot, which is already warming at the side of the stove, and swirl it around several times to heat the inside of the pot. Throw the water away or put it in the teacups to heat them—completely unorthodox, but I like scalding tea and the cups are invariably cold unless the temperature is in the hundreds. Measure the tea leaves into the heated pot—1 heaped teaspoon for each person and 1 for the pot is the rule of thumb—and pour the boiling, bubbling water onto the leaves, strictly observing the old British rule "Take the pot to the kettle, not the kettle to the pot." Stir well. Put a tea cozy over the pot and leave it for 6 minutes for the tea to draw. If you are heating the teacups, pour the hot water into the slop basin—you'll need a big one unless you have an open window nearby. Pour a little good cold whole milk—not skimmed or boiled milk, which give a bad color and flavor to the tea, and not cream, which is far too rich—into each cup. Give a final stir to the tea (not done in polite society) and pour. Add a little more hot water to the pot as necessary, as the tea will be strong and you don't want to exhaust it first time around. When you have finished pouring, add more water for the second round.

BRITISH SAVANTS DISCOVER HOW TO BREW TEA

LONDON (AP)   The Queen of England, it must be said, does not pour a perfect cup of tea.

In fact, that much was implied Friday by the British Standards Institute, whose scientists have been at work on one of this country's great questions:

What comes first—the milk or the tea?

Queen Elizabeth II, Buckingham Palace sources disclose, always pours the tea into the cup and then adds the milk.

Institute scientists, however, have now laid down unanimously that the milk must be poured first. Otherwise, they state, the milk is scalded and that affects the taste of the tea.

The ideal teapot is made of earthenware or white porcelain; tea must be two per cent of the total mass of the pot; the water must be freshly boiled and filled to within four to six millimeters of the brim, beneath a loosely-fitting lid with a hole in it; and the filled pot must stand for exactly—repeat, exactly—six minutes before pouring commences.

Cucumber Sandwiches   ABOUT 18 SMALL SANDWICHES

There is no doubt that when you think of England and sandwiches you think of cucumber sandwiches, which were launched into literary fame by Oscar Wilde. They are refreshing and crunchy when well made and insipidly soggy if made with indifference.

Whenever cucumber sandwiches are mentioned, I think of tea in the garden on a summer afternoon. The weather-beaten outdoors table was hidden under a fresh, starched colored cloth—not white, because it was outdoors—and covered with plates of bread and butter, scones, sandwiches, jam pot, cakes, and biscuits. The tea trolley was lifted cautiously over the lawn to where a hammock was slung under some trees, and deck chairs—excruciatingly uncomfortable to eat in—set around the table. It was always a juggling act to keep a napkin, plate, and knife on your knee while balancing a full cup and saucer, taking sips and bites, and brushing off an angry wasp attracted to the jam. It was indeed a full tea (not high tea, which indicates a late tea—a substitute for the evening meal—with a more substantial savory meal, either hot or cold) and even on the hottest of days everyone drank several cups of steaming Indian tea and felt refreshed.

There was something very special about tea in the garden when the whole family came together in peace. There was an aroma of freshly mown grass and the first birdsong of the evening from the apple tree, and if we were late enough, church bells in the distance swelling and fading as the breeze changed direction. Nostalgia? I wouldn't go back to those days for anything, but perhaps the world would be a better place if everything would slow down and we would take time to feel and think, drink tea, and dream a little.

Commercially grown cucumbers in the United States have been a disaster: they are tough-skinned, overfertilized, and tasteless. To make matters worse, some misguided vegetable makeup artist has decided that they should be waxed—what a ridiculous waste of effort and money! But now many markets across the United States are carrying the more delicately flavored long, thin European-type cucumbers—the type that is always used in England. (They usually come in plastic shrink-wrap in the United States.) Of course, if you live near a country vegetable stand and can buy them freshly picked, better still. If the cucumbers have a trace of wax on them, they will have to be peeled; but if not, they should be scored lengthwise with the tines of a sharp fork. Leaving the skin on makes for a better flavor and texture, which is important to these sandwiches. The bread should be either white or whole wheat, salty and with a tough crumb—far too many breads are sweet and doughy and should be shunned for everything, but particularly sandwiches.

½ **European-type cucumber** (*see note above*)
   Sea salt and freshly ground black pepper to taste
3 **tablespoons strong, unseasoned malt vinegar** (*optional*)
   Bread (*see note above*)
   Salted butter, slightly softened

Score the cucumber lengthwise and cut in paper-thin slices. Put the slices in a bowl. Season with the salt, freshly ground pepper, and vinegar. Set aside while you cut the bread and butter it. (The bane of my existence when I was growing up—the bread was always falling apart as I attempted to butter it.)

Cut the end crust off a loaf of bread and lavishly butter the cut surface. Slice thin. Repeat until enough bread has been buttered and cut for the sandwiches. Drain the cucumber a little, and put a thin layer between 2 slices of the bread. Trim off the crusts, if you wish—depending on how fancy you want to be—and cut into triangles or rectangles. (I personally dislike all those fancy little pinwheel things.) Eat very soon after making, as these sandwiches are apt to become soggy.

Egg and Anchovy Sandwiches

If you are on a salt-free or low-cholesterol diet, turn the page quickly, for these sandwiches can become addictive. As usual, the essentials for making good sandwiches are very good bread without the slightest hint of sweetness, a good serrated knife to cut it with, and plenty of good fresh, unsalted butter to spread it with.

This should be enough filling for 8 small slices of bread, depending, of course, on how heavy-handed you like to be with this rich filling.

> 2 **hard-boiled eggs, peeled and mashed while still warm**
> 2 **scant tablespoons unsalted butter, at room temperature, plus extra to butter the bread**
> 4–5 **teaspoons anchovy paste, or to taste—less if using Crosse & Blackwell's highly concentrated anchovy essence**
> **About 8 slices bread**

After mashing the eggs, allow them to cool off completely—but do not refrigerate. Mix well with the butter and anchovy paste and layer between 2 slices of well-buttered bread, preferably whole wheat.

If you want to be extra fancy, then cut the crusts off the bread when the sandwich is made and cut it into different shapes.

Yogurt Scones

These scones have a nice short texture, and the acidity of the yogurt gives an unusual flavor. The recipe is an adaptation of one from the cookbook I have called *Definitely Different*. I have tried making it with whole wheat flour, but the result is not as pleasing. However, the scones are very good with the addition of a little bran, about 1 ounce, reducing the flour accordingly. You can also use buttermilk instead of yogurt; ⅓ cup should be sufficient.

    4 ounces unbleached, all-purpose flour, plus extra for rolling out the dough
    2 ounces cornstarch
    ¾ teaspoon double-acting or 1 teaspoon single-acting baking powder
    ¼ teaspoon sea salt
  2½ ounces (5 tablespoons) unsalted butter, at room temperature
    ½ ounce (1 tablespoon) good pork lard, at room temperature *(optional)*
    ¼ cup yogurt, diluted with enough milk to make just over ⅓ cup

Preheat the oven to 350° F and place the oven rack at the top of the oven. Lightly grease a cookie sheet.

Mix the flour, cornstarch, baking powder, and salt together well. Cut the fats into small pieces and, with the fingertips, rub them into the flour mixture until it resembles coarse bread crumbs. Stir in the yogurt and milk until you have a fairly stiff dough. Put the dough on a lightly floured surface and handle it very lightly and as little as possible. Press it out with a rolling pin until it is about ½ inch thick and cut the scones out with a 2-inch biscuit cutter. Gather up the remaining dough, pressing the pieces together, and roll out again. Repeat. My very last scone always turns out to be a funny shape because I use up every scrap of the dough.

Bake the scones for about 20 minutes, raise the heat of the oven to 400° F, and bake for about 5 minutes more, or until well risen and a golden brown. Transfer them to a wire rack and allow to cool. You can split them open and butter them, but I find they are quite rich enough and prefer them just with a good jam.

TIP If scones become the slightest bit stale or dry in the freezer, revive them by quickly dipping them in whole milk and heating in a very hot oven (450° F) for 5 minutes.

Whole Wheat Scones I

This is my preferred, and more earthy, version of whole wheat scones. I developed the recipe in New York, where for the first time I could find good, unbolted whole wheat flour *(see note page 15)*.

> 5 ounces whole wheat flour, plus extra for rolling out the dough
> 3 ounces unbleached, all-purpose flour
> ⅛ teaspoon finely ground sea salt
> ½ teaspoon baking soda
> ¾ teaspoon cream of tartar
> 2 ounces (4 tablespoons) unsalted butter, slightly softened
> 1 ounce (2 tablespoons) pork lard, slightly softened
> About ⅓ cup buttermilk, or 2 tablespoons yogurt and ¼ cup whole milk

Preheat the oven to 425° F, setting the oven rack in the top part of the oven. Lightly grease a cookie sheet.

Put the 2 flours in a bowl and mix in the salt, baking soda, and cream of tartar. Cut the butter and lard into the flour mixture and then rub lightly with the fingertips until the fats are well incorporated. Stir in the buttermilk, a little at a time—always reserving some until you see just how much the flours will absorb. At first the dough will be rough and lumpy. At this stage, turn out the dough onto a very lightly floured working surface and press the lumps together lightly. If they do not adhere with a little coaxing, add a little more of the buttermilk—but do not allow the dough to become too wet and sticky, as this will make the scones too heavy. Press the dough out lightly with a rolling pin until it is between ½ and ¾ inch thick. Cut the scones out with a 2-inch fluted cookie cutter, or cut into rough triangles. Bake until deep golden and crusty on the outside and spongy inside, about 25 minutes. Transfer to a wire rack to cool.

NOTE These scones are best eaten the day they are made. Just split them open horizontally and serve with butter, or thick cream and jam. The scones also freeze very well providing they are frozen as soon as they have cooled off after baking.

TIP To reheat stale scones, dip quickly in whole milk and put into a 425° F oven for about 10 minutes.

Everyday Scones

Last minute teatime eats nearly always include these particular scones, which we hastily conceived one hectic afternoon in the peaceful Michoacán countryside.

> 8 ounces all-purpose, unbleached flour, plus extra for the board and cutter
> 1 pinch salt
> 1 teaspoon cream of tartar
> ½ teaspoon baking soda
> ⅓ cup sultanas *(optional)*
> 2 ounces unsalted butter, plus extra for greasing baking sheet
> ¼–½ cup whole milk

Heat oven to 425° F. Lightly grease a baking sheet. Place rack on top rung of the oven.

Sieve together the flour, salt, cream of tartar, and baking soda into a mixing bowl. Cut the butter into the flour mixture and rub lightly between your fingers until it resembles coarse breadcrumbs. Stir in the sultanas. Quickly and lightly mix in ¼ cup of the milk, the rest if necessary, to make a fairly soft, sticky dough. Pat the dough into a flat, circular shape with your hands (about ¾ inch thick). Dip the cutter into the extra flour as you cut each scone and place them about 1½ inches apart on the greased baking sheet. Gather up the remaining pieces, pat smooth and cut into shape.

Bake until puffy and golden, about 10 minutes. Transfer onto a wire rack to cool.

Eat fresh, cutting them open horizontally and spreading with butter or thick cream.

The scones can be frozen while fresh. To reheat, defrost, dip quickly into milk and put into a preheated 400° F oven for a few minutes.

Drop Scones, or Scotch Pancakes*

I was indoctrinated into the lore of scones when I lived in Scotland for two years. As an assistant housing manager, I helped to administer low-income housing estates in both rural and mining areas of Dumfriesshire. Apart from my interesting working day, my baking apprenticeship was unwittingly continued there, for every woman I knew was an accomplished home baker. Teatime came into its own, and not only were there several types of cake on the table but at least two different types of scones: dark brown treacle and light fruity girdle (griddle in the United States) potato scones and these little drop scones. (We also had crumpets; quite unlike those farther south, they resembled thin pancakes and were buttered, rolled up, and eaten cold.) Drop scones are, of course, akin to the American breakfast pancake but much smaller and buttered when cold. They can be prepared several hours ahead and kept moist in a tea towel, but they should be eaten the same day they are made.

> 8 ounces unbleached, all-purpose flour
> Scant ½ teaspoon baking soda
> Scant ½ teaspoon cream of tartar
> Scant ¼ teaspoon double-acting or ½ teaspoon single-acting baking powder
> 1 tablespoon granulated sugar
> 1 tablespoon unsalted butter, at room temperature, plus extra to grease
>   the griddle
> 1 egg
> 1¼ cups whole milk
> 1 tablespoon cane or corn syrup (Lyle's golden syrup, preferably)

Sift together the flour, baking soda, cream of tartar, and baking powder. Mix in the sugar, and then rub the butter into the mixture with your fingertips. (No, it doesn't resemble bread crumbs, since there's not enough fat.) Beat the egg into the milk by hand (not with an electric beater) and stir into the flour mixture alternately with the syrup. The mixture should resemble a thick batter—don't worry if it is slightly lumpy because you shouldn't overbeat it. Set the mixture aside for at least 10 minutes, but never more than 15; it should be slightly bubbly.

Meanwhile, heat the griddle over a medium flame and smear with buttered paper just before you begin cooking the pancakes and again before each batch is cooked. Drop a large spoonful of the batter onto the griddle—there should be a slight sizzle if the griddle has reached the right temperature, and the batter should not spread out more than about 2¾ inches. Repeat as many times as there is room on the griddle. Cook the pancakes for about 2 minutes, or until the underside is a pale golden color and the top bubbly but not dried out, as if you were cooking crumpets. Flip them over and cook the second side for a further 2 minutes, or until golden. As soon as they are cooked, transfer them to

*This recipe is based on the best one I know, from The Constance Spry Cookery Book.

a tea towel—they can be stacked on top of each other—cover and let them cool off in the towel until ready to use. Grease the griddle again and cook the next batch of pancakes. The first cooked side will be the face that is buttered—the public side, as Julia Child would say. Butter rather thickly and serve just like that or with jam.

Date and Walnut Loaf
ONE 9-INCH CAKE

Thickly buttered slices of date and walnut loaf appeared with some regularity on the tea table at our house. This was one of Mother's favorite recipes. While you can eat it the day it is made, I prefer to let it cool off, wrap it tightly, and let it mature for a day or two. (*See note about buying dates, page 15.*)

- 1 pound pitted dates, roughly chopped
- 1 teaspoon baking soda
- 1 cup boiling water
- 8 ounces (2 cups) unbleached, all-purpose flour
- ¼ teaspoon sea salt
- 3 ounces soft brown sugar (½ cup, firmly packed)
- 3 ounces walnuts, roughly chopped (¾ cup chopped)
- 1 large egg
- 1½ ounces (3 tablespoons) unsalted butter, melted, plus extra for greasing the pan

Preheat the oven to 350° F. Butter a 9 × 9-inch cake pan.

Put the dates in a mixing bowl. Dissolve the baking soda in the boiling water and immediately mix it into the dates while it is still effervescing. Set aside for 10 minutes. Mix the flour, salt, sugar, and ½ cup of the chopped walnuts together. Beat the egg and add with the melted butter to the dates. Stir into the flour mixture until well incorporated; the mixture will be soft and sticky.

Pour the batter immediately into the prepared pan. Sprinkle the top with the remaining nuts and bake for about 2 hours. By that time the loaf will be shrinking slightly from the sides of the pan. (Obviously the usual skewer test will be deceptive, as the dates remain sticky and can stick to the skewer.) Set the loaf aside to cool before attempting to unmold. Slice and butter liberally.

NOTE Dates are much easier to chop if you add a tablespoon or two of flour before you begin.

My Rock Cakes

Rock cakes are as English as the White Cliffs of Dover and as craggy. Quick and easy to make at the last minute, they were a standby at home if anyone came to tea unexpectedly. Mother would quite often use the fat drippings from the beef roast for rock cakes, and for what she called her "rubbed in" fruit cake. It was delicious but did not keep quite as moist as that made with butter.

    8 ounces unbleached, all-purpose flour, or 7 ounces flour and 1 ounce bran
      Large pinch of sea salt
    ½ teaspoon double-acting or teaspoon single-acting baking powder
    2 ounces light brown sugar, preferably turbinado
    ½ heaped teaspoon mixed powdered spices: cinnamon, cloves, and nutmeg
    2 ounces (4 tablespoons) unsalted butter, plus 1 tablespoon for greasing the baking
      sheet
    1 ounce (2 tablespoons) good pork lard
    4 ounces mixed dried fruit: currants, sultanas (or golden raisins), and raisins
      (about ⅔ cup)
 1½ tablespoons citron, finely chopped
    1 large egg
    ¼ cup milk

Preheat the oven to 375° F and place the oven rack at the top of the oven. Lightly grease a baking sheet.

Mix the flour, salt, baking powder, sugar, and ground spices together well, or toss in a plastic bag. Cut the fats into small pieces and add to the flour mixture. Rub the fats into the flour until the mixture resembles rough bread crumbs. Stir in the dried fruit and citron. Beat the egg into the milk and stir into the flour-fruit mixture—the dough should be rather stiff and sticky. Do not overwork the dough. Put the dough, by large spoonfuls, onto the cookie sheet—allowing about 1 inch between them—and form into rough pyramid shapes. Bake for about 20 minutes, or until cooked through and browned on top. Transfer the rock cakes to a wire tray to cool off. Store in an airtight container. These are best eaten fresh.

If the cakes are getting a little dry and tired-looking, quickly dip them into whole milk and bake again in a 375° F oven until well heated through and crisp on the outside.

Matrimony Cake

I hadn't made this recipe for years until now and had forgotten about this rather luscious date-filled oatmeal slice—probably there is a recipe for it in most home cookbooks, but this one was given to me when I was traveling across Canada in 1955 by a Mrs. McPherson who lived in the Okanagan Valley. Health food devotees might be tempted to put whole wheat flour into it, but don't: it makes it too stodgy, like far too many of the cookies and bars sold in health food stores.

date filling

> 8–12 ounces pitted dates (see note page 15)
> ½ cup cold water
> 3 tablespoons light brown sugar
> 2 tablespoons lemon juice

cake

> 1 cup rolled oats
> 1 cup unbleached, all-purpose flour
> ½ cup light brown sugar
> ¼ teaspoon baking soda
> ¼ teaspoon double-acting or ½ teaspoon single-acting baking powder
> ½ cup unsalted butter plus extra for greasing pan

Put all the filling ingredients together in a saucepan and cook gently until the dates have softened, about 7 minutes. Set aside to cool.

To make the cake Mix the dry ingredients well together. Cut the butter into small pieces and rub with the fingertips into the flour mixture until it resembles rough bread crumbs.

Preheat the oven to 350° F and put the rack at the top of the oven. Butter well an 8 × 8 × 2-inch pan.

Divide the oat mixture in 2. Press one half into the prepared pan, spread the cooled date filling over it evenly, and spread the remaining oat mixture over the top, pressing it down very lightly. Bake for about 25 minutes, by which time the bottom should be well cooked and the top lightly browned.

MATRIMONY CAKE VARIATION This is also delicious with a sharp apricot filling. I suggest the proportion of 6 ounces dried apricots plus 4 ounces dates; 4 heaped tablespoons light brown sugar; ⅔ cup water.

Duck eggs were cheap and plentiful in the stores when we were growing up, and Mother always used to buy them for her baking. Father liked to eat them for breakfast, poached, but their strong yolks and half-transparent whites—although cooked—did not appeal to my sister and me. I remember the shells as that beautiful pale bluey green and was disappointed when the duck eggs at San Pancho turned out a dirty cream color.

I remember years ago eating a duck-egg sponge that I loved at the home of a friend. It was chewy and delicious. You never find sponges like that anymore because it is the fashion, as with laundry, to have cakes "soft and downy," with far too much double-acting baking powder to boot. When my ducks started to lay, I decided to make the recipe again. Elisorio, who with his family looks after my *ranchito,* decided otherwise and seemed reluctant to hand over the eggs. I was very surprised at his reaction because I knew that he rather despised ducks; he didn't like the flavor of the meat, which ruled out all other considerations— nothing should be kept that wasn't good to eat was his rule of thumb. And then the ducks always escaped from any enclosure and raided the newly sown alfalfa, and in any case they laid their eggs all over the place. "No," he said, "the ducks look broody. They are making the right noises" (and he imitated them). They began to sit. One duck broke her eggs two by two, the other he put into a box and tied it down with cord. Two weeks later he arrived at the kitchen door smiling and holding out six duck eggs. "They are perfectly all right to use," he assured me.

I greased and floured the cake pan, measured out the ingredients, and broke open the eggs . . . every one had the yolk sticking to the shell and smelled, to say the least, gamey. It was months before I could find some duck eggs again. I went all over town to anyone who kept ducks. Either the neighborhood dogs had eaten them, or the local bakeries had bought them all up, or the ducks weren't laying. And so the pan and the ingredients sat waiting in the refrigerator. Then the deluge began. I was stopped in the street a dozen times and offered duck eggs because all the ducks in Zitácuaro had begun to lay again.

If carefully stored, or frozen, this sponge keeps for a long time, and even if it does get stale, you can always use it for a trifle. I use a 10-inch springform pan for this recipe.

> Unsalted butter for greasing the pan
> 5 ounces unbleached, all-purpose flour, plus 1 tablespoon for the pan
> 8 ounces (1 cup) granulated sugar plus 1 tablespoon for the pan
> ½ teaspoon double-acting or ¾ teaspoon single-acting baking powder
> Pinch of sea salt
> 4 duck eggs, weighing about 9½ ounces together, at room temperature
> Finely grated rind of 1 lemon

Grease well a 10-inch springform pan, sprinkle with 1 tablespoon of the flour, and tap the sides of the pan, turning it in circular fashion so that the bottom and sides become evenly coated. Discard the loose flour that does not adhere. Repeat with 1 tablespoon of the sugar. **Preheat the oven to 350° F** and set the rack in the top half of the oven.

Put the flour, baking powder, and salt into a plastic bag and shake well. Separate the eggs. Put the yolks in a mixing bowl and beat with the sugar until the mixture hangs in thick strands from the beater. Gradually add the flour mixture and lemon rind, beating well after each addition.

In a separate bowl, beat the egg whites until fairly stiff but not dry. Add one quarter to the flour mixture and stir well. Fold in the remainder of the egg whites. Turn the mixture into the prepared pan and make a slight well in the middle so that it will rise evenly. (The batter will look lost, but it will rise up to about two-thirds the height of the pan.) Bake until the top is a pale gold and firm, but the cake is springy to the touch—about 1 hour. Turn the oven off, open the oven door, and allow the cake to sit in the cooling oven for about 15 minutes. Remove and allow to cool for a further 10 minutes before unmolding.

Coffee Sponge

ONE 8-INCH CAKE

This is one of my most favorite cakes, and I make it when I feel in need of a little self-indulgence—besides it reminds me of Mrs. Parker's delicious cake *(see page 166)*.

cake

- 2 tablespoons instant coffee
- 1 tablespoon hot water
- 6 ounces unsalted butter, at room temperature, plus extra for greasing the pan
- 6 ounces unbleached, all-purpose flour plus ½ tablespoon for the pan
- 1 scant teaspoon double-acting or 1½ teaspoons single-acting baking powder
  Pinch of sea salt
- 5 ounces granulated sugar
- 3 large eggs (each weighing about 2 ounces)
  Milk as necessary

decoration

- ¾ cup whole hazelnuts
- 3 tablespoons hot water
- 2 tablespoons instant coffee
- 1 ounce (2 tablespoons) unsalted butter, softened
- 1½ cups confectioners' sugar, sieved
- ⅓ cup apricot glaze *(see page 213)*

Dissolve the 2 tablespoons instant coffee in the 1 tablespoon hot water and set aside to cool.

Preheat the oven to 350° F and place the rack in the top part of the oven. Choose either a round baking pan—8½ inches in diameter and at least 2 inches deep—or a square one 8 × 8 inches and at least 2 inches deep. Butter the pan well, sprinkle the flour over the inside, and tap, turning it around so that there is a light coating of flour around it. Turn upside down and tap out any excess flour.

Mix together in a plastic bag the flour, baking powder, and salt. With an electric beater, beat the butter and granulated sugar together until light, about 2 minutes. Add 1 of the eggs and a little of the flour and beat just until well incorporated, no more; repeat for the other 2 eggs. Gradually mix in the flour and coffee essence; mix only until just incorporated, do not overbeat. The mixture should just fall off the spoon with a plop. If it appears too dry, then add a little milk. Transfer the mixture to the prepared pan, smooth over the top of the dough, and make a slight well toward the center. Bake about 25 minutes, or until the sides of the cake shrink away from the pan and the center is spongy but firm to the touch. Remove the sponge from the oven and let it sit for 5 minutes before unmolding. Gently loosen the sponge around the edges with a palette knife and turn onto a wire rack, then reverse it by using another rack so that the top is on top. Set the sponge in a place free from drafts until completely cool.

Preheat the oven to 400° F. Place the nuts on an ungreased baking sheet in one layer and bake until lightly toasted. Remove and cool. Place them in a tea towel and rub them hard so that the papery skin is released—if it won't all come off, don't worry. Choose the cleanest ones for the top of the cake and chop the others roughly to press around the sides.

Stir the 3 tablespoons hot water into the 2 tablespoons instant coffee, and when it has dissolved, add it to the butter and confectioners' sugar. Mix well, smoothing out any lumps with the back of a wooden spoon, and continue working it until it is smooth and shiny.

If the apricot glaze is still a little stiff and cold, warm it slightly. Spread the glaze over the surface and down the sides of the cake with a broad palette knife. Set aside to dry off for a few minutes while you prepare the icing (frosting).

Have ready a pot of boiling water for your palette knife. As soon as the glaze has dried, pour the icing over the surface of the cake, and with a warm palette knife spread it evenly over the surface and sides. Set the cake aside for about 15 minutes for the icing to set a little, press the chopped nuts around the sides of the cake, and decorate the top with the whole nuts. Take care not to let the icing become too hard before doing this.

VARIATION You could, of course, gild the lily by making a double sponge and putting a thick layer of buttercream flavored with coffee between the two, as well as the icing.

Gingerbread

This is a wonderfully sticky, rich gingerbread, so different from the usual spongy ones that have far too much soda in them.

You can decorate the top with preserved ginger cut into thin slices, and if you do that, then put it on after about 1 hour of baking, otherwise it might get lost when the batter rises so precipitously.

½ **pound unbleached, all-purpose flour**
2 **tablespoons powdered ginger**
1 **tablespoon powdered cinnamon**
3 **ounces (about rounded ½ cup) sultanas or golden raisins**
½ **pound unsalted butter, plus extra for greasing pan**
½ **pound dark brown sugar (about 1¼ cups, firmly packed)**
½ **pound (about ¾ cup) dark molasses**
2 **eggs, lightly beaten**
1 **teaspoon baking soda**
⅓ **cup warm whole milk**
  Several slices of preserved ginger to decorate the top *(optional)*

Preheat the oven to 325° F and place a cookie sheet on the middle rack of the oven. The batter foams up and sometimes overflows a little; however, do not choose a larger pan. Lightly grease a 9×9-inch cake pan at least 3 inches deep. Measure the bottom of the pan, not the top.

Put the flour, ginger, cinnamon, and sultanas into a plastic bag and shake them around thoroughly. Cream the butter with the sugar until fluffy. Beat in the molasses by degrees, followed by the eggs and then the dry ingredients. The batter will be soft and sticky. Dissolve the baking soda in the warm milk, stir briefly, and add to the mixture. Stir until all the ingredients are thoroughly blended. The batter will now be very loose. Pour the batter into the prepared pan and bake for about 1½ hours. The gingerbread will be cooked when a slight crust has formed around the edge, which has pulled away from the sides of the pan. Set aside to cool completely before attempting to unmold. With a spatula, carefully loosen the sides and as much of the bottom of the gingerbread as you can without breaking it and then unmold. Wrap the gingerbread in greaseproof or waxed paper and then foil and store for 2 days in an airtight tin—of course, you can eat it right away, but it gathers flavor with keeping.

Dundee Cake

ONE 7-INCH ROUND CAKE

Day in, day out, this is my favorite teatime cake. Dundee cakes were originally made in the Scottish town of Dundee about two hundred years ago, or so it is said. During the years, as with all recipes, this has undergone many changes, as it used to be made with a lot of chopped orange rind and sugared caraway—how I hated the sandy-textured caraway cakes that Mother made when we were young! Now it is a luscious, fruit-filled cake with halved almonds over the top. Even today, when it is so expensive, there is no stinting on dried fruit in breads and cakes in Britain, and you can still get an excellent commercially made packaged or tinned Dundee cake.

My sister makes the best Dundee cake that I have tried, and she beats hers by hand—bare hand, not hand beater—which makes for a moister, more porous texture.

6 ounces unsalted butter, softened, plus extra for greasing the pan
8 ounces unbleached, all-purpose flour
Large pinch of sea salt
⅔ teaspoon double-acting or 1 teaspoon single-acting baking powder
⅛ teaspoon powdered cinnamon
⅛ teaspoon ground cloves
⅛ teaspoon freshly grated nutmeg
3 ounces (rounded ½ cup) raisins or seeded muscats
3 ounces (rounded ½ cup) sultanas or golden raisins
3 ounces (scant ¾ cup) currants
2 ounces (⅓ cup chopped, loosely packed) glacé cherries, roughly chopped
2 ounces (scant ½ cup) citron, chopped into small cubes
2 ounces (rounded ⅓ cup) almonds, blanched and slivered
Finely grated rind of ½ lemon
6 ounces light brown sugar (about 1 scant cup, firmly packed)
3 large eggs
2 tablespoons medium dry sherry *(optional)*
About 2 tablespoons milk
12 almonds, blanched and split
1 egg white, beaten until frothy

Prepare a cake pan about 7 inches in diameter and a minimum of 3 inches high, buttering it well and sprinkling with flour. Turn upside down to shake out excess flour. Wrap a double layer of brown paper around the outside of the pan, at least 1 inch above the rim, and secure it with string. **Preheat the oven to 350° F** and place the rack in the center of the oven.

Mix together the flour, salt, baking powder, and spices and set aside. In a separate bowl, mix the dried fruits, citron, slivered almonds, and lemon rind. Stir in 2 tablespoons of the flour mixture and mix well—this ensures that the fruit does not sink to the bottom of the cake. Set aside.

Beat the butter and sugar until well creamed but not fluffy; continue beating while you add the eggs one by one, alternating with a spoonful of the flour mixture to prevent curdling. Do not overbeat. Fold in the flour mixture, the dried fruits, the sherry, and 2 tablespoons milk. The mixture should be moist but neither too runny nor too stiff. Add a little more milk if necessary.

Turn the mixture into the prepared pan, smooth over the top, and then make a slight well in the middle so that it rises evenly. Place the almond halves around the top and brush with the beaten egg white. Bake for about 1½ to 2 hours; during that time, if you see that the surface is browning too much, cover with a double layer of brown paper. Test at 1½ hours by inserting a skewer; if it comes out perfectly clean, the cake is cooked. Turn the oven off, leave the door open, and let the cake sit for 15 minutes more. Remove from the oven and allow the cake to cool on a rack for a further 20 minutes in its pan. Unmold onto a rack and wait until it is completely cool before wrapping. Pack, wrapped in several layers of waxed paper, in an airtight tin, and try not to eat it until at least 4 days have passed, as it improves in flavor.

They are known by all three names, but they are not tarts in the strict sense of the word. They are short, crumbly cakes, wickedly rich, and I love them, although I haven't eaten one since I was last in England and having tea with a neighbor and friend of my late mother. I had never made them myself and the recipes in print just didn't work, so I wrote to Hilda. She is an immaculate baker, whose kitchen is always spotless, and her cakes a work of art that not only look but taste wonderful. She sent me her recipe and I began cooking from it. It just didn't work with American ingredients; obviously the flour, butter, and icing (confectioners') sugar were different. There is not much you can do about the butter short of thumping some of the water out of it, but I changed the flour, using part granular—i.e., Wondra—(also suggested by Peter Kump), and by grinding granulated sugar to a powder instead of using confectioners' sugar. It worked, just as I was about to give up in despair. With this same mixture you can make "shortbread fingers," which I have called Viennese Fingers. Hilda sandwiches these together with a buttercream before dipping the ends into chocolate, but I have substituted a thick apricot glaze *(see page 213)*.

You may like to attempt the second recipe, Viennese Fingers, first, as it is more straightforward.

½ **cup granulated sugar**
½ **pound unsalted butter, softened**
4 **ounces Wondra flour**
6 **ounces unbleached, all-purpose flour**
  pinch of salt
1 **egg yolk**
8 **drops vanilla extract**
  About ⅓ cup raspberry jam

Line a muffin tin with paper cupcake holders about 2½ inches in diameter. Have ready a large pastry bag for cake decoration and the largest star nozzle, #9. **Preheat the oven to 375° F** and place the rack in the center of the oven.

In the coffee/spice grinder, reduce the sugar to a fine powder. Measure 5 tablespoons into a bowl and reserve the rest. Add the softened butter to the sugar and beat very thoroughly until smooth and fluffy. Mix the flours together. Beat in the egg yolk and vanilla and continue beating, gradually adding half the flour. Beat only until mixed in. Stir in the rest of the flour with your hands (this is a very important point for the correct texture) just enough to mix and distribute evenly. The mixture should be moist and slightly creamy. Put half of the mixture at a time into the pastry bag and pipe a circle into each of the paper cups. Bake until a pale golden color and cooked completely through, about 30 minutes. Transfer to a rack and allow to cool. Put a dot of jam in the center of each cake, and just before serving dust with the remainder of the powdered sugar.

I personally prefer the fingers, as they cook more evenly. You can freeze them successfully or just keep them in an airtight tin in a cool spot—not the refrigerator—and they improve in flavor after the first day.

Preheat the oven to 375° F. Lightly butter 2 baking sheets. Set the racks in the center of the oven.

Follow the recipe for Viennese, Swiss, or Sand Tarts *(see page 184)* for the mixture, use the star nozzle as in that recipe, and pipe the mixture into 2 to 2½ inches in length onto the baking sheets, leaving a space of about 1 inch between them to allow for expansion. Bake for 25 minutes, or until a pale golden brown and crisp right through. Allow to cool on the sheets for about 10 minutes and then very carefully transfer them to wire racks to cool off completely.

> **7–8 ounces semisweet couverture chocolate** *(see page 15)*
> **1 cup thick apricot glaze** *(see page 213)*

Put the chocolate in a double boiler, making sure that the level of the water is as high as possible without spilling over. Melt over a very slow flame. Stir until smooth, and then dip the ends of the cakes into the mixture to cover lightly. Set aside to dry off in the refrigerator. When the chocolate is completely set, sandwich the fingers together with the apricot glaze.

ALTERNATIVE Instead of sticking them together with glaze, dip the ends into chocolate, and when it is nearly set, sprinkle the ends with chopped nuts—anything but peanuts. Dust with confectioners' sugar. For petit fours use a smaller nozzle and make them about 1½ inches long.

CRISPY THINGS

Biscuits belong to the class of unfermented bread, and are, perhaps, the most unwholesome of that class. In cases where fermented bread does not agree with the human stomach, they may be recommended: in many instances they are considered lighter, and less liable to create acidity and flatulence. The name derives from the French *bis cuit* "twice baked."

—Mrs. Beeton

These are not biscuits as they are known in the United States, of course, but crackers. But Mrs. Beeton's reasons are not my reason for liking them. Be they rye crisp or breadsticks, crackers are wonderful for snacking on—and less fattening than peanuts—especially when made of whole wheat and rye flour, to accompany cheese, soup, what you will. Commercial crackers are nearly always too salty, or too sweet and salty at the same time; devoid of salt, they are just plain uninteresting. Although rolling them out is time-consuming, it is worth the effort and you can adjust the ingredients to suit your taste.

Crackers to eat with cheese have always been a big thing in Great Britain. When it comes to French cheeses, I am completely in agreement with Craig Claiborne about crusty bread being the best and only accompaniment, but crackers go very well with the solid, blander English cheeses. We always had a large variety of them to eat at home: water biscuits, thin Romary biscuits, rusks, Bath Olivers (which were considered a treat), rye crisp, minute biscuits flavored with cheese and celery seeds, and, of course, semisweet wheaten (sweetmeal) or digestive biscuits.

With the rising cost of packaged crispbreads—most of which, I fear, goes into the packaging—you can certainly come out ahead making your own. Another important factor is that you can control the amount of salt you use and eschew that sugar, subtle though it is, that creeps more and more into our everyday food. But above all you can make crackers into low-calorie snacks with new dimensions of tastes and crunchiness from whole or partially ground grains that to me are so much more satisfying in texture and nutrients. I know that crunchiness is a passion with me that perhaps only the psychologists could explain!

I know how much the basic ingredients—flours and butters, etc.—vary over the country, as I have cooked these recipes in various places, so be prepared to make slight adjustments, and please *weigh* your ingredients where indicated—it can make a world of difference in this sort of cooking. I have spent many hours developing these recipes, the sort of cooking I love—I always think of it as a culinary exercise—because one slightly wrong proportion can put the flavor or texture off track. It presents a fine challenge and not a little sleuthing.

NOTE When dough is short and difficult to handle use a double thickness—a plastic bag—to roll it out thinly and evenly without using a lot of extra flour. Plastic wrap tends to be too thin and uncontrollable.

Wheaten Biscuits

I suppose the custom still exists in a few hotels, and most certainly when staying with friends, that you are awakened with an early morning cup of tea—"knocked up" is the British expression! It is a cup of strong Indian tea with milk, and on the saucer, more often than not, is a "rich tea biscuit"—actually a semisweet, very crisp cookie, or a digestive biscuit sometimes called wheaten. I remember that when I went to stay with my rich godmother, the first thing I investigated in my luxurious chintz-filled room was a matching chintz-covered box filled with fresh digestive biscuits. I miss them when I am in Mexico, and so does my friend Alan Riding, *The New York Times*'s correspondent who used to cover my late husband Paul's old beat, so I will dedicate this recipe to him. It has taken hours of cooking to approximate the really excellent commercial ones. Worth it? Of course.

⅔ **cup quick oats**
4 **ounces whole wheat flour, plus extra for rolling out the dough**
4 **ounces unbleached, all-purpose flour**
½ **teaspoon cream of tartar**
½ **teaspoon baking soda**
¼ **teaspoon sea salt**
2–3 **tablespoons, or to taste, granulated brown sugar (turbinado or Demerara, *not* Brownulated)**
7 **tablespoons unsalted butter, plus extra for greasing the cookie sheets**
1 **tablespoon good pork lard**
2 **tablespoons whole milk**
1 **tablespoon Lyle's golden syrup or cane syrup**
1 **egg, well beaten**
¼ **teaspoon vanilla extract**

Put the oats, one half at a time, into the blender jar. Blend briefly until they are just broken up, not reduced to a flour. Put the oats into a mixing bowl, add the flours, cream of tartar, baking soda, salt, and brown sugar, and mix well together.

Preheat the oven to 375° F and set the rack in the top of the oven. Lightly butter 2 cookie sheets.

Put the butter, lard, milk, vanilla, and syrup in a saucepan and heat through until the butter is melted. Set aside to cool. Stir in the beaten egg and beat briefly. Gradually add this mixture to the flour mixture in the bowl; you should have a somewhat stiff and sticky dough. Dust the working surface very lightly with a little whole wheat flour. Pat dough out flat, cover the surface with a plastic bag *(see note on page 188),* roll out to about 3/16 inch—not thinner—and cut into rounds with a 2½-inch cookie cutter. Prick the dough well and bake on the cookie sheets until cooked through and golden brown, about 20 minutes. Transfer to wire racks and allow to cool off completely.

Store in an airtight container. If the biscuits lose their crispness, I reheat them in a 375° F oven for about 10 minutes. (I also do this to commercial digestive biscuits, as they are not packed to stay fresh unless they are in a tin.)

Digestive Biscuits

No sooner had I developed a recipe that I liked for digestive, or wheaten, biscuits than I stumbled across a clipping in one of Mother's old cookbooks. I have no idea where it came from, but the recipe makes a very crunchy, satisfying cookie.

> **4** ounces (about ¾ cup) steel-cut oats *(see note below)*
> **4** ounces unbleached, all-purpose flour, plus extra for rolling out the dough
>   Large pinch of sea salt
> **½** teaspoon double-acting or 1 teaspoon single-acting baking powder
> **1** ounce (3 tablespoons) Demerara or turbinado sugar
> **2** ounces (4 tablespoons) unsalted butter, at room temperature, plus extra for
>   greasing the baking sheet
> **¼** teaspoon baking soda
> **2** tablespoons whole milk
> **½** teaspoon strong malt vinegar

Mix together the oats, flour, baking powder, salt, and sugar. Cut the butter into small pieces and rub it into the flour mixture with the tips of your fingers. Dissolve the baking soda in the milk and stir well, and add this along with the vinegar to the flour mixture. Mix the dough quickly and lightly, forming it into a flat, round cake. It will be quite stiff and slightly sticky.

Preheat the oven to 350° F. Lightly butter a large baking sheet. Press the dough out flat, cover the surface with a plastic bag, and *(see note on page 188)*, roll it out onto a very lightly floured surface—try not to incorporate a pinch more flour than absolutely necessary—to about ⅛ inch thick. Cut with a 2½-inch cookie cutter, prick well with a fork, and place about ⅓ inch apart—they do not expand much—on the prepared sheet. Bake for 15 to 20 minutes, or until a deep golden color. Transfer to a rack to cool.

Lower the oven temperature to 300° F. When the cookies are completely cool, turn them over and bake on the same baking sheet for a further 15 minutes, or until thoroughly crisp right through.

These are better eaten the following day and keep very well if stored in an airtight container.

NOTE The most widely distributed steel-cut oats are packed under the label Arrowhead Mills. These need to be ground finer: 10 to 15 seconds in a coffee/spice grinder will do the trick, but be sure to grind a small amount at a time.

These crackers lend themselves to variations: Parmesan cheese and/or celery seeds, or any other flavors that you can come up with. The crackers should be very crisp but not too short—make cheese pastry if you want something richer. Do not handle the dough too much or the crackers will be tough.

  2 tablespoons hulled (cream colored) sesame seeds
  4 ounces unbleached, all-purpose flour, plus extra for rolling out the dough
  ¼ rounded teaspoon finely ground sea salt
  ¼ teaspoon double-acting or ½ teaspoon single-acting baking powder
  1 rounded tablespoon unsalted butter, plus extra for greasing the baking sheet
  ½ tablespoon good pork lard
  ¼ cup whole milk

Preheat the oven to 375° F and put the oven rack in the top part of the oven. Have ready a lightly greased baking sheet.

Put the sesame seeds in an ungreased frying pan and cook over a medium flame, turning them almost constantly, until they turn an even golden brown. Set aside to cool.

Mix well together the flour, salt, and baking powder. Cut the fats into small pieces, add to the flour, and rub between the fingertips until the mixture resembles coarse bread crumbs. Mix in the cooled sesame seeds and milk. Keep mixing until all the flour is incorporated; have patience, and don't add more milk unless absolutely necessary.

Very lightly flour your work surface. Flatten the dough and cover the surface with a plastic bag *(see note on page 188)*. Roll out the dough as thin as possible— until almost transparent. Cut the crackers out—I use a 2¾-inch cutter—prick the dough all over, and place on the baking sheet. Bake the crackers until very lightly browned, about 15 to 20 minutes. Remove and cool on a wire rack.

Store in an airtight container. If the crackers lose their crispness after a few days, reheat in a 400° F oven for about 10 minutes.

Whole Wheat Crackers

Whole wheat crackers are usually far too sweet, and then again you can find the insipid unsalted ones. This recipe corrects both tendencies and lends itself to a lot of variations with a mixture of different flours.

Do not overwork the dough because it will make tough crackers. These crackers should be crisp but not greasy, and, done this way, they can be buttered and eaten with cheese. If you use more fat, they will resemble pastry.

> 1½ tablespoons wheat berries
> 2 ounces whole wheat flour, not too finely ground, plus extra for rolling out the dough
> 2 ounces unbleached, all-purpose flour
> Rounded ¼ teaspoon double-acting or rounded ½ teaspoon single-acting baking powder
> Rounded ¼ teaspoon finely ground sea salt
> 1 tablespoon unsalted butter, plus extra for greasing the baking sheet
> 1 tablespoon good pork lard
> ¼ cup whole milk and water mixed in equal quantities

Put the wheat berries in an ungreased frying pan and toast over a low flame, shaking them and turning them over from time to time until they start to pop around and act like popcorn. Set aside to cool. They should be quite crisp. Put them in the blender jar—not the spice grinder or the processor—and blend briefly just to break them up roughly. Mix together the 2 flours, crushed wheat berries, baking powder, and salt. Cut the butter and lard into small pieces, add to the flours, and rub the mixture between the fingertips until it resembles coarse bread crumbs. Mix in the milk and water. The dough will be fairly stiff.

Sprinkle the work surface with whole wheat flour. Flatten the dough and cover the surface with a plastic bag *(see note on page 188)*. Roll out the dough as thin as you can —¹⁄₁₆ inch if possible.

Preheat the oven to 375° F and place the rack at the top of the oven. Lightly grease a baking sheet. Cut the crackers into rounds or whatever you like, prick well all over, and place on the baking sheet. Bake until the crackers are crisp through, but not too brown, about 25 minutes. Transfer to a wire rack and allow to cool off before storing in an airtight tin.

If they lose their crispness, then reheat in a 350° F oven for about 10 to 15 minutes.

Plain Puffy Crackers

You can vary this recipe by adding wheat berries (see Variation I below) or Parmesan cheese, celery seeds, etc. This dough can and should be worked well.

> 4 ounces high-gluten bread flour *(see note page 124)* plus extra for rolling out the dough
> ¼ rounded teaspoon finely ground sea salt
> 1 heaped tablespoon unsalted butter, softened but not melted, plus extra for greasing the baking sheets
> About 4 tablespoons cold water

Preheat the oven to 400° F and place the rack at the top of the oven. Butter well 2 baking sheets.

Put the flour, salt, and butter in the container of the food processor and process with the steel blade for 2 seconds. Gradually add the water and continue processing until the dough forms a ball around the blade. Continue processing for 2 minutes more. Remove the dough, which will be warm, and divide into 3 parts. Put 2 parts in a plastic bag to keep moist while you work the other third. Work on a wooden, not marble, surface (marble is too cold, and you want to keep the dough as warm and pliable as possible). Roll out the dough as thin as you can—it should be almost transparent—and cut into different shapes. Do not prick the dough. Place on the baking sheets and then work the second piece of dough. Each piece should yield about one dozen small crackers. Bake, turning them over once during the baking time, until they have puffed up and are a pale biscuit color, about 10 to 15 minutes. Cool on a wire rack and store in an airtight container.

NOTE This dough is best rolled without the plastic bag trick since it has a different consistency.

Variation I

> 1½ tablespoons wheat berries
> ½ tablespoon unsalted butter, softened but not melted

Put the whole wheat berries in an ungreased frying pan and heat over a medium flame, turning them over occasionally until they swell up and open like popcorn. Set aside to cool. Put the cooled berries in the blender jar and blend briefly until they are just broken up. Add this and the butter to the basic dough.

Variation II

> 2 tablespoons finely ground Parmesan cheese
> ½ tablespoon unsalted butter, softened but not melted
> ¼ teaspoon cold water

Add to the basic dough.

Oatcakes

I would hazard a guess that there are very few cooks in Scotland or Ireland today who still make their own oatcakes. Most people buy the commercial ones, and as a rule they are of a very high quality. They are not so easy to come by in the United States outside of specialty shops, and not to be found at all in Mexico. One day when I had a yearning for oatcakes I went into the kitchen and made them. They are undoubtedly better in flavor and texture made with the rougher steel-cut oats, but in case you can't find them, then you can also use quick Quaker oats *(see recipe page 195)*. At home there was always a package of oatcakes in the biscuit tin, either the little round ones or the large triangular ones called farls—derived from an Anglo-Saxon word meaning a fourth part, and these are a quarter of a circular cake. If they were not absolutely fresh we would toast them lightly before eating them with butter and honey, or just with cheese.

There are varying grades of steel-cut oats, and if you cannot find the finest grind, then grind them yourself in a coffee/spice grinder, which is more efficient for this task than the blender.

> 1⅓ **cups (about 8–8½ ounces) steel-cut oatmeal, plus extra for kneading and rolling out the dough**
> ¼ **teaspoon baking soda**
> **Rounded ¼ teaspoon finely ground sea salt**
> 1½ **tablespoons unsalted butter**
> ⅓ **cup water**

Divide the oats roughly into 2 parts; put one half—⅓ cup at a time—into the coffee/spice grinder and grind for 10 seconds. Grind the other half for 15 seconds. The oats should still have a nutty texture, but if they are too coarse they will not stick together when the water is added.

Mix the ground oats together with the baking soda and salt and set aside. Melt the butter in the water, and when the water is very hot pour it onto the oats—it is best to use ¼ cup at first and then the rest if necessary. Knead the mixture into a cohesive mass—it will be stiff and very slightly sticky. Use the extra oatmeal or some whole wheat flour for kneading if necessary. Divide the mixture into 2 parts and cover one of them with plastic wrap while you work with the other.

Heat a griddle (ordinary metal, but soapstone is preferable) over a medium flame, but do not grease. Roll the first batch of dough out thin—about ⅛ inch but not thinner. Cut the oatcakes out; do not make them too large or they will break easily. I find the 2½-inch or 2¾-inch cutter ideal. Carefully transfer them on a spatula to the heated griddle. Cook for about 7 minutes on the first side— it should be lightly browned—then turn and cook for a further 7 minutes on the second side, or until crisp right through. If you get impatient, start them on the griddle and then transfer them to a baking sheet and finish them off in a **preheated 375° F oven.** I do not advise cooking them in the oven for the entire time, as they tend to steam and stay damp, and you have to keep turning them.

Helen's LaVosch

Or that's how the recipe was given to me by Betty Levin, a friend who lives in San Miguel d'Allende and who knows my predilection for crisp snacks. And there is no better snack than these uneven sheets of crisp bread.

The recipe could also be varied to include whole wheat flour—¼ of the quantity—or caraway, or celery seeds, etc. It may seem like a lot, but it is not worth making in any smaller quantity. Besides, it will keep and can also be crisped up in a 350° F oven for 5–10 minutes if it becomes soft.

> 2½ cups unbleached, all-purpose flour, plus extra for working surface
> 2½ teaspoons crumbled cake yeast—½ package dried
> Scant ½ teaspoon sugar
> Approximately ¾ cup warm water
> 1 rounded teaspoon salt
> 2½ tablespoons safflower oil or melted butter, plus extra for greasing the bowl
> Approximately 4 tablespoons sesame seeds

Sieve the flour into a bowl. Mix the crumbled yeast and sugar with 2 tablespoons of the warm water and form a thin cream, pressing out any lumps with the back of a wooden spoon. Add the yeast mixture to the flour. Dissolve the salt in the remaining water and stir in the oil. Gradually add to the flour mixture and stir until all the ingredients form a cohesive mass.

Lightly flour your working surface, turn the dough out onto it, and knead into a cushion shape. Continue kneading until the dough—which is fairly stiff—is beginning to become spongy and elastic, about 3 minutes. Let the dough rest while you grease the bowl. Replace the dough in the bowl, cover with greased plastic wrap, and wrap in a towel. Set aside in a warm place—70° F is ideal—to rise to about double its bulk, about 1–1½ hours. Meanwhile heat oven to **350° F** and have ready 2 baking sheets. At the end of the rising period turn the dough out onto your working surface and cut into 4 equal pieces—each one will weigh just over 4 ounces. While you work with one of the balls, cover the rest with plastic wrap to prevent the surface from drying out.

Sprinkle the working surface with 1 tablespoon of the sesame seeds. With your hands press one of the balls of dough out on top of the seeds into a rough rectangle, then roll out until very thin. Carefully transfer the dough to an ungreased baking sheet reversing it so that the sesame seeds are on top. Bake on one side until golden and slightly blistered, about 10 minutes. Turn the dough over and bake until crisp through, about another 5 minutes. Transfer to a rack to cool. Continue with the rest of the sheets, taking care not to let the one that is baking overcook.

Rye Crisp

There is no rye crisp available where I live, but even where it is available, most commercial brands tend to resemble cardboard or are far too salty—so I have no choice but to make my own.

To obtain the right consistency for the rye crisps, you will need a coarsely ground, unbolted rye flour. If you cannot find it, then buy the brand available and grind some of the whole grains to give more texture. A Mexican hand corn grinder will grind the grains very satisfactorily *(see illustration page 11),* although it is slightly laborious.

The dough for this recipe should be rolled out as thin as possible, or the "crisps" will be more like tough hardtack.

The yeast will not leaven the dough in the usual way for yeast breads, but it will give the dough a more stretchy consistency and, of course, add flavor.

    4 ounces stone-ground, unbolted rye flour
    2 ounces unbleached, all-purpose flour, plus a little extra for working the dough
        only if necessary—the less the better
 1½ tablespoons gluten flour *(see note page 124)*
    About 6 tablespoons warm water
  ¼ ounce cake yeast (about 2 teaspoons crumbled)
  ½ teaspoon medium-grind sea salt
    3 tablespoons lard or vegetable shortening, melted
    Butter to grease the baking sheets

Mix the 3 flours together in a bowl. Add 1 tablespoon of the water to the yeast, and cream, pressing out the lumps with the back of a wooden spoon. Make a well in the flour and add the creamed yeast. Dissolve the salt in the rest of the warm water and stir well. Add this gradually to the flour, along with the melted lard, reserving 2 tablespoons of the water until you see how much water the flour is absorbing. The dough should be stiff and very slightly sticky. Knead for about 3 minutes and set aside in a greased plastic bag for about 2 hours.

Preheat the oven to 375° F. Have ready 2 lightly greased baking sheets.

Cut the dough into half and set one half aside in the plastic bag while you roll out the first part as thin as you possibly can—I find a thin rolling pin or dowel better for this *(see page 12)*—and cut into shapes or strips as desired. A convenient size for me is 4 × 1 inch and less than ¹⁄₁₆ inch thick, if possible. Bake the crisps for about 8 minutes on one side, turn them over, and continue baking until very lightly browned and crisp right through, about 5 minutes. Cool on a wire rack and store in an airtight container.

Whole Wheat Crisp

A very rough, unbolted flour should be used for this recipe *(see note page 15)* to obtain the right crunchy texture.

> 6 ounces whole wheat flour *(see note above)*
> 2 tablespoons gluten flour *(see note page 124)*
>   About 5 tablespoons warm water
> ¼ ounce cake yeast (about 2 teaspoons crumbled)
>   Rounded ¼ teaspoon sea salt
> 2 tablespoons lard or vegetable shortening, melted
>   Butter to grease the baking sheets

Follow the instructions for the Rye Crisp recipe *(see page 196)*. The dough will be a little softer than it is with rye flour.

DRINKS
AND NATURAL
REMEDIES

Somebody is going to say that it is a far cry from my personal soul food to remedies for flatulence and insomnia, but—in the great tradition of Mr. Beeton—I couldn't resist putting them in, and besides, these remedies are so much a part of my life here in rural Mexico.

I haven't taken a pill for indigestion or sleeplessness for years. That is not to say I never suffer from them, but I have learned to cure them without medicine from the drugstore. For instance, if I have a headache or feel restless at night, I go to the garden just outside the front door and pick a bunch of *myrto,* which, incidentally, I have seen growing profusely in Texas. It has a small, highly aromatic leaf and small salmon-pink flowers. I place it in a large handkerchief under my head. Efigenia (that's how she spells it), my daily help, says that I can do the same with basil leaves and that in an infusion they will help a cold. In fact, I haven't had enough headaches or nervousness to try out all the soporifics at my door. The *zapote blanco (Casimiroa edulis)* grows wild all over the property, and its leaves are said to act like a sedative when infused in water. (The pits are said to be hypnotic, but also poisonous if taken in large quantities.) I have cultivated several passion fruit vines. Their leaves and flowers are much sought after here as a cure for nerves—in fact, I have to firmly curb my Mexican visitors from deflowering and stripping my vines of their leaves, since they cannot understand that I grow the vines only to eat the fruit. There are lemon and orange leaves, dried orange flowers as *calmantes* (sedatives) and pomegranates, an infusion of the tough skin of which makes an effective cure for light cases of diarrhea. The corn silk is used as a diuretic and restorative after kidney ailments.

The other day I passed by Señorita Esperanza's house to pick up some cream that I had ordered and she handed me a tot glass full of a light brown liquid. It tasted very pleasant. She had a look of triumph on her face. "It will cure cancer," she proclaimed. "I am giving everyone a little to try, *por si las dudas* [just in case]." She then began to explain that her sister, also a devotee of herbal medicine, had sent her a "certain type of mushroom" (which turned out to be a fungus just like a vinegar mother) with instructions for its use. Señorita Esperanza had made a decoction of it and diluted it with weak tea sweetened with brown sugar, to make it more palatable.

When I come to think of it, we used to have a lot of natural remedies in the bathroom medicine cabinet at home in England. There were senna pods to make a tisane for constipation; Epsom or Glauber's salts as a purge, or to use in a hot tub for aches and pains; oatmeal for a footbath for tired feet; and oil of eucalyptus for a stuffy nose. Mother always made a superb lotion out of equal parts of well-refined olive oil, glycerine, and lemon juice to prevent our hands from chapping in the winter and keep them soft. There was always a chamomile rinse for fair hair and a special shampoo made from Aunt Bertha's recipe. She had deep auburn hair, which was always slightly untidy but wonderfully sleek, and she used this shampoo on it. I remember I made it for years from soft soap, oil of lavender, and henna. The details escape me, and alas, nobody in the family seems to remember. Perhaps, then, it is little wonder that now, living so near to the earth for much of the year, I have come to adopt these natural "medications."

HOMEMADE DRINKS

When I was growing up, our favorite summer drinks were lemon barley water and, for a special Sunday treat, ginger beer. In any Mexican home, if you are offered "water" with your meal it will turn out to be an *agua fresca*. These refreshing drinks are based either on a seasonal fruit such as melon, pineapple, and watermelon, or on chia seed, the flesh of tamarind pods, or Jamaica flower *(Hibiscus sabdariffa)*—although it is actually the calyx of that flower that is used to stain the water deep red and give it a unique acidy flavor. At home, my favorite *agua* is made with Seville oranges *(see page 16)*, while in a Mexican restaurant I often order a *limonada preparada* made with lime juice, soda water, and a little sugar. You can always use brown sugar or honey in your fruit drinks, and if they're made with citrus fruits, thinly pared rinds always give extra flavor. The variations are endless—use your imagination.

Epazote Tea

Epazote (Chenopodium ambrosioides)—known in the United States as Mexican tea or wormseed—that most Mexican of cooking herbs, about which I have written almost *ad nauseam* in my Mexican cookbooks, has other uses. I am told that in the American Deep South a vermifuge was made for children from the tiny round green seeds mixed with molasses. In Mexico also the herb is believed to dispel internal parasites, and a cup of strong *epazote* tea should be taken every morning before breakfast. It is very effective against stomach gases.

Ants cannot stand *epazote*. If you pick a large bunch of the herb, crush the leaves between your hands, and throw them down where the ants are invading, they will disappear within two minutes.

Epazote does grow wild in the southern and central part of the United States—I have even seen it in Central Park in New York—but there the flavor is not as strong. Parking lots seem to be its favorite haunt, and indeed it does taste vaguely of petroleum. To grow some for yourself, write for seeds to: Horticultural Enterprises, P.O. Box 34082, Dallas, Texas 75234.

Always use herbal teas in moderation, especially if they are made with "whole" herbs, either fresh or dried, because you never know their strength and potency when taken over long periods. The packaged commercial varieties are much less potent.

To make the tea Add 2 large stems and leaves of fresh *epazote* to 2 cups boiling water and let it simmer for about 2 minutes. Leave to steep for a further 3 minutes. Strain and drink.

Chamomile Tea

If you have any sort of stomach upset, take a cup of strong chamomile *(Anthemis nobilis)* tea. Try to buy the dried herbs loose in a health food store or at a herbalist's, or, if packaged, those with whole flower heads. They are stronger and more effective than the powdered, bag-packed herbal teas.

As in every case of herbal teas, one shouldn't overdo the dose, especially in this case if one is a ragweed allergy sufferer.

To make the tea, add 1 heaped tablespoon of the herb to 2 cups boiling water and allow to boil for about 2 minutes. Leave to steep for another 3 to 5 minutes. Strain and serve; you'll have a couple of cups.

Lemongrass Tea

Lemongrass *(Andropogen citratus),* which is used as a flavoring in certain oriental dishes, is used in Mexico as a light sedative "to calm the nerves," as they say. The narrow, stringy, mid-green leaves, which are creamy-colored at their base, are easy to grow in a fairly warm climate. They have a strong lemony fragrance that lingers long after the leaves have been cut.

For 2 cups of tea, cut 2 leaves and tie them into a small bundle. Add them to 2 cups boiling water and boil for about 2 minutes. Allow to steep for about 3 minutes more. The tea takes on a delicate, lemony-green color and strong flavor.

NOTE It is advisable with herbal teas of this type not to drink them too strong nor in large quantities.

Ed Holler's Frothy Milk for Cappuccino without a Machine

FOR 2 CUPS CAPPUCCINO

¾ cup whole milk (or part half-and-half)

Pour 1 cup boiling water into the blender jar, cover, and set aside to heat through. Bring the milk to a frothing boil. Discard water from jar, add milk, and blend at high speed for 1–1½ minutes, covered. Set aside still covered so that the foam rises up, about 1–2 minutes more. Spoon out the froth onto the cups of espresso coffee. (Drink coffee through it—do not stir.)

Señorita Esperanza's Cure for Insomnia

One day in April last year, Señorita Esperanza hailed me in the street. "I hope you are picking your citrus blossoms," she shouted. Frankly, the idea hadn't occurred to me, so I went over to her to find out what it was all about. "Well, I can tell you how to make the best cure for insomnia out of them." She went on to tell me that a tree cannot produce fruit for every blossom that it bears, so pick those that are not attached securely to a strong stem. Collect from all your trees: *limón, lima, cidra, naranja, naranja agria, limón real, mandarina* (lime, sweet lime, citron, orange, bitter orange, [no translation], and tangerine).

- **1 cup citrus flowers**
- **1 cup boiling water**
- **3 tablespoons pure cane alcohol (if not available, use vodka)**

Put the citrus flowers in a small jar and pour the boiling water over them; add more water if necessary so that they are completely but *just* covered, no more. Leave them to soak overnight. The following day, strain through a fine strainer, reserving the water and discarding the flowers. Add the alcohol to the flower-scented liquid and put into a small bottle with a tightly fitting top. It will last many months in the cupboard without anything happening to it.

If you find you are unable to sleep or are very restless, then do the following.

Make an infusion of orange leaves and linden blossoms to take twice a day, morning and evening, with 1 drop of the citrus flower essence. The next day do the same with 2 drops, and every day increase the dosage until you reach 8 drops. By that time you should be cured. If not, then go backwards, 8, 7, 6, etc., until you reach 1 again. She didn't tell me and I forgot to ask her if anyone had gone that far!

Linden trees line the sidewalk along Riverside Drive in New York City and are in full bloom in June. They have an almost overpowering fragrance. You are advised in England never to leave your car under a linden tree because there is a strong liquid that drips from the trees that can destroy the paint.

Mung Bean Tonic

Last summer I arrived at a friend's apartment in London tired and stale after a long-overdue flight. I was talking about how I felt when a visiting Chinese student, Jingxia Yang, went into the kitchen and started to cook some mung beans. An hour or so later she handed me a small glass of brownish liquid. I drank it, as she prescribed, three times daily for a few days and felt completely refreshed after the "hangover" of traveling. Later on, she sent me the recipe:

"Moong Bean has been used not only as a food but also as a traditional cure by Chinese for a long time. In the summer, Chinese people always like to drink moong bean juice to keep their body in comfortable condition."

    1 cup mung beans
    4 cups cold water

Rinse the mung beans and put them in a saucepan. Cover with the water and cook over a gentle heat for about 15 minutes. The juice will become a deep greenish brown at the end of this time and remain clear. Set aside to soak for about 2 hours, then strain and reserve the juice—use the beans for some Chinese food. A small glassful is the right dose.

Barley Water

I can still see the pitcher of barley water standing on the garden table on a summer morning. It was covered with a white gauzy top edged with a crochet pattern from which hung small blue beads. They acted as weights to keep the top in place in the summer breeze and protect the barley water from wasps. Barley water was our favorite summer drink—next to ginger beer, of course.

It is a particularly refreshing drink, said to be very good for washing out the urinary tract.

    2 ounces (about ¼ cup) pearl barley
    1 quart cold water
      Juice of 1 lemon, or more, to taste
      Sugar or honey to taste
      Lemon slices (optional)

Put the barley in a pan and cover with cold water; bring to a boil. Strain and discard the water. Add the 1 quart fresh water, cover, and cook over a very low flame or in a double boiler—it should hardly simmer—for about 1½ hours. Stir well and allow to stand for another 40 minutes. Strain, pressing the barley gently; add the lemon juice and sugar to taste. Serve cold, with slices of lemon if desired.

Ginger beer is enjoying a revival in the United States today. And well it might, for it is a very refreshing nonalcoholic drink that looks like a glamorous pearly-grey champagne.

Ginger beer was our weekend treat when we were young. It used to come in heavy stoneware bottles with white ceramic stoppers held tightly in place with a rubber washer and thick wire spring—the type still used by some German beermakers today. You can easily make your own ginger beer.

This recipe is one I found and adapted very slightly from *West Indian Cookery* by E. Phyllis Clark.

Serve it very cold in a bulbous wineglass with a sprig of mint and a thin slice of lime. It can also be served over a little shaved ice.

> **2-ounce piece of fresh ginger root**
> 4 **quarts boiling water**
> **Juice and rind of 2 limes**
> 2 **ounces cream of tartar**
> 2 **ounces fresh cake yeast**
> ⅓ **cup warm water**
> 1¼ **pounds granulated sugar**
> **About ½ cup dark Jamaican rum** *(optional)*

Wash the ginger root but do not peel it. Chop roughly and process in the food processor until reduced to a textured paste.

Put the ginger in a large container and pour the boiling water over it. Stir in the juice and rind of the limes and the cream of tartar, cover, and stir from time to time. When the mixture is lukewarm, mix the yeast together with the ⅓ cup warm water, pressing the lumps out with the back of a wooden spoon, and add it to the container. Cover and leave to stand for 6 hours. Stir the sugar into the ginger beer until completely dissolved and bottle immediately, making sure that the stoppers are well sealed and airtight. The ginger beer will keep for 3 to 4 days in a cool place. If you wish to keep it longer, then add about ½ cup dark Jamaican rum.

Remedy for Light Cases of Diarrhea

I remember that when I first went to Mexico in 1957 I clipped this remedy from a little magazine put out by the British Chamber of Commerce. I should also explain that the magazine then was extraordinary. It was edited—and largely written—by a retired military attaché to Mexico. He knew the country like the back of his hand and wrote fascinating articles on its wildlife and plants, particularly orchids, on which he was an acknowledged expert.

    1 (6-ounce) glass of distilled water
    ½ teaspoon bicarbonate soda
    3 tablespoons lime juice
    1 white of egg, beaten until frothy
      Sugar to taste

Mix all together well—the blender would be best for this—and drink down immediately.

Garlic Cure

Garlic has been used for centuries as a cure—almost a panacea—for many ailments, including circulatory problems and parasites. However, if taking large doses of it continuously, one runs the risk of being ostracized! A friend of mine in Mexico City was given this recipe by a veterinarian, and it works very well.

    1 pound garlic, unpeeled and lightly crushed
    2 cups pure cane alcohol or vodka

In a blender, blend together the garlic and alcohol until they form a paste. Store in a jar of dark-colored glass with a tightly fitting top. Set aside in a cool, dark place for 1 month. At the end of that time drain off the liquid into another bottle. Take 10 drops of the liquid before breakfast each morning.

Elder Flower Champagne

During the latter years of the Second World War all my spare time was spent with friends who lived in a Wiltshire farmhouse. I remember that one cold night they opened some aged bottles of elder flower champagne and we all drank several glasses. I had to cycle ten miles back to where I was billeted but they seemed to pass in ten minutes, as though I had wings.

This is a delicate and lovely drink and is still made in the West Country by many country housewives, each of whom has her own recipe. This one was given to me many years ago by Barbara Aldridge, then of Home Farm, Stourton, in Wiltshire.

> 2 **large heads elder flowers**
> 1 **tablespoon strong white vinegar**
> 1¾ **pounds (3½ cups) sugar**
> 1 **gallon cold water**
> **Rind and juice of 1 orange or lemon**

Mix all the ingredients together well and set aside, covered, to stand for 48 hours in a warm place. Bottle and allow to age for at least 1 month before drinking.

PRESERVES

When I see those chic packaged jams and jellies in specialty food stores, I am filled with admiration for their "designer" labels and fancy covers but aghast at the prices. All my frugal instincts are aroused and I think back to my mother's constant plentiful stock of superlative jams produced for mere pennies. The cupboard at home was usually cold and damp, with a wire-netting window on the outside wall of the house. What a variety of jams there were: dried apricot, beautifully orange, flecked with the ivory-white of split almonds; two types of plum, densely purple and red; greengage with its large pieces of greeny yellow flesh; strawberry, with the fruit still whole; raspberry with its myriad seeds—it must have been someone with illfitting dentures who first advocated taking the seeds out of raspberry jam! My particular favorites were made of the little wild black damson plum, which stained your mouth dark blue, and black currant with its intense flavor and small chewy berries. There was always a small quantity of jam made from the deep red loganberries from the vines that fanned out over the wires on the garden wall.

There was far too great a quantity as well of the jams I didn't like: stringy rhubarb that set your teeth on edge; gooseberry jam with its rather tough and gluey texture; and marrow—that tasteless nonsense squash so beloved by the British—which has always to be "tarted up" with ginger. There were endless pots of bitter orange marmalade to last the year round, and if you looked hard enough, somewhere near the back was a lonely pot of mincemeat or lemon curd. Tucked away out of sight also there was always a cloth-covered Christmas pudding left over from the holidays.

No commercial pectin was used to set those jams—just equal amounts of sugar to fruit in most cases. There was no wax on top either, merely a little circle of cellophane covered with kitchen parchment and held down with a rubber band. Since the cupboard was a damp, cold place, one often had to peel off a layer of mold or dig through a sugary topping before one got down to the real jam, and scooped it out into the cut-glass teatime jam pot that was always accompanied by a fancifully worked silver spoon.

In the same cupboard, alongside the jams, were bottled fruits: large oval Victoria plums, greengages, gooseberries, and blackberries with sliced apples, which would eventually go into a deep-dish pie, or under a thick, thick layer of baked sponge pudding, which always came out of the oven with a crisp browned crust. And then, of course, there were always red currant jelly for roast lamb, and chutneys of apple, plum, or green tomato to perk up the cold leftover Sunday roast. Every weekend there was a great shuffling around of jams in that cupboard to find a different one for the coming week of teas. It was never a very orderly place at the best of times, but delectable and intriguing.

During those seemingly endless summer and fall days of our youth there was a lot of work to do picking colandersful of white, red, and black currants before the birds beat us to it, and then coaxing them off their long, stringy stems with the tines of a fork. There were gooseberries to "top and tail"—we always hunted for the sharpest nail scissors for this task; there were strawberries to hull, and raspberries to remove gently from their prickly stalks.

My small store of jams is never very orderly, either. For one thing, the pots are of all shapes and sizes: recycled mayonnaise and pickle jars that my city friends save for me, along with old tin cans, plastic bags, and the like. And how frustrating it is when you can never find the matching top just as the jars have been sterilized and filled with hot jam! My repertoire is much more limited than my mother's. I now make only the jams that I particularly like from fruits that are readily available at the different seasons of the year. Small, sweet strawberries grow in my garden for at least five months of the year; blackberries are prolific in the late spring, just before the rains, and sold at the curbside of the town by peasants from the surrounding hills; and small, tough peaches ripen in the orchard at the end of May. The winter months bring the biggest crop of firm and perfumed guavas, and there are *tamarillos (see page 214)* throughout the summer and fall. I am almost sure to find a few bitter oranges from neighboring trees, until mine come into their own in November and last well on into the New Year.

From one year to another I have bottles of untouched jam stored away and forgotten until visitors drop in unexpectedly, or for special teatimes that call for a vintage jam: plum made in New York in 1975, strawberry, spring 1980—the first hectic spring in my new house. How on earth did I find time to make jam in spring 1980?

Apricot Jam

Sharp apricot jam with a few split almonds in it is one of my favorites. It immediately brings back memories of teas after school on a wintry afternoon, with thick brown (whole wheat) bread and butter and apricot jam. I remember I used to get home first, and it was my job to start the fire in the living room grate. It would never light, despite the carefully rolled newspaper spills and carefully pyramided sticks. (This was before the days of the now-popular "firelighters.") I was almost in tears by the time my sister and mother arrived, as I was always scolded for not having a cheery fire and a warm room. (It was easy for my sister, who had been a Girl Scout—I couldn't bring myself to join because I would never salute anyone—and for this reason also during the war I had perforce to join the Land Army). Well, to get back to apricot jam: Choose the sharpest dried apricots you can find; generally that means the smallest and darkest in color. They are sometimes hard to find, as there is a preponderance of large, fleshy, light-colored ones. Don't overdo the almonds.

Apart from eating this jam *as* jam, we used to use it as a topping for semolina pudding, Queen of Puddings, or steamed sponge puddings. Besides, it made a very good apricot glaze *(see page 213)*.

START TWO DAYS AHEAD

- 1 **pound dried apricots** *(see note above)*
- 7 **cups hot water**
- 3 **pounds granulated sugar**
- 3 **tablespoons lemon juice**
- 25 **almonds, blanched and split**

If the apricot halves are small, cut them again in halves; if large, into quarters. Do not chop. Put the apricots in a china or glass bowl, cover with the 7 cups hot water, and leave to soak for 36 hours, moving them around every 8 hours or so.

Sterilize preserving jars and keep them warm.

Strain the fruit, reserving the juice. Add water to make 3½ cups of juice. Put the juice and fruit in a preserving pan (or heavy shallow saucepan) and simmer until soft but not falling apart—this could take 40 minutes from the time the mixture starts to simmer. Take care not to let the fruit boil or it will lose its setting properties. Stir the sugar into the softened fruit and cook over a low flame until it has completely dissolved, stirring constantly. You will need to keep pressing the fruit down into the liquid with a large wooden spoon. Bring the mixture up to a fast boil, add the lemon juice, and cook until the setting point is reached, about 30 minutes. (I find most cookbooks are far too optimistic on this and greatly underrate the cooking time.) When the jam is beginning to jell, stir in the split almonds—they should cook only briefly or they will become too soft. Pot the jam immediately, and seal.

Apricot Glaze

For the recipes in this book you will not need a fine, clear glaze; a thicker one is more suitable for sandwiching the Viennese Fingers together or spreading under the icing of the Coffee Sponge. It is, of course, better made with home-made dried apricot jam. Apart from richer flavor, you will get a better yield than if it is made with a commercial brand of apricot jam.

> 1 **cup apricot jam**
> ⅓ **cup cold water**
> 1 **scant teaspoon lemon juice**

Remove any almonds from the jam and eat them.

Put all the ingredients in the blender jar (the blender is better than the food processor for this) and blend until smooth. Transfer the puree to a small, heavy saucepan and cook over a medium flame. When it comes to a boil, continue cooking at a brisk pace for about 7 minutes, stirring most of the time. Seal in a sterilized jar and store away in a cool place until needed.

Tamarillo or Tree Tomato Jam ABOUT 6 CUPS

In the New York fruit stores there is usually a small section devoted to boxes of exotic (fashionable) fruit imported from New Zealand, passion fruit and kiwi, for example. Another fruit called *tamarillo* has joined their ranks. It has a smooth, matte, mulberry-red skin, and an average size would be 2½ inches long and 1½ inches at its widest part. And every time I see it I wonder if anybody, except a Sri Lankan or New Zealander, knows how to use it!

When I first bought my land in San Pancho I was fascinated by a rangy shrub with large elongated, heart-shaped leaves. Its small white flowers hang in clusters at the ends of its branches. The fruit is oval in shape—a stylized tear-drop—slightly pointed at the tip, and before it ripens, it is a light green color flecked with dark green that turns to purple. It then ripens to an appetizing red. Locally it is called *merenjena* (not *berenjena,* which means eggplant), but nobody could identify it for me or knew anything about it. Two years ago I was teaching in Hawaii and met a botanist from Sri Lanka who solved the mystery for me. Its botanical name is *Cyphomandra betacea;* it's a member of the Solanaceae family—and a native of Peru. It was introduced in 1882 into Ceylon (now, of course, Sri Lanka), where it flourished and is known as tree tomato.

In San Pancho the fruit is usually eaten raw. You bite off the tip and suck out the fleshy, dark red core, which contains many little seeds, and discard the outer peach-colored, rather acrid flesh.

It is also made into an *agua fresca* (a fresh drink made in Mexico like limeade and orangeade). My botanist friend told me that in Ceylon they make jam out of it, but he didn't have a recipe. I invented one. The fruit jells very well and has a flavor and texture somewhere between red currant and raspberry, with a touch of gooseberry.

60 ripe red *tamarillos*
5 cups granulated sugar

Remove the stems from the fruit and rinse them. Cover the *tamarillos* with hot water and simmer just until the skins can easily be sloughed off—about 3 minutes; do not overcook, or the flesh will become too mushy. Drain and allow to cool. When cool enough to handle, remove the skins and discard. Chop the flesh and core together, or process briefly—the pulp should have some texture. This quantity should yield about 6 cups pulp.

Sterilize the preserving jars. Put the pulp (no water) into the preserving pan together with the sugar and heat through, stirring until all the sugar has dissolved. Bring to a boil and cook fast, stirring frequently, until the setting point is reached—about 35 to 40 minutes. Pot and store as for any other jam.

There was always a pot of lemon curd in the pantry at home—before any of us had refrigerators—and it was used in many different cakes and puddings: to fill small lemon curd tarts, as a topping for Queen of Puddings—a favorite—and as a filling for a Victoria sponge sandwich. It is best, of course, made with lemons, but in Mexico I make it with the local small limes, which are the same as the key limes of Florida.

Some people like to use lemon curd for lemon meringue pie, but it is very rich and should be used much more sparingly than the usual lemon filling. I sometimes add beaten egg white and use it as a cold lemon sauce for a dish such as poached pears, and sometimes just leave it around to eat a spoonful of now and again.

> ¼ **pound (8 tablespoons) unsalted butter**
> ½ **pound (1 cup) gradulated sugar**
> **Rounded ¼ teaspoon finely grated lemon rind**
> 6–7 **tablespoons lemon juice**
> 3 **large eggs, at room temperature**

Sterilize preserving jars and keep warm.

Put the butter, sugar, and lemon rind and juice in the top of a double boiler and heat through, stirring the mixture from time to time until the sugar has dissolved. Break the eggs into a bowl and remove the white cord attached to the yolks. Beat the eggs together well. Stir about 3 tablespoons of the hot mixture into the eggs and, when thoroughly amalgamated, add the egg mixture to the contents of the pan. Lower the heat so that the water at the bottom of the double boiler is just simmering. Cook the mixture, stirring constantly, and scraping the bottom of the pan until the mixture thickens and coats the back of a wooden spoon, about 12 to 15 minutes. Pour the lemon curd into the warm jars, cool, and seal.

Lemon curd should last about 2 weeks in the refrigerator.

Bitter-Orange Marmalade

I am a dyed-in-the-wool conservative when it comes to breakfast fare: toasted whole wheat bread or English muffins, unsalted, *unmelted* butter, and bitter-orange marmalade—although it has to take its turn with home-produced honey, organic at that, because I don't believe in harmful sprays and most of my neighbors can't afford to buy them. You can keep all your kumquat, grapefruit, sweet orange, and lemon marmalade—I will unswervingly stick to mine.

Marmalade making was almost a ritual at home. Every February the brightly colored little Seville oranges would appear in the greengrocers' shops and we were all put to work cutting the thick skins and removing the pips and tough membranes of the oranges before washing those endless jam jars, sorting out the covers, and writing labels. We would make enough marmalade to last the year, and so it was made in two batches because the large but shallow preserving pan did not hold quite enough. When we finished, our hands were sore, we were bored and tired, but when that wonderfully sharp aroma filled the kitchen and wafted through the house announcing that the marmalade was finished, we would wipe our fingers around the edge of the empty pan, savoring that first taste of the new season's marmalade, and all the pain and boredom was forgiven and forgotten. As the year progressed, the marmalade, rather like wine, took on deeper color and rounder flavor as it matured and thickened.

One year when I went back to England, I was somewhat shaken when I saw that Mother had put the rind of the oranges through the mincing machine, the marmalade wasn't the same. And when she was older, poor dear, and couldn't even manage that—but persisted in making marmalade up until her ninetieth year—she bought, as did her younger neighbors, a commercial marmalade base, prechopped and seeded all ready for the sugar and cooking. I could easily forgive her, but when I read a serious recipe for that concentrate in a well-known food magazine—it came from a noble Scottish home—you can just imagine, can't you, how I raised my eyebrows!

I have been making bitter-orange marmalade ever since I first came to Mexico. There are Seville oranges available the year round, but here, as elsewhere, they are at their best and most plentiful during the winter months. I am now the proud possessor of one large tree, which has been badly neglected over the years, and many small ones grown from seeds that have been planted around the kitchen terrace. Luckily, many of my neighbors have prolific trees, and when I came to San Pancho to build a home the fruit fell unused and rotting on the ground. My promotion of English marmalade among my neighbors has had a mixed reception. Most of them pull a wry face, while a few others eat it by the spoonful instead of candy.

One day I took a pot of my marmalade along to Señorita Esperanza, my arbiter on all things sweet. Her father owned small sugar mills in the hot country a few miles away, and she studied herbal medicine. She sells cream, cheese, and *ates* (see recipes later in this chapter), hands out herbal remedies, and rents out property for a living.

She took a small spoonful of the marmalade and, with the air of a connoisseur, took a little on her tongue and then rolled it around her mouth. She carefully put the spoon down, threw her hands into the air, and with a note of triumph loudly announced, *"Para la bilis, ahaa, para la bilis!"* So when next you eat bitter-orange marmalade at breakfasttime, think of Señorita Esperanza and appreciate what a lot of good the marmalade is doing your bile duct.

One of my favorite little cookbooks had a recipe for bitter-orange marmalade that dispensed with all that cutting through tough skin, and later on I saw that they had taken the idea from the estimable Mrs. Beeton. Well, now I'll give you my versions of that recipe. It makes a strong, thick marmalade with large strips of chewy rind in it.

> **4 pounds Seville oranges** *(see note, page 16)*
> **4 quarts water**
> **7 pounds granulated sugar (or brown sugar if you like a really dark marmalade)**
> **3 tablespoons lemon juice** *(optional)*

Rinse the oranges well and put them whole into a large stainless-steel or enamel pan. Cover the oranges with the 4 quarts water and cook them over a medium flame until tender—when the handle of a wooden spoon can easily pierce the rind. (Do not let the oranges boil, as this will impede the setting later on.) This should take about 1¼ hours, depending on how ripe the oranges are. Remove the oranges and measure the cooking water. There should be 1½ quarts. Add more water to make up to that amount if necessary. If you have too much, then reduce over a high flame to the correct amount.

Sterilize 8 (1-pint) preserving jars and keep them warm.

Put the cooking water into a preserving pan, add the sugar, and stir well over a low heat until it has dissolved. Meantime, cut the oranges into halves and scoop out the pulp. Discard any very tough membrane and separate out the seeds (sometimes they are so flat you can hardly see them), which should then be tied in a small bag of cheesecloth. Add the pulp to the pan along with the bag of seeds. Cut the rinds up into thin slices and add to the pan. Bring the marmalade up to a fast boil and continue cooking it over a high flame, stirring well and scraping the bottom of the pan almost constantly once the mixture starts to thicken. After about 30 minutes test for setting point: Put 1 teaspoon of the mixture on a cool plate and almost immediately a skin will form; it holds its shape. Pot while still hot, stirring the marmalade well before each jar is filled. Seal and store in a cool, dry place.

NOTE If lemon juice is used add when marmalade is boiling.

SHORT CUT If you find that separating the seeds and tough membrane is too much of a chore, pass all the pulp through a coarse sieve or strainer. Then put the debris into a bag of cheesecloth and boil it with the rest of the fruit. (The seeds provide pectin for setting the marmalade.)

Bitter-Orange Marmalade with Honey

If you are swearing off sugar and like a really acidy marmalade, you might like to try this one, based on a recipe from Mrs. Beeton's *Household Management*. I tried it one year when I had an extra big honey yield, and had to make some adjustments to the original recipe.

> **3 pounds Seville oranges** *(see note, page 16)*
> **4 cups water**
> **3 pounds honey**

Cut the oranges into halves horizontally, scoop out the insides, and reserve. Weigh out 1 pound of the rinds and cut them into thin strips. Cover with water and cook until soft, this should take about 40 minutes from the time they come to a boil. Sterilize the preserving jars and have the covers ready.

Meanwhile, remove all the seeds from the pulp and put into a small cheesecloth bag; reserve the pulp and membranes. When the skins are tender but not too soft, add the honey, bag of seeds, and all the remaining fleshy part and membranes, as well as any juice that has exuded. Bring to a fast boil, and boil, stirring, until setting point is reached—about 40 minutes. Pour the hot marmalade into the sterilized jars and store in a cool, dry place.

SHORT CUT If you find that separating the seeds and tough membrane is too much of a chore, pass all of the pulp through a coarse sieve or strainer. Then put the debris into a bag of cheesecloth and boil it with the rest of the fruit. (The seeds provide pectin for setting the marmalade.)

Guava Jelly

Jelly making is a rather frustrating business—you start with so much and end up with so little. But it is worth it, at least in this case. (But surely never in the case of that nonsense horseradish jelly that I saw in a recent article.)

Of all the jellies I have eaten, there are only two that I consider sublime: red currant and guava—well, perhaps crab apple as a third. After all, there is never enough time to eat everything, so you have to choose, and why not pick out the best?

At home in England there was only a small quantity of red currant jelly made, mainly because the birds got to the currants first, despite the netting over the bushes, and partly because of the work involved. It was a laborious job to remove the currants from their stringy bunched stems, and after all that, there was so little to show for it. We used to eat the jelly in the fall with roast lamb or use it as a glaze over a fruit tart, and very occasionally with scones at teatime.

Guava jelly provided another treat, and to my sister and me it was a very exotic one. Mother's oldest sister, Aunt Maud, lived for many years in Jamaica and every other year would make a trip home. To us at the time she was a rather glamorous figure; although short and dumpy, she was very handsome in her big floppy hats and chic dresses of the finest materials. Her greying hair was slightly tinged with lavender and a delicate perfume always wafted after her— that is, when she wasn't smoking one of her flat Turkish cigarettes. When she visited us the whole household deferred to her—she had quite a regal presence— and total quiet reigned while she had her afternoon nap, followed by her maté tea, before gathering up anyone she could get hold of to play bridge for the rest of the evening. We would go to the railway station to meet her, and it was quite a sight to see her walking along the platform with soft colorful baskets crammed full of goodies from Jamaica. She always somehow managed to preserve some huge and delicious Bombay mangoes in the ship's cold room. There were large bags of cashew nuts, large floppy panama hats, and tins of guava jelly. (I shall always remember those hats with some embarrassment. During the summer term at school, students had to wear panama hats, well blocked and respectable, with a band of the school colors around the crown. But since the family didn't have money to spare, Mother made us wear those wide-brimmed unblocked panamas. I can still hear the snickers of our classmates when we wore them.) Anyway, Aunt Maud's visits started off my passion for cashews and guava jelly, so little wonder that when I first arrived in Mexico and saw real guavas my enthusiasm knew no bounds. I started to make guava jelly galore, for friends and acquaintances alike, whether they wanted it or not.

I prefer to use small jelly glasses because, once they have been opened and are sitting around, the jelly tends to lose its texture. I prefer to eat the jelly when it is about one month old, or even more. The jelly is then quite firm without being rubbery, like the commercial brands—they probably have gelatin added to them. A Jamaican cookbook that I have in my library suggests that a small piece of alum should be added to the jelly to help it set faster. I have tried it both ways and don't find much difference. (Señorita Esperanza throws up her hands in horror at the suggestion. "It will eat all the enamel off your teeth," she warns.)

> 6 pounds slightly underripe guavas
> About 7 cups water, or to cover
> 1½ pounds (about 3 cups) granulated sugar
> 1 (¼-inch) piece of alum *(optional; see note above)*

Just rinse the guavas, do not even bother to remove the shriveled flower at the tip of the fruit. Chop the guavas roughly and put them in a stainless-steel or enamel pan with water to cover them. Cook over medium heat—do not let the fruit boil hard, or it will lose its setting properties—stirring from time to time. Continue cooking the fruit until the contents of the pan have reduced by about one-third—this can take up to 1½ hours.

Have ready a jelly bag, or a double layer of cheesecloth tied firmly at the corners to form a bag. While the fruit is still hot, pour it into the jelly bag (held in a frame or slung between the legs of an upturned kitchen chair) and leave it to strain into a stainless-steel or enamel pan for about 18 hours (24 hours is an absolute maximum because after that time the juice starts losing its setting strength). If you want a perfectly clear jelly, do not squeeze the bag. There should be about 3¾ cups of juice.

Sterilize the jelly glasses and keep them warm.

Put the strained juice back in the cooking pan and heat. When it has just about reached boiling point, stir in the sugar and keep stirring until it has dissolved. If using alum, add it at this time. Boil the sugar and juice together fast and test with a thermometer: it will have reached the correct setting point at 220° F. If you do not have a candy thermometer, test by holding up the wooden spoon with which you are stirring the jelly. The jelly should form a light coating on the back of the spoon and hang in a thin string from it. The boiling stage will take about 15 to 20 minutes.

Remove jelly from heat and pot immediately. I do not skim. If any froth has formed, it will rise to the top of the pot and I like to eat it.

Ate de Guayaba

Guavas grow profusely in the state of Michoacán, as do quince, figs, and peaches, while in the higher altitudes there are apples, pears, and crab apples, to name only a few. It is hardly surprising, then, that Michoacán is well known for its fruit pastes, *ates,* as they are called in Spanish. In Morelia, the beautiful state capital, *láminas*—thin layers of fruit pastes ranging in color from brown to reds and greens—are made. The layers are lightly sugared, rolled, and cut into several different sizes. They are then packed attractively into cellophane-topped boxes and sent to markets and candy stores all over the country. Perhaps the most popular of the *ates* is that made of guava, *guayabate* as it is known locally, with its distinctive rich flavor and slightly grainy texture.

As winter approaches and the guavas are ripening, Michoacán cooks and housewives take down their copper *cazos*—deep preserving pans mostly made in nearby Santa Clara de Cobre—and clean them up with lime or bitter orange juice and rough salt or wood ash. Then *ate* making starts in earnest, and in large quantities to last the year round—or almost the whole year.

There are many types of guava, and like so many other fruits, the larger and more showy they are, the less flavorful. For making jelly or *ate* I choose the little round ones with pink or yellow flesh and a highly perfumed skin—you can always tell when you are within range of a guava tree when the fruit is ripening, as a wonderful aroma emanates from it in the hot winter sun.

> 6 **pounds ripe guavas**
> 6 **cups cold water**
> 4½ **pounds granulated sugar**

Rinse the guavas and remove the small, black shriveled flower at the base; do not peel. Cut each guava into halves horizontally and remove the fleshy center with a small spoon. Put the hollowed-out "shells" in one pan and the fleshy part with seeds in another. Add 4 cups of water to the shells and 2 cups to the pulp. Cook both saucepans over a medium flame; they should simmer, not boil fast, or the setting quality of the fruit will be impaired. Simmer the pulp for 5 minutes. The shells should be quite soft in anywhere from 5 to 10 minutes, depending on the thickness, ripeness, etc. Strain the shells, reserving the cooking water. Blend or put in the food processor until they are reduced to a puree— do not overblend and lose all the texture. Return the puree to the cooking water in the preserving pan. Press the pulp and liquid through a fine sieve or the fine disk of a food mill—theoretically the seeds should not go through the sieve, but if a few do, don't worry; they will add character. The debris should be almost dry by the time you have finished. Add the sieved, gelatinous pulp to the pan with the other puree. Stir in the sugar and cook over a low flame until dissolved. Increase the heat and cook fast, stirring from time to time at first and then constantly as the mixture begins to thicken. Use a wooden spoon with a very long handle, as the mixture tends to splutter. When the mixture shrinks away from the sides of the pan and hangs thickly from the spoon, it is ready—this will take a laborious 1½ hours, approximately.

While the *ate* is cooking, you can prepare the molds. I use wooden cheese hoops, but anything will do. A metal mold will have to be lined with greased parchment paper or the *ate* will stick. Use a glass cup to ladle the *ate* into the molds; it will, ideally, be 2 inches thick. Leave the *ate* in a warm, dry place to dry off completely and become firm, you can then unmold it. Wrap in grease-proof paper and store in a dry, airy place.

Stored in a cool, dry place, the *ate* will keep for a year. It is a delicious snack when you feel like something sweet and, of course, it is most popularly served with a piece of creamy cheese (not strong in flavor) as a dessert.

Membrillate (Quince Paste)   6 OR 7 CAKES

Quinces have a delicate, intriguing flavor. The paste is made in much the same way as the guava paste, except that the cores and seeds are first ground and soaked to extract the highly gelatinous juice, which provides the pectin for the high setting point of the fruit.

Señorita Esperanza gave me this recipe, and when I brought her some of my paste to try, she nodded her head thoughtfully and gave me a piece made by her cronies—it was reddish in color and did not have such a strong taste of quince. After many days of prodding she admitted that they added crab apple jelly to help along the setting point. . . . It works perfectly well without.

In New York I bought huge, blown-up quinces that were called Chinese apples. They were much rounder than those I am accustomed to in Mexico and England, and they did not have the same downy skin, or, for that matter, such an intense flavor.

START THE DAY BEFORE

    5 **pounds quinces**
    9 **cups cold water**
3½ **pounds granulated sugar (use 3¾ pounds in Mexico)**

Rinse the quinces in cold water and remove the withered remains of the flower if they are still attached. Do not peel. Cut the fruit into quarters and cut out the center core with all the seeds attached. Set aside the fruit and cover tightly with plastic wrap. Put the cores together with 3 cups cold water into the blender jar or food processor and blend briefly so that they are well broken up. Leave them to soak for a minimum of 2 hours.

The following day, put the debris of cores and seeds into a fine strainer and press down hard to extract all the gluey substance exuded overnight. Add this with the sugar and 2 cups cold water to the preserving pan and set over a low flame, stirring from time to time until the sugar has melted. Raise the flame and cook until the sugar has turned to a light brown caramel color—this will take about 20 to 30 minutes, depending on the quality of the sugar.

Meanwhile, put the fruit in a heavy saucepan with 4 cups cold water, cover, and cook over a medium flame until soft—about 20 minutes—but do not boil fiercely, or the setting point of the fruit will be impaired. In small batches, transfer the cooked fruit to the food processor and process until it is a thick puree, without adding more water. Keep the puree warm. Add the warmed puree to the caramelized sugar and stir thoroughly. Cook over a high flame, stirring constantly, until the setting point is reached and the paste shrinks away from the sides of the pan and hangs in thick lumps from a wooden spoon, about 25 minutes. Follow instructions for molding in the recipe for Ate de Guayaba *(see page 221)*. If the atmosphere is moist, the paste will remain a little sticky. Keep turning it over for several days in a dry, airy place or in the sun—if you don't have bees near at hand.

NOTE Cooking time will be affected by altitude; allow almost double time for altitudes over 5,000 feet (for example, Central Mexico).

Easy Peach Jam

At the risk of having the whole of the state of Georgia up in arms, I have to say that American peach jam is the most boring of jams and too sweet. Who gave people the notion that peaches have to be peeled, anyway? If you leave the skins on, not only do you have a much better texture, but the flavor is enhanced. Also, by allowing the pits to boil with the fruit, you get another dimension of flavor.

    4 **pounds slightly underripe peaches**
        About 8 cups water, or to cover
    3½ **pounds granulated sugar**
    3 **tablespoons lemon juice**

Rinse the peaches well, especially around the base of the stalk—traces of spraying chemicals tend to concentrate there as the fruit grows. Do not peel the peaches. Score them right down to the pit. Put the fruit and water to cover in a preserving pan and cook over a medium flame—on no account let the fruit boil hard, or some of its setting properties will be destroyed—until soft, about 20 to 25 minutes, depending on the size and ripeness of the peaches. At this point the flesh should be falling away from the pits.

Sterilize the preserving jars and keep them hot.

Add the sugar to the pan and stir over medium heat until dissolved. Then boil over a high flame, adding the lemon juice, and removing the pits as they float to the top. Test for the setting point, about 40 minutes after the jam has started to boil. Put 1 teaspoon of the mixture on a cool plate and almost immediately a skin will form; it holds its shape. Pot in the usual way while the jam is still hot, stirring it from time to time, as the flesh tends to congregate at the bottom.

Señora Lucinda's Peaches

The market of the small town where I live boasts of several stands that specialize in fruits cooked to a dark brown stickiness, but in such a way that they keep their form despite the long cooking. While they are generally eaten for breakfast with a glass of milk, for some reason unbeknown to me and others I have asked, they are considered a Lenten food and sold along the sidewalks just before Easter stuffed into fresh crusty rolls. The fruits include crab apples, figs, sweet potatoes, peaches, pumpkin, and the rind of sour grapefruit and Seville oranges. Here was something new and I was fascinated.

Two years ago, when we had an abundance of peaches in the orchard—small, hard, white-fleshed peaches that I happen to love—I asked a neighbor, Señora Elia, how to prepare them *en dulce,* as they do in the markets. She told me to put them in a solution of lime and water for three days and then to cook them in very little water and not too much sugar. I did what she said and they turned out rather like tough-skinned prunes and not oversweet. I was satisfied. A few days later I was chatting with another neighbor, Señora Lola, and gave her one of my newly cooked peaches to try. She took one bite and her nose turned up perceptibly. "These are too *correoso* [chewy]," she said; "my mother knows how to prepare them much better than this. I'll take you to her house and she will tell you how to cook them."

The recipe was rather vague, but I checked with Señora Lucinda (Lola's mother) every step of the way to avoid making a mistake; besides, the peach season was almost at an end. "How long do they take to cook? How do you know *when* they are cooked?" I asked Señora Lucinda. "Oh, they will tell you when they are ready," was her reply. It was eight hours!

I ate one the day after they were cooked—they were indeed a very good texture, but I found them far too sweet, so I put them away and forgot about them. Six months later I came across them in my store cupboard and tried one—it was deliciously mellow by now and not too sweet. A year passed, and again I tried one: it was a little drier but still had a wonderful flavor and a very slight sugary texture. Lola had been right—the others were *correoso* beside these.

Don't be put off by the time of cooking. Get a fascinating book, or wait until there is a special on TV, or invite a talkative person to keep you company. If you hurry the peaches along and boil them too fast, the syrup will harden too quickly before the peaches are thoroughly cooked inside.

50 small, firm, underripe peaches (about 5 pounds)
¼ cup wood ash★
Cold water
4½ pounds granulated sugar

★*Sift some of the ashes from a wood fire through a fine strainer. Increase quantity for soft wood like pine and fir.*

Rinse the peaches well, but do not in the process rub the fine down off the skin. Prick each peach with a fork 3 times, making sure that the tines reach down to the pit. Put 3 quarts of water in a glass or stainless-steel or hard-baked stoneware receptacle, stir the wood ash into the water, and allow the grey particles to settle on the bottom. In about 20 minutes the water should be comparatively clear. Place the peaches in the water, which should cover them, and leave them to soak overnight. While they are soaking and while you are still awake, gently tilt the pan from time to time so that the peaches change position slightly, but without disturbing the ash particles that have settled at the bottom of the container.

The following day, remove the peaches carefully, again trying not to disturb the ash too much. Rinse them well in fresh water and then with your fingers gently rub the downy surface from the skin in a bowl of water. Meanwhile, put the sugar and 5 cups water in a preserving pan and bring to a boil; lower the flame, stir well until all the sugar has melted, and then put the peaches into the syrup one by one—the water should come only about three quarters of the way up the peaches. Cook over a low flame—they should just barely simmer—tilting the pan gently from time to time. (Señora Lucinda said "no spoon," but I used a large wooden one . . . very gently.) Continue simmering until the syrup begins to thicken, about 6 hours—and the peaches take on a greenish hue. As the syrup thickens more and more, it will form a coating around the peaches and gradually they will become a deep brown color. They are done when the syrup hangs in a thin string from the spoon. Test a peach anyway by opening it up; you will see that it is colored right through to the pit. The peaches will begin to resemble prunes, so don't expect them to keep a perfectly round, smooth shape. Carefully remove the peaches with a slotted spoon and place them on a drying rack to drain. In very humid weather, dry the peaches in the oven at a very low setting—200° F or "warm." Leave them to finish drying in an airy, dry place—in the sun, if you don't have beehives around. Can be eaten right away or stored for several months. They will simply become dryer and less sweet.

There will probably be quite a bit of syrup left over. It can be used to sweeten a fruit salad, eaten on top of yogurt, or instead of honey on bread and butter.

Green Tomato Chutney 5 TO 6 CUPS

Despite Mother's busy schedule when we were young, she somehow always managed to keep a store cupboard full of jams, preserves, salted-down string beans, eggs (bought in bulk when they were cheap) preserved in isinglass, and, of course, chutneys. I say "of course" because it was unthinkable then to eat the leftover Sunday roast on Monday without chutney—and a large baked potato in its leathery skin. Chutney—served from its proper cut-glass jar with a special fork with a long, thin bone handle—would accompany cold ham for high tea, and it was one of our favorite fillings for school lunch sandwiches: thinly sliced Cheddar cheese and chutney between thickly buttered whole wheat bread. I never really liked the very sweet chutneys and much preferred the sharp green tomato chutney with its crunchy mustard seeds.

One year when Mother was getting on in years, I returned to England for a holiday. She had made some green tomato chutney, but it wasn't the one I had remembered; she had no recollection of the original and we couldn't find her recipe. One day last summer when my Mexican garden was full of unripe tomatoes—and there was no hope of their ripening in the heavy summer rains—I started to experiment, to try and recapture the flavor and texture of the green tomato chutney I remembered.

The skin of the tomatoes does become a little stringy; personally, I don't mind it but if you do, you can always peel the tomatoes.

Chutney should be cooked in a stainless-steel or enamel saucepan, and I suggest potting it in 1- or 1½-cup jars because, once the jar is opened, the vinegar evaporates very quickly and the chutney dries out—unless you have a family with enormous appetites for chutney.

- 3 **pounds unripe green tomatoes, not Mexican★**
- 2 **large onions (about 10 ounces)**
- 4 **small dried red chilies**
- 2 **tablespoons coarse sea salt, or to taste**
- 1 **tablespoon mustard seeds**
- 2 **cups white vinegar**
- 10 **ounces light brown sugar**
- ¼ **cup finely chopped fresh ginger root**
- 8 **cloves garlic, peeled and finely chopped**
- 2 **whole allspice**

Sterilize jars for 5–6 cups chutney and keep warm.

Rinse the tomatoes, remove the stalks, and core and slice them fairly thick without peeling. Slice the onions thin and put them together with the tomatoes in a heavy pan—a preserving pan is ideal. Cook over a medium flame, covered, until the onion is soft, scraping the bottom of the pan with a wooden spoon from time to time, to ensure that the mixture does not stick to the bottom of the pan. This should take 15 to 20 minutes. Add the rest of the ingredients, mix well, and cook over a medium flame, stirring from time to time and scraping the bottom of the pan so that the mixture does not stick. In about 30 minutes the chutney should begin to reduce and thicken. Cook for 5 minutes more. Fill the jars while the chutney is still hot. Seal the jars tightly and forget about the chutney for 2 months. It will then be ready to eat.

★*This is not a recipe for the Mexican* tomate verde *or tomatillos.*

Dill Pickles in Brine

When dill pickles are so easy to make I wonder why anyone would buy them. Try if you can—depending on how good-tempered your produce man is that day—to choose pickling cucumbers that are between 3 and 4 inches long and not more than 1 inch in diameter. The rye bread helps the fermentation to start in the pickles and gives them a pleasant sour taste. Crusts are better, as they tend not to fall apart so easily in the brine. If you do not have any 1-quart jars available, or the cucumbers are large so that you need larger jars, then increase the amount of brine so that it comes up to the top of the jars. Allow 2 tablespoons salt to every quart of water.

This recipe is one given to me by Inge Lotwin, my one-time neighbor in Mexico City.

> 2 **pounds pickling cucumbers** *(see note above)*
> 1 **large bunch fresh dillweed (if not available, then 1 tablespoon dried)**
> 8 **cloves garlic, peeled and left whole**
> 3 **tablespoons coarse-grained sea salt**
> 6 **cups water** *(see note above)*
> 2 **small slices sour rye bread (end crusts if possible:** *see note above***)**

Sterilize 2 (1-quart) jars and keep them warm.

Scrub the cucumbers so that no grit or sand remains in the ridges. Lay them in crisscross horizontal fashion in the jars, with dill between the layers. Add the whole cloves of garlic. Add the salt to the water and bring to a boil. Put a metal spoon (Inge specifies silver) in one of the jars and fill with the hot brine; remove the spoon and repeat with the second jar. Put a piece of bread in the liquid at the top of each jar, cover loosely, and place on a tray in the sun. Depending on the heat of the sun, the pickles will start to ferment by the second day. Turn the jars around a little each day for 5 days. If the sun is not shining, then place the jars near a warm stove or in an oven that has a pilot light to provide a low and gentle warmth. Or you can leave them at room temperature, but the pickling will take about 3 days longer.

Cover and refrigerate to stop the fermentation. The pickles are now ready to eat. Discard any soft ones at this point. If you do not like the look of the disintegrated bread, etc., in the brine, then you could remove and strain the liquid. I never do so: it looks more picturesque with all the bits in.

Pickled Onions ABOUT 6 CUPS

Not so many years ago, the *sine qua non* of a British pub lunch to accompany a glass of ale—they have become much more fancy now—was a thick slice of bread, a hunk of winy Cheddar cheese, and some pickled onions. They were not pearl onions but slightly larger and more robust—or you can use shallots, which to my mind have by far the best flavor for this recipe, or small white onions.

The onions will take on a brownish hue from the malt vinegar as they age. Start at least one month ahead, preferably two.

> 2 **pounds small round onions or shallots, peeled and left whole**
> 1 **scant cup coarse sea salt**
> 8 **cups hot water**
> 4 **Turkish or 8 California bay leaves**
> 4 **small dried red chilies** *(optional)*
> 12 **whole peppercorns (omit if spiced vinegar is used)**
> **About 3 cups good malt vinegar or prepared spiced vinegar** *(see recipe page 230),* **at room temperature**

Trim the onions and put in a large glass or stainless-steel bowl. Dissolve the salt in the hot water and set aside to cool. When cool, add to the onions and set aside to marinate for 2 days, stirring the onions occasionally and pushing them down in the water, since they tend to float to the top.

Sterilize the preserving jars. Drain the onions and pack them into the jars, leaving room for about 1 inch vinegar above the level of the onions. Divide the bay leaves, chilies, and peppercorns equally among the jars. Pour the cold vinegar over the onions so that they are completely covered by about 1 inch. Seal tightly and set aside in a cool place to ripen.

Alice Crang, in her little book on the subject of jams and pickles, *Preserves for All Occasions,* insists that, if properly stored, "they can last for years."

Spiced Vinegar for Pickling

This is based on a recipe by Alice Crang in her little paperbook *Preserves for All Occasions*.

It is better to use whole spices if possible; they impart a better flavor, since they keep fresher longer, and powdered spices make the vinegar cloudy. A good malt vinegar is preferable for this type of pickling, and it should be poured over the vegetables—onions, cauliflower, beans—cold or, more accurately, at room temperature. It should always stand in the jars at least ½ inch above the level of the vegetables.

    4 cups malt vinegar
    1 rounded tablespoon whole allspice or 1 teaspoon ground
    2 (2-inch) sticks cinnamon or 1 teaspoon powdered
    1 (1-inch) piece dried ginger or 1 teaspoon powdered
    1 tablespoon whole cloves or 1 teaspoon ground
    1 tablespoon whole peppercorns or 1 scant teaspoon ground

Put the vinegar and spices in a china or glass receptacle and place in a water bath on top of the stove. Heat gently until the vinegar is breaking into a simmer. Remove and allow to steep a minimum of 6 hours.

CHRISTMAS

CHRISTMAS FOOD

In my childhood it seemed that no sooner was the summer vacation over, and the evenings drawing in, than preparations for Christmas began. Mother would buy huge quantities of raisins, sultanas (white raisins derived from a white grape of that name grown in the Mediterranean countries), currants, and large shiny muscats. First they had to be washed and then dried off on large baking sheets in a very slow oven. Pounds of sticky, too-brilliantly-red glacé cherries had to be chopped; almonds blanched (there was always a small proportion of bitter almonds among them); candied orange and lemon peel, which was covered with a solid white coating of sugar, cut up together with citron; and all the small seeds removed from the very sticky muscats. Hunks of dried beef suet had to be grated—a job I hated because I was always grazing my knuckles—and dried crusts of bread put through the mincing machine. The work seemed endless.

When all the ingredients were ready, we would start with the puddings. Mother would climb the kitchen stepladder to bring down the huge mixing bowl from the top shelf of the pantry where it was stored from one year to another. It was one of those unmistakably English ceramic mixing bowls, white inside and yellow ocher outside. There were two greyish veins running from top to bottom where it had been cracked at one time—but nobody in those days would have thought of discarding a mixing bowl of that dimension because of a gentle crack—it had stood the test of time. The ingredients were put in one by one and mixed together until the eggs and ale transformed it into a sticky mass that squelched as you stirred. And every one of the family came to give a final stir as small silver trinkets—thimbles and horseshoes and sprigs of holly—and real threepenny bits were added. That was the time to wish. . . . I can only imagine, because I do not remember, that my wishes in those days were for something extravagantly unattainable, like a handsome prince who would marry me and cherish me ever after, or some such absurdly romantic notion with which we were brought up.

The pudding basins were lined up—at least ten of them—plain white ceramic basins, quite unlike those fancy fluted molds depicted in Mrs. Beeton's book. These were filled and covered with several layers of greaseproof paper, which was then topped with a cotton pudding cloth held in place by a tightly tied drawstring.

Earlier in the day a fire had been lighted under the "copper" (the name came originally from a ship's boiler, used in the galley for cooking), which was in fact a square solid table of masonry built into the wall of the scullery—outer kitchen—with a hollowed-out cement bowl in the center of it and a small firebox underneath. Every Monday the fire was lit to heat water for the laundry, and as the clothes bubbled away they had to be pushed down time and time again with the stout wooden "copper" stick. The soapy-lye smell that filled the kitchen was synonymous with Monday lunch, concocted of leftover Sunday roast: cold sliced roast beef with chutney, shepherd's pie, or a lamb curry.

As the water was bubbling away, the Christmas pudding basins were gently lowered into it. Halfway through the cooking time a rich aroma wafted from the scullery, and everyone who approached the house knew that Christmas puddings were being cooked. After a few more hours they were removed, and cooled, and their fresh, dry tops were put on before they were stored away in the coolest part of the pantry to ripen.

The cake came next. In fact, Mother always made two: the large one to be decorated for Christmas Day and the smaller one to be left plain, a good heavy fruitcake to be eaten with a glass of sherry on a wintry Sunday morning. The baking pans for the cakes were always round and deep. They were lined and wrapped about with several layers of buttered brown paper to protect the cakes in the long baking, and even then, in the slowest of ovens, some of the dried fruit around the edges was a little scorched. When they had finished cooking and had cooled off on racks, the smaller cake was packed away, well wrapped in several layers of greaseproof paper before it went into the tin. The other one was turned upside down, the bottom pierced with a slim skewer and a wineglassful of brandy or rum poured through the holes. It was then carefully wrapped in several layers of cheesecloth, also moistened with brandy, and put away in a tin.

Last of all came the mincemeat, always made in large quantities. It, too, was liberally laced with rum, potted in one-pound jars that were covered with cellophane secured with rubber bands and left alongside the other Christmas fare to ripen during the months ahead.

As Christmas Eve approached, even the butcher shops took on a festive air, as they were hung around with enormous turkeys and geese, their fluffy neck feathers still unplucked and large red or blue rosettes stuck into their breasts. Strings of extra-slim pork sausages—erroneously called chipolatas—were woven into braids around the white-tiled counters. There large, bread-crumbed York hams were displayed alongside more prosaic but fragrantly smoked pieces of gammon. (They were really smoked in those days, but smoked ones are hard to find now, when most are artificially colored and injected with smoke flavor.) The poultry was "undressed" (there were no overly protective health inspectors to prevent the poultry innards being touched by human hand), and it was Father's job—and later, after his death, mine—to pluck, draw, and truss the bird. By that time, luckily, I had been well drilled in the markets of Mexico. It was customary then to stuff the neck cavity with a pork stuffing while the inside was filled with a herb-bread and bacon forcemeat.

I must confess I am almost passionately fond of a well-roasted turkey *if* it has plenty of crisp brown skin and a large parson's nose to which I lay claim as soon as decently possible on Christmas morning. (One kind hostess, knowing this, placed a particularly succulent parson's nose—roasted, of course—prettily wrapped with colored paper and ribbons under the Christmas tree.) I am appalled at what most people accept as turkeys today in the United States. The poor things look as though they have died from overexposure, with their blue-hued flesh and fatless skin. Then, of all the most ridiculous nonsense, the packers insert that tasteless vegetable fat, colored and flavored with "butter buds," between the fillets of the breast. What an insult to human intelligence and palates . . . off with their heads!

On Christmas Eve, when Father came home with a large string bag full of unshelled brazil nuts, filberts, almonds, and walnuts, the nutcrackers were brought out and some of the nuts cracked open to be stuffed into large, spongy dates from North Africa. Pounds of rough puff pastry were rolled out to make small mince pies for the carolers who came to the door that week, as well as for Christmas dinner, and, of course, for sausage rolls—no festive food was complete without sausage rolls in those days. Meanwhile, my sister would set to and ice the cake. Almond paste that had been made the day before was now rolled out in a thick circle to cover the top of the cake. This, in turn, she covered with a thick layer of white royal icing, piped around the sides and whipped up over the top for the traditional family snow scene with Santa Claus, reindeer, and sprigs of holly.

When Christmas Day at last arrived, it was always impossible for me to tear myself away from the kitchen. I loved to hear the turkey fat splattering away in the oven and smell that enticing aroma. Besides, there was a lot of work to be done. My sister and I would roll the rashers of thick, well-smoked, lean bacon, trim the brussels sprouts, and peel the potatoes that were to be roasted. There was bread sauce to stir, chipolatas to fry, and at the last moment the gravy to be made from the drippings in the pan. The last details were always helped along by a glass or two of deep brown sherry that had been aged in the cask.

My father always prided himself on his carving, and on Christmas morning, as on every Sunday throughout the year, he would bring out his long, bone-handled carving knife and lovingly sharpen it on the long, thin steel with a matching handle. He carved with the precision of a surgeon—or almost—and to this day I shudder as I see someone hacking away clumsily at the turkey—often removing the crisp brown skin, which is the best part—or sawing it with an electric knife, which instantly transports me to the dentist's chair.

We invariably spent Christmas and Boxing Day with cousins, and about ten of us would sit down to dinner at one o'clock sharp. All was ready, but first we had to pull the party favors we called crackers: everyone crossed his arms and linked up with his neighbors, a cracker end in each hand—how I dreaded putting on those silly hats that fell out and always hoped that mine would be lost in the commotion. The food was served and passed around far too slowly, and every gluttonous instinct came out as I swallowed that first bite, and then the whole plateful, hardly stopping to drink the good dry claret that was always served with Christmas dinner. I thought how glorious it was to have a real turkey dinner, and still to this day wish that someone would invite me to one every three months—no fun cooking a turkey when you are alone!

As the youngest member of the group I had to gather up the plates—which gave me a good opportunity to go to the kitchen and sneak a few more delectable bits of the turkey—while Mother unmolded the Christmas pudding, sprinkling it with sugar, sticking a sprig of holly on the top, and then dousing it with brandy: she carried it flaming to the table. Along with it went hot mince pies and a sauceboat of hard sauce, which even in those days I thought was overkill. Nuts were cracked, and stuffed dates, dried figs and apricots, almonds, muscats and chocolates were consumed before the meal was ended, just in time to raise our glasses to "the King" as three o'clock struck and George V's Christmas message came over the radio. Another Christmas dinner was over.

After all those dishes had been scraped, stacked, and washed, the more energetic of us would go for a brisk walk in the murky afternoon light while the rest dozed by the fire in armchairs, burping discreetly once in a while.

By five o'clock the kettle was singing and the cheery clink of teacups sounded in the kitchen and "Well, just a cup of tea, then . . ." turned out to be a full-fledged affair. "After all, it only comes once a year," was the predictable comment. The toasting fork came out and slices of bread were toasted over the glowing coals, then to be smothered with turkey drippings and sprinkled with salt. The tea trolley was wheeled in with plates laden with chocolate biscuits and shortbread. There was always a cry of "What a shame!" as the cake was cut into and the snow scene dismantled. Tea was followed by parlor games, Christmas carols from King's College, Cambridge, over the radio, and the evening broke up some hours later with a light supper of turkey and ham sandwiches, mince pies, and coffee.

There was always too much turkey and ham left over for Boxing Day, while my father laid claim to the turkey giblets for his favorite of all food— giblet pie. You know the rest: fricassee of turkey, turkey and ham pie, minced turkey, rissoles (breaded ground meat patties), turkey soup . . . while the rest of the stuffing was put out for the birds who hopped around the kitchen door expectantly as the frosts of January hardened the ground and painted the bushes and trees a silvery white.

Christmas Pudding

Many Christmas puddings turn out to be smooth and black; mine are lumpy and brown. They were always brought to the table flaming in brandy or rum, with a sprig of holly on top and well covered with fine granulated sugar, and accompanied by hard sauce (but see the recipe for Christmas Pudding Sauce on page 238). Although they were made ostensibly for Christmas, there were always some extras for the occasional midyear treat, and I can see my mother now, asking on a cold summer day if we wouldn't like to have a Christmas pudding for lunch. My father was always happy when some was left over because he liked to finish it up for breakfast, thickly sliced and fried in butter.

> **Butter to grease the pudding basins and parchment**
> 4 ounces unbleached, all-purpose flour
> ⅔ teaspoon double-acting or 1 teaspoon single-acting baking powder
> ½ teaspoon sea salt
> Scant ½ teaspoon ground nutmeg
> ¼ teaspoon powdered cinnamon
> ¼ teaspoon ground cloves
> ¼ teaspoon ground allspice
> 6 ounces roughly ground white bread crumbs
> 6 ounces (about 1½ cups, closely packed) grated suet
> 6 ounces (about 1 cup, lightly packed) soft brown sugar
> ½ pound (about 1⅔ cups) currants
> ½ pound (about 1⅓ cups) sultanas or golden raisins
> ½ pound (about 1⅓ cups) seeded muscat raisins *(see page 15)*
> 1½ ounces citron, cut into small cubes (about ¼ cup cubed)
> 1 ounce blanched almonds, shredded (heaped ¼ cup shredded)
> 1 large, sour cooking apple (such as a greening) grated
> 3 tablespoons thick-cut bitter-orange marmalade
> 2 teaspoons finely grated orange rind
> 3 eggs, lightly beaten
> ¼ cup brandy or rum
> ¼ cup orange juice
> About ¼ cup heavy, dark beer (British stout or brown ale preferred)

Have a pan of boiling water ready—the pan should be large enough for the basins to fit easily on the bottom, and the water should come two thirds of the way up the sides of the filled basins. Keep another kettle of water simmering on the side to replenish the water as it boils down.

Butter 2 (1-quart) pudding basins. Have ready rounds of cooking parchment heavily buttered to cover the top—2 for each basin—and pudding-basin covers. If you do not have covers, improvise with a tea towel cut to shape so that the circles cover the top of the basin and overlap by at least 1½ inches all the way around. Tie them down with string just below the rim.

Mix well together the flour, baking powder, salt, and spices and then stir in the bread crumbs, suet, and sugar. Next add the dried fruits, citron, almonds, cooking apple, marmalade, and grated orange rind and stir well. Beat the eggs together well and add the brandy or rum, orange juice, and ¼ cup beer. Mix all together very well. The mixture will be stiff and sticky. If it is a little dry, then add more beer.

Divide the mixture in 2 and transfer to the prepared basins, allowing room for expansion at the top. Cover with the buttered paper and then with the pudding covers.

Put the basins in the pan of boiling water, cover, and boil for at least 5 hours. Take care that the water does not go off the boil, or the puddings will become sodden.

At the end of the cooking time, replace the pudding covers with fresh ones and set in a cool, dry place for at least 2 months. The puddings will, in fact, last for over a year, providing they are well stored.

When ready to use them, boil the puddings again in the same manner for about 3 hours and serve warm, with Christmas Pudding Sauce.

NOTE Beef suet is the solid membranous fat that encases the kidneys of the animal. It is easier to grate, whether by hand on an ordinary grater or in the food processor, if it is partially frozen first. The fine connective tissue will pull away from the fat and should be discarded.

Christmas Pudding Sauce

Eating hard sauce over Christmas pudding, or, worse still, with mince pies, seems to me like gilding the lily. My sister, Jean Southwood, has for some years made this sauce at Christmastime, and I think it is an excellent one for those of us whose livers can't take fat on fat on fat.

    2 tablespoons unsalted butter
    2 rounded tablespoons potato starch
 1¼ cups warm whole milk
    3 tablespoons soft light brown sugar, or to taste
      Grated rind of 1 lemon
      Grated rind of 1 orange
      Large pinch of powdered cinnamon
  ¼ cup orange juice
  ¼ cup lemon juice
    2 tablespoons heavy cream
    2 tablespoons (or more) brandy, rum, or Irish whiskey

Melt the butter in a heavy saucepan, and when it is hot and foaming add the potato starch, stirring vigorously to keep it smooth. (I much prefer a wooden spoon for this rather than a whisk.) Gradually add the warm milk, stirring constantly. When all the milk has been absorbed and the sauce is smooth, add the sugar and rinds and cook for a further 3 minutes, stirring all the time. Add the cinnamon and juices and continue cooking for 5 minutes more. The sauce should have thickened to the point where it easily covers the back of a wooden spoon and should have no trace of raw starch in it.

At this stage it can be put aside for an hour or so, providing you cover the surface with a buttered paper and put the lid on the pan. I reheat the sauce over a double boiler and adjust seasonings at this stage before adding the cream and brandy at the last minute before serving.

Mincemeat

Most commercially made mincemeat is far too sticky and sweet. This English version is spicy, rough-textured, and not too sweet. The fruit must remain whole and should not be ground or chopped.

Beef suet is the solid membranous fat that encases the kidneys of the animal. It is easier to grate, whether by hand on an ordinary grater or in the food processor, if it is partially frozen first. The fine connective tissue will pull away from the fat and should be discarded.

- ½ pound shredded suet (about 2 cups shredded)
- ½ pound (about 1¼ cups) dark brown sugar
- ½ pound (about 1⅓ cups) seeded muscat raisins *(see page 15)*
- ½ pound (about 1⅓ cups) sultanas or golden raisins
- ½ pound (about 1⅔ cups) currants
- 1 large cooking apple (such as a greening—but the sourest you can find), finely chopped
- 4 tablespoons bitter-orange marmalade, with the peel chopped, or, if not available, 2 ounces candied orange peel, chopped
- 2 ounces blanched almonds, roughly chopped
- 2 ounces citron peel, finely chopped
- 2 teaspoons finely grated lemon rind, closely packed
- 10 tablespoons lemon juice
- 2 teaspoons mixed ground spices: allspice, cinnamon, cloves
- ½ teaspoon nutmeg
- ¾ cup dark Jamaican rum

Have ready 6 (1-pint) preserving jars.

Mix all the ingredients except the last 5 together well in a large mixing bowl. Add the lemon rind and juice to the spices and stir thoroughly. Add this together with the rum to the mixed fruits and keep turning and mixing everything together—with your hands is best—for about 3 minutes. Set the mixture aside overnight to season (not absolutely necessary if you are short of time, but I like to do it).

The next day, sterilize the jars and allow to cool. Give the mixture several more turns so that the moisture is evenly distributed and pack tightly into the jars. Seal and store in a cool, dry place.

This lasts for at least a year, depending on how cool and dry the place really is.

Christmas Cake

I love this fruity, not-too-sweet Christmas cake—which can also be used for a wedding cake—with its customary thick layer of almond paste topped by a much thinner layer of royal icing. Although I generally forgo them, these layers not only give the cake extra sweetness and an interesting texture as you bite through the three contrasting layers, but help to keep it moist. It is still the custom in England to send small pieces of the wedding cake in special little boxes through the mail to relatives and friends who were unable to attend the wedding.

I always think that a recipe like this sounds formidable, but if you plan ahead and have all the fruits ready and the pan lined, the assembling of the cake is simple.

½ pound unsalted butter, plus extra to grease paper and pan
½ pound (about 1⅓ cups) raisins
½ pound (about 1⅓ cups) sultanas or golden raisins
½ pound (about 1⅓ cups) seeded muscat raisins *(see page 15)*
½ pound (about 1⅔ cups) currants
3 ounces glacé cherries, roughly chopped (rounded ⅓ cup chopped)
2 ounces citron, finely diced (rounded ⅓ cup diced)
2 ounces (rounded ⅓ cup) candied orange and lemon peel (or substitute coarse-cut bitter-orange marmalade)
2 ounces almonds, blanched and slivered (scant ½ cup slivered)
10 ounces unbleached, all-purpose flour, plus 2 tablespoons for the dried fruit
½ pound (1¼ cups, lightly packed) dark brown sugar
1 tablespoon molasses
⅛ teaspoon ground cinnamon
⅛ teaspoon ground cloves
⅛ teaspoon ground nutmeg
⅛ teaspoon powdered ginger
⅛ teaspoon ground mace
2 teaspoons finely grated orange rind
1 teaspoon finely grated lemon rind
4 large eggs
½ teaspoon vanilla extract
⅓ cup brandy or rum

You will need a cake pan, either round or rectangular, of at least 10-cup capacity and at least 2½ inches deep. Line the pan with 2 layers of well-greased paper (brown bag or cooking parchment) and wrap the outside with 3 layers of brown-bag paper secured with string—all that dried fruit tends to scorch on the outside during the long cooking period.

Mix together all the dried fruits, cherries, candied peels, and almonds with at least 2 tablespoons of the flour—this will prevent the fruit from sinking to the bottom of the pan.

Place the oven rack in the center of the oven and **preheat the oven to 325° F.**

In a separate bowl, beat the butter and sugar together until creamy and light. Add the molasses, spices, and fruit rinds and beat well. Add the eggs one by one, with 1 tablespoon of flour after the first 2 to prevent curdling. Beat well and add the vanilla. Gradually stir in the flour, then the dried fruits, and finally the brandy or rum. It will be a heavy, sticky mixture that plops heavily off a wooden spoon. Transfer the mixture to the prepared pan and bake for 1½ hours. Cover the top with brown paper if it is coloring too fast, lower the oven temperature to 300° F and continue cooking for a further 1½ to 2 hours—very much will depend on your oven and the depth of the cake. If you are cooking in an electric oven, I suggest lightly covering the top of the cake from the beginning, since the heat is often boosted from the top. Carefully check the temperature of your oven and lower heat before the given time if you think the cake is cooking too fast. To test for doneness, insert a thin metal skewer, which should come out clean.

At the end of the cooking period, turn off the heat, open the oven door, and let the cake sit for a further 20 minutes. Allow to cool off for another 40 minutes out of the oven but still in the cake pan. Remove the cooking paper, turn out onto a wire rack, and pierce some holes in the bottom of the cake. Pour the rest of the brandy through the holes. Soak a piece of cheesecloth in more brandy. Wrap it around the cake, then cover with several layers of foil and store in a cool place in an airtight tin. The cake should not be eaten for 3 or 4 weeks (although it should keep up to a year if well wrapped). During that time you can pour more brandy through the bottom of the cake, this is a matter of taste.

Almond Paste

This amount of almond paste is sufficient for covering a small cake or for filling about 25 stuffed dates.

    4 ounces blanched almonds
    1 medium egg, well beaten
    2 ounces confectioners' sugar
    2 ounces granulated sugar
    ½ teaspoon almond extract
    ¼ teaspoon lemon juice

Grind the almonds in a coffee/spice grinder to a fairly grainy texture—do not overgrind to a coarse powder.

Put the egg and sugars in the top of a double boiler and stir until the sugar has dissolved. Then beat over a low heat until fluffy, about 5 minutes. Set aside to cool. When cool, stir in the almonds, almond extract, and lemon juice and allow to cool off in the refrigerator overnight. (This will freeze well once it is made.)

stuffed dates

    25 large dates with pits
       Almond Paste (see preceding recipe)
    25 almond halves or walnuts

Carefully remove the pits from the dates, trying to keep the ends intact. Stuff with a small amount of the almond paste and place an almond or walnut half on top. (Some people sprinkle the dates with finely granulated sugar, but that is too sweet for my taste.)

Shortbread

Shortbread, or something akin to it, probably dates back to the Roman occupation of Britain, when it was the custom to break a brittle wheat cake over the head of the bride during the wedding ceremony.

In some ways it is still a festive "bread." Tins of commercially made shortbread are a very acceptable gift at Christmastime, and it is always to be found on the Christmas tea table. It is more often than not referred to as Scots or Scottish shortbread.

One period of my life after the war, in the late forties, took me to Dumfriesshire in southern Scotland. Although the area my colleagues and I covered as housing managers was mainly rural, there were some mining villages in it. The mining families there were very hospitable, and at Christmastime everyone expected us to stop and drink "a wee drappie" and eat some shortbread with them. Every housewife made her own. I asked one particularly good baker among them how she made her shortbread: "Two gowpens full of flour, one of butter"—she saw I was nonplussed and relented (*gowpen,* in Scottish dialect, means the hollows of both hands put together)—"to one pound of flour, half a pound of butter and a quarter of sugar, rub together and press into a tin, cook until golden. . . ."

Ingredients are entirely different now, especially in the United States, and this balance just doesn't work, so I have made the necessary adjustments.

It is traditional, although hardly ever done these days, to add some chopped almonds and citron to the dough. The top may also be decorated with thin slices of citron, although I prefer to do as my sister does and put halved almonds over the top.

IT IS BEST TO WEIGH INGREDIENTS FOR THIS RECIPE

- 5 ounces unsalted butter, slightly softened, plus ½ tablespoon extra to grease the pan
- 6 ounces unbleached, all-purpose flour
- 2 ounces Wondra quick-mixing flour
  Large pinch of sea salt
- 2½ ounces superfine sugar
- ⅓ cup roughly ground almonds
- 15 whole blanched almonds, halved horizontally

Preheat the oven to 350° F and set the oven rack at the top of the oven. Have ready a shallow pie pan with straight sides and about 8 inches in diameter, lightly buttered.

Mix the flours together with the salt, sugar, and ground almonds. Cut the butter into small pieces. Add to the flour mixture and rub in lightly with the fingertips until well incorporated—the dough will have a crumbly, uneven texture. Press the mixture firmly but lightly into the greased pan. Mark the dough with a sharp knife into thin triangular segments, decorate with the halved almonds, and prick well with a sharp fork. Bake until a pale golden color and crisp all the way through, about 45 minutes.

Wassail Bowl

IO TO I2 SMALL SERVINGS

This is a delicious festive drink, originally made to be offered to wandering carolers at Christmas or at Twelfth Night festivities. It is certainly a welcome change from the cloying richness of eggnog. I was given this recipe many years ago in Toronto (where I lived for three and a half years) from a couple of extraordinary cooks, Bon and Maurice, whose last names have escaped me.

When I test-cooked this again in Jerrie Strom's home in Rancho Santa Fe, the temperature was about ninety degrees outside. After discreet, approving sips, at her suggestion we put the rest of it into the ice cream machine to make an unusual and delicious sorbet.

> 1 teaspoon freshly grated nutmeg
> ½ teaspoon powdered ginger
> ⅛ teaspoon ground mace
> ½ teaspoon powdered cinnamon
> 3 whole cloves
> ½ cup cold water
> 2 egg whites
> 3 egg yolks
> 1 quart medium dry sherry (a good Amontillado is best), warmed
> 3 apples, cored but not peeled
> ½ cup light brown sugar

Put the ground spices and cloves with the water in a saucepan and boil for 3 minutes. Keep warm. In a large bowl, beat the egg whites and yolks together very thoroughly and gradually stir in ½ cup of the warmed sherry. Gradually add 1 more cup of sherry and set aside.

Add the remaining sherry, apples, and sugar to the boiled spices, bring to a simmer, and continue simmering until the sugar has dissolved, stirring from time to time. Gradually stir this into the egg-wine mixture and heat through, but do not allow to boil. Serve hot.

NOTE If I am making a large quantity, I like to put a few whole soft Ceylon cinnamon sticks on top.

244   CHRISTMAS

Burnt Almond Chocolate

I am not a great chocolate lover, but just occasionally I crave a piece of that thick, bitter chocolate crammed with burnt almonds—whole, mind you, and unskinned, like Bourneville best (and late-lamented, since I couldn't find it anywhere on my last visit to England). It was something we liked to eat with after-dinner coffee, and I always hoped to find some in my stocking at Christmas-time. Well, I suppose I just have to make my own. . . .

The type of chocolate used for a sweet of this kind is very much a matter of individual taste, and if you don't like it quite as bitter as I do, you can alter the proportions to suit yours. But leave the nuts whole! (I fail to see why American manufacturers have taken all the joy out of perfectly good English Cadbury chocolate bars by chopping the nuts up until they are practically unidentifiable—off with their heads!)

For this recipe, buy the best semisweet couverture chocolate *(see page 15)* you can find; to complement it, Baker's unsweetened cooking chocolate adds just the right bitter touch. You can add raisins, too, if you like; they add a nice chewy touch.

> Butter for greasing baking sheet
> 5 ounces semisweet couverture chocolate
> 3 ounces unsweetened chocolate, preferably Baker's
> 40 unskinned almonds
> ½ cup raisins *(optional)*

Butter a small baking sheet well. **Preheat the oven to 350° F.** You can use a toaster oven for this.

Break the chocolate up into 1-inch pieces and put into the top of a double boiler. Fill the bottom with as much water as it will hold—with the top pan in place, of course—without overflowing. Cover the pan and melt the chocolate over hot, but not boiling, water; it will take about 30 minutes.

Meanwhile, place the almonds on a baking sheet lined with foil and toast them until they are a dark golden brown right through, about 10 minutes. If you are using a toaster oven, watch closely and keep turning them. Set aside to cool.

Remove the top pan and stir the chocolate until it is perfectly smooth, allowing it to cool and thicken but not set. At this stage stir in the almonds and raisins. Using a wide palette knife, smooth the chocolate over a 7 × 5-inch area on the baking sheet—it should be about ½ inch thick. Put into the refrigerator to cool off; before it hardens completely, with a sharp knife score the surface, going a little way into the chocolate, into squares—this will make it easier to cut when cold. Allow to harden thoroughly before eating.

BIBLIOGRAPHY

ALLMAN, RUTH. *Alaska Sourdough*. Anchorage: Alaska Northwest Publishing Co., 1976.

AYRTON, ELISABETH. *The Cookery of England*. Harmondsworth, England: Penguin Books, 1977.

BEARD, GLASER, AND WOLF. The Great Cooks Library series. New York: Random House, 1977.

BEETON, MRS. ISABELLA. *Household Management*. 1861.

BRILLAT-SAVARIN, JEAN-ANTHELME. *The Philosopher in the Kitchen*. Anne Drayton, trans. Harmondsworth, England: Penguin Books, 1970.

CLARK, E. PHYLLIS. *West Indian Cookery*. New York: Thomas Nelson, 1945.

CRANG, ALICE. *Preserves for All Occasions*. Harmondsworth, England: Penguin Books, 1944.

DAVENPORT, RITA. *Sourdough Cookery*. Tucson, Ariz.: H.P. Books, 1977.

DAVID, ELIZABETH. *A Book of Mediterranean Food*. New York: Knopf, 1980.

_____. *English Bread and Yeast Cookery*. London: Penguin Books, 1977.

_____. *French Country Cooking*. London: MacDonald, 1958.

_____. *French Provincial Cooking*. London: Michael Joseph, 1960.

GRIGSON, JANE. *Charcuterie and French Pork Cookery*. Harmondsworth, England: Penguin Books, 1970.

HIBBEN, SHEILA. *American Regional Cookery*. Boston: Little, Brown, 1946.

KENNEDY, DIANA. *Recipes from the Regional Cooks of Mexico*. New York: Harper & Row, 1978.

————. *The Cuisines of Mexico*. New York: Harper & Row, 1972.

LUCAS, DIONE. *The Cordon Bleu Cook Book*. Boston: Little, Brown & Co., 1947.

SPRY, CONSTANCE, AND ROSEMARY HUME. *The Constance Spry Cookery Book*. London: J.M. Dent & Sons, Ltd., 1956.

TOKLAS, ALICE B. *The Alice B. Toklas Cookbook*. New York: Harper & Row, 1954.

Definitely Different. Published by *Daily Telegraph,* London (no date).

INDEX

Bijol, 107
Biscuits
  digestive, 190
  wheaten, 189
  See also Crispy foods
Bitter-Orange Marmalade, 216–17
  with Honey, 218
Blackberry Ice Cream with Hot
    Blackberry Sauce, 159
Braised Corned Beef, 114
Bread crumbs, 12
  toasted, 13
Breads. *See* Yeast breads
Bread Sauce for chicken or turkey,
    110
Breadsticks
  grissini, 133
  sourdough, 132
Brewer, Sam, 4, 45
Bridge, Fred, 10
Brillat-Savarin, Jean-Anthelme *(The
    Philosopher in the Kitchen)*, 9
British-Style Roast Potatoes, 54
Brito, Señora María Alejandre de,
    115
Brochette of Monkfish, 104
Broth, chicken, 37
Brown, Howard, 161
Brown and Wild Rice Salad, 60–61
Brown Rice, 74
  "risotto," 75
Bulgur, 72–73
  in fish kibbe, 95–96
Buns, hot cross, 134–35
Burnt Almond Chocolate, 245

Cactus (nopal) salad (Ensalada de
    Nopal), 58–59
Cake(s)
  Christmas, 240–41
  coffee sponge, 179–80
  date and walnut loaf, 175
  Dundee, 182–83
  gingerbread, 181

matrimony, 177
  meringue layer, 148–49
  pastel alemán (German), 146–47
  rock, 176
  Ruth's duck-egg sponge, 178–79
  Viennese fingers, 185
  Viennese tarts, 184
Caldeirada de Belmondo, 102–3
Cappuccino, frothy milk without a
    machine for, 202
Caribbean foods and drinks
  Arroz con Pollo a la Cubana, 107
  Ginger Beer, 205
  Guava Jelly, 219–20
Carrot and Coriander Soup, 39
Cazuelitas (Little Cazuelas), 21
Chamomile Tea, 202
Champagne, elder flower, 207
Cheese, melted, dried chile ancho
    with, 29–30
Chicken, 106–13
  arroz con pollo a la cubana, 107
  broth, 37–38
  fat, 14–15
  lemon, 111
  liver and gizzard hors d'oeuvre,
      Chinese, 22
  liver pâté, 28–29
  Pierre Franey's ragoût toulousaine,
      112–13
  roast, with bread sauce, 110
  salad, 70, 71
  stuffed, braised, 108–9
Chicken fat, 14–15
Child, Julia, 121, 124, 175
Chile Ancho con Queso (dried chile
    ancho with melted cheese), 29–
    30
Chile con queso, 29
Chilies, 13–14
  ají dulce, 107
  ancho, 14
  congo, 14
  flame-peeling, 13–14
  habanero, 14
  jalapeño en escabeche, 14
  poblano, 13–14

Pommes de Terre au Grain de Sel,
   Sauce Bouillade, 53
Pommes Soufflées, 55
Terrine de Campagne, 26–27
Tian, 65
Fruit
   dried, data on, 15
   salads, 153–54
   slice, Mother's, 145

García Muñoz, Paco, 71
Garlic
   cure for internal parasites, 206
Gazpacho, 45
Gelatin, meat, 92
Ginger, 155
   beer, 205
   gingerbread, 181
   gingersnap dessert, 157
   gingersnaps, 156–57
Graham, Mymie, 146
Green Tomato Chutney, 226–27
Grigson, Jane (Charcuterie and French
   Pork Cookery), 87
Grissini (Breadsticks), 133
Guadalupe's Pigs' Feet, 90–91
Guava
   ate, 221
   jelly, 219–20

Hazan, Marcella, 76
Hazelnut dessert fingers, Bernese,
   150–51
Headaches, myrto for, 200
Headcheese, 30–31
Heatter, Maida, 156
Herbs
   data on, 16
   omelette ouverte (André
      Claude's), 79
Herb teas
   epazote, 201

chamomile, 202
lemongrass, 202
Hibben, Sheila (American Regional
   Cookery), 40
Honey
   bitter-orange marmalade with, 218
   pineapple in, 151
Hors d'oeuvre, Chinese chicken liver
   and gizzard, 22
Hot Cross Buns, 134–35

Ice cream
   blackberry, with hot blackberry
      sauce, 159
   mango, 160
Ingredients, advice on, 12–17
Insomnia, linden blossoms for, 203
Iranian Broiled Lamb, 121
Italian foods
   Grissini (Breadsticks), 133
   Lemon Chicken, 111

Jam
   apricot, 212
   peach, 224
   tamarillo or tree tomato, 214
Jelly
   guava, 219–20
Jenkins, Fran, 76
Jicama in Lime Juice (salad), 60
Jingxia Yang, 204

Kennedy, Paul, 3, 4, 8
Kibbe, fish, 95–96
Kokotxas, 100
Kump, Peter, 184